The Writer as Witness:
literature as historical evidence

The Writer as Witness:
literature as historical evidence

Edited by
TOM DUNNE

HISTORICAL STUDIES XVI

Papers read before the Irish Conference of Historians,
held at University College, Cork
23 - 26 May 1985

Charles Doherty
Donnchadh Ó Corráin
John Scattergood
Katharine Simms
Brendan Bradshaw
Seamus Deane

Oliver MacDonagh
Tom Dunne
Eda Sagarra
David Hempton
Owen Dudley Edwards
Lawrence J. McCaffrey

Cork University Press
1987

First published in 1987 by
Cork University Press, University College, Cork

British Library Cataloguing in Publication Data
The Writer as witness: literature as historical
evidence
1. History in literature   2. Literature —
History and criticism
I. Dunne, Tom
809'.93358   PN50

ISBN 0-902561-49-9

Printed in the Republic of Ireland by Tower Books,
86 South Main St., Cork

In Memory of T.W. Moody

Contents

Preface..ix

Historical Studies: Publishing History........................... x

Contributors...xi

A polemical introduction: literature, literary
   theory and the historian 1
   Tom Dunne

The Irish hagiographer: resources, aims, results.................... 10
   Charles Doherty

Legend as critic.. 23
   Donnchach Ó Corráin

Winner and Waster and the mid-fourteenth
   century economy 39
   John Scattergood

Bardic poetry as a historical source.................................. 58
   Katharine Simms

Edmund Spenser on Justice and Mercy.............................. 76
   Brendan Bradshaw

Irish national character 1790-1900 90
   Seamus Deane

Sanditon: a Regency novel? 114
   Oliver MacDonagh

Fiction as 'the best history of nations': Lady
Morgan's Irish novels...133
   Tom Dunne

Jewish emancipation in nineteenth-century
Germany and the stereotyping of the Jew in
Gustav Freytag's *Soll und Haben* (1855) 160
   Eda Sagarra

Popular religion and irreligion in Victorian
fiction..177
   David Hempton

Mark Twain: historian of a lost world 197
   Owen Dudley Edwards

Fictional images of Irish-America....................................227
   Lawrence J. McCaffrey

Preface

The biennial Irish Conference of Historians has been organised by the Irish Committee of Historical Sciences since 1953, and since 1955 the Proceedings have been published as *Historical Studies*, being devoted to a single theme from 1975. A full list is appended. The present volume, the sixteenth in the series, arises from the Conference held 23-26 May 1985 at University College. The Irish Committee of Historical Sciences is grateful to University College Cork for its hospitality, and for a generous grant in aid of this publication. As Conference organiser and as editor, I am indebted to my colleagues on I.C.H.S. for their support and advice; to Charlotte Wiseman who coped so admirably with the secretarial work involved; to the Chairmen of the two general sessions on the Conference theme, Nicholas Canny and Roy Foster; and to Donal Counihan of Cork University Press.

Tom Dunne

Historical Studies:
Publishing History

T.D. Williams (ed.)	*Historical Studies I* (London, Bowes and Bowes, 1958)
M. Roberts (ed.)	*Historical Studies II* (London, Bowes and Bowes, 1959)
J. Hogan (ed.)	*Historical Studies III* (London, Bowes and Bowes, 1961)
G.A. Hayes-McCoy (ed.)	*Historical Studies IV* (London, Bowes and Bowes, 1963)
J.L. McCracken (ed.)	*Historical Studies V* (London, Bowes and Bowes, 1965)
T.W. Moody (ed.)	*Historical Studies VI* (London, Routledge & Kegan Paul, 1968)
J.C. Beckett (ed.)	*Historical Studies VII* (London, Routledge & Kegan Paul, 1969)
T.D. Williams (ed.)	*Historical Studies VIII* (Dublin, Gill & Macmillan, 1971)
J.G. Barry (ed.)	*Historical Studies IX* (Belfast, Blackstaff Press, 1974)
G.A. Hayes-McCoy (ed.)	*Historical Studies X* (Dublin, I.C.H.S., 1976)
T.W. Moody (ed.)	*Nationality and the Pursuit of National Independence* (Belfast, Appletree Press, 1978)
A.C. Hepburn (ed.)	*Minorities in History* (London, Edward Arnold, 1978)
D.W. Harkness & M. O'Dowd (eds)	*The Town in Ireland* (Belfast, Appletree Press, 1981)
J.I. McGuire & A. Cosgrove (eds)	*Parliament and Community* (Belfast, Appletree Press, 1985)
P.J. Corish (ed.)	*Radicals, rebels and establishments* (Belfast, Appletree Press, 1985)

Contributors

Charles Doherty: Lecturer in Early and Medieval Irish History, University College, Dublin

Donnchach Ó Corráin: Associate Professor of Irish History, University College, Cork

John Scattergood: Professor of Medieval and Renaissance English, Trinity College, Dublin

Katharine Simms: Lecturer in Medieval History, Trinity College, Dublin

Brendan Bradshaw: Fellow of Queen's College, Cambridge

Seamus Deane: Professor of Modern English and American Literature, University College, Dublin

Oliver MacDonagh: W.K. Hancock Professor of History, The Institute of Advanced Studies, Australian National University, Canberra

Tom Dunne: Lecturer in Irish History, University College, Cork

Eda Sagarra: Professor of German, Trinity College, Dublin

David Hempton: Lecturer in Modern History, Queen's University, Belfast

Owen Dudley Edwards: Reader in American History, University of Edinburgh

Lawrence J. McCaffrey: Professor of History, Loyola University of Chicago

A polemical introduction:* literature, literary theory and the historian

TOM DUNNE

Historians have made surprisingly little contribution to the extensive modern theoretical debate about the nature of historical understanding, which has been conducted instead mainly by philosophers, anthropologists and, increasingly, literary theorists. There are some important exceptions, such as the *Annales* group, and some American intellectual historians,[1] but the general lack of theoretical reappraisal has been a damaging feature of Irish, as of British historical writing, and this narrower context informs much of the argument which follows. There is a growing recognition that traditional demarcations in cultural studies are inadequate and restrictive, and in particular that the scope and importance of historical inquiry can no longer be defined in terms of the work done in academic history departments. The majority of historians in the fuller sense, are to be found elsewhere, and not least in language and literature areas. These scholars concentrate on particular forms of evidence, and use specialised techniques and vocabularies, but they share with their colleagues, more specifically designated as 'historians', basic concerns with understanding past cultures, and common problems in relation to evidence, interpretation and analysis. What is required is a new appreciation by all of the full range of cultural studies and of the potential for interaction between different approaches and disciplines. As part of this process, the range of academic history needs to be extended, and if they wish to retain the central role implied in their traditional title, 'historians' have a particular responsibility not only to absorb, but to integrate and develop all the relevant approaches and skills available in related disciplines.

History has already absorbed much from economics, sociology, anthropology and other areas, and in the process it has been greatly expanded and renewed. Modern literary theories have the potential to transform

---

* The phrase is Northrop Frye's, in *Anatomy of Criticism* (Princeton, 1957). I am indebted to Kevin Barry, Pat Coughlan, Oliver MacDonagh, Clare O'Halloran and Dorinda Outram for their comments on different drafts of this introduction, and for advice on reading.

1

historical scholarship even more radically, because as well as questioning its subject matter and techniques, they demand a fundamental reassessment of its very basis, of all its component elements, whether of the structures of language and of narrative, or of the nature of interpretation. Their impact must ultimately be felt on all levels — on the historian's reading, understanding and use of sources (non-literary as well as literary), as well as on the processes involved in the writing of historical texts. An excessively narrow empiricism in modern historical research, and especially in dominant British modes, has been a major factor in the tendency to recoil in some distaste from theoretical debate. Historians have also been put off by the impenetrable jargon, the unreality and preciousness of some literary theory, a factor cited by one of the founding editors of *Literature and History,* to account for the failure of historians to contribute significantly to this important interdisciplinary journal.[2] It would appear to be equally ture that 'history' is offputting to many literary specialists, who perceive it wrongly as a kind of empirical depository, too complex and detailed to master, instead of recognising in it a literary form which they are admirably equipped to interpret. How often at conferences like the one which gave rise to this volume, do literary critics preface their remarks by saying, 'I am no historian', before going on to demonstrate that the opposite is true, while historians struggle with the unfamiliar concepts of structuralism, deconstruction and the rest, only dimly aware how historically conditioned and historically relevant are the theories involved.

Despite the predictions of Barthes and the ambition of the *Annales* school,[3] narrative history, far from dying, is assuming more sophisticated and complex forms — some of them, indeed, devised by its severest critics. The essentially fictive nature of historical narrative has long been recognised and is now common ground for a wide variety of philosophers and literary theorists. One of the most important analyses is that of Paul Ricoeur, who argues that history and fiction are related and comparable forms of discourse, in terms both of their narrative structures and the location of each in historical time. While fiction is mimetic, history writing is, in the well known phrase of Hayden White, 'a literary artefact',[4] that is, involving processes which are essentially literary, and constructed from figurative language. Such an argument is not altogether shocking to the many historians who recognise that their work is, of necessity, characterised by a form of imaginative reconstruction, and that commitment to objectivity and empirical method can do little more than operate as constraints on what, in the last analysis, is a statement as personal in its way as that of the poet or novelist. What is lacking is some structured reflection by historians on the implications of this instinctively understood feature of what they do, not least a greater awareness that they share with imaginative writers basic structures and techniques of language and narrative. This will also aid the realisation that, if all history is a form of ficiton, so too, all literary fictions are a form of history, and constitute indispensable historical evidence. Thus, for example, however committed the novelist may be to producing a work of the individual imagination, transcending particular circumstances, even perhaps to the point of ignoring the actual social world altogether, the end product will inevitably be a personal 'history' of the writer's time and place.

The intimate relationship between literature and history has particular historical roots in the eighteenth century, when the development of the modern novel was the product, not only of general social and cultural circumstances, but also of earlier developments in historical narrative.[5] Novelists, indeed, found that their readers demanded that they disguise their fictions as histories; while historians continued to regard themselves as involved in a branch of literature, or at least of the establishment of high culture, known as polite letters. Critical attitudes to sources and documentation were slow to develop and slower to take root. Jane Austen's heroine in *Northanger Abbey* wondered how, 'history, real solemn history . . . should be so dull, for a great deal of it must be invention'.[6] Forty years later, while working to change that perception of his subject, Macauley still felt that the ideal historian should 'give to truth those attractions which have been usurped by fiction'.[7] This symbiotic relationship between history and fiction in a formative period for both, was eroded gradually by romanticism, which sought to transform rather than reflect reality, and which, as Eagleton has argued, in stressing the autonomy of the imagination, became 'a comfortingly absolute alternative to history itself'.[8] The long dominance of romanticism has been a major factor in the historian's enduring distrust of imaginative literature, particularly as it has coincided with the growing empiricism of historical studies, and the false self-image which this produced for historians. Much of the theoretical groundwork has now been laid, however, to reverse this unreal and damaging polarisation.

The attack by the *Annales* school on narrative history was on the basis that it was 'novelistic' and 'dramatising' rather than 'scientific', and drew on the more fundamental critique of narrative by structuralist and poststructuralist writers. The philosophic attack on the objectivity of historical narrative as simply a western bourgeois myth was summarised elegantly in Barthes' key essay, 'Historical discourse'.[9] In arguing that there was no 'specific difference between factual and imaginary narrative', Barthes dismissed 'historical discourse' as 'essentially a product of ideology, or even of imagination', and greeted what he perceived to be the tendency to abandon 'historical narrative' as a 'fundamental ideological transformation'. The implication of this kind of analysis is that the fictive nature of historical writing constantly undermines its claims to depict 'reality', and that what is required instead is a new kind of history concerned with underlying structures. Partly in reaction, a strong defence of the role and potential of narrative, and its particular appropriateness for historical inquiry has come from American analytical philosophy and modern hermeneutic theory. For the former the case has been made particularly well by Hayden White, whose view of 'the historical text as literary artefact',[10] far from being a reproach to historians, is a reaffirmation of the value of their work. White, in effect, stands the structuralist and post-structuralist arguments on their head, in claiming that the fictive basis of history is — or ought to be — its great strength rather than its weakness. In such operations as the selection and repression of evidence, the development of plot by variation in emphasis, tone and perspective, the historian applies what are essentially literary techniques, and in this way constructs his narrative in a manner that will be meaningful to the reader. However, this 'in no way detracts from the status of historical narratives in providing a kind of knowledge', because, 'the encodation of events in terms of such plot-structures is one of the ways a culture has of making sense of both personal and public pasts'. Such a widening of the perspective by White, making history one of several literary means by which a culture understands itself and its past, is potentially liberating. Historians, he argues, 'succeed in endowing sets of past events with meaning . . . by exploiting the metaphorical similarities between sets of real events and the conventional structures of our fictions'. Indeed, 'our understanding of the past increases precisely in the degree to which we succeed in determining how far that past conforms to the strategies of sense-making that are contained in their purest form in literary art'. White concludes that, 'history as a discipline is in a bad shape today because it has lost sight of its origins in the literary imagination. In the interest of appearing objective and scientific, it has repressed, or denied to itself, its own greatest source of strength and renewal'. This seems revolutionary in terms of academic history's normal perception of itself, yet it probably involves for many historians little more than working through the implications of their private estimations of what they do when they write history. It also points to a way of jettisoning some of the more negative aspects of the Rankean legacy.

Given its basic concern with the relationship between past and present, it is not surprising that what Hans-Georg Gadamer has called the new 'historical hermeneutics', has begun to revolutionise approaches to intellectual history, partly as an alternative to Marxism.[11] The synthesis in this area achieved by Ricoeur, has been described as 'surely the strongest claim for the adequacy of narrative to the realisation of the aims of historical studies'. Ricoeur has defined as 'the ultimate problem', the need 'to show in what way history and fiction contribute, in virtue of their common narrative structure, to the description and redescription of our historical condition'. What binds together 'true history' and 'fictional history' is 'the basic historicity of human experience', and this can only be articulated by 'the mutual interplay of two narrative genres'. Through such a 'dialectic', he believes, 'the "true" histories of the past uncover the buried potentialities of the present'.[12] For Ricoeur, therefore, as for White, however different their general philosophical approach, 'real history' must engage fully with 'fictional history' if it is to fulfil adequately its central cultural role.

Of all the factors which shape the production of historical texts, perhaps none has received less attention from historians than the basic matter of language. The long search for a more scientific history has been frustrated, in part, by the lack of a specialised language, and the historian's dependence on 'ordinary educated speech'[13] means that his reading and writing of texts is powerfully conditioned by the complex of social, cultural and psychological codes of which such language is composed. The underlying structures of language have been the concern of semiotics, which can be used to enrich the sociological study of fiction, as in Umberto Eco's analysis of *Les Mystères de Paris*.[14] He described his method as 'circular', moving 'from the external social context to the internal structural context of the work', in order 'to bring out parallelisms between the ideological and rhetorical aspects'. The historian's special task, the interpretation of evidence, needs to be extended to some understanding of the significations and patterns involved in the range of 'languages' through which evidence is transmitted, as well as those in which history is written. Perhaps the most stimulating study of the historical dimensions of language is Bakhtin's dazzling tour-de-force on the novel, *The Dialogic Imagination*.[15] The historian will recognise the raw material here assigned to the novelist as his own — the flux of competing and interacting languages, evolving in ever-changing social and idelogical contexts. Bakhtin links the origins of fiction and history in a particular way, making the ancient novel responsible for the growth of historical consciousness, by developing 'a new way of conceptualising time'. The basic difference between them lay in the fact that history developed a closed form of narrative, while the novel remained experimental and open-ended. Bakhtin's view of history, in this comparison, is traditionalist, and there are now a growing number of historians who would be happy if they could claim for their form of writing, what Bakhtin considered the basis of the greater strength of the novel, that 'it dramatises the gaps that exist between what is told and the telling of it', and is 'constantly experimenting with the social, discursive and narrative asymmetries'.

Other areas of literary theory are of major relevance for history, most notably that concerned with reception, which examines the role of the reader in shaping the writing as well as the interpretation of texts.[16] It has only been possible here to indicate some of the implications of history being 'a literary artefact', and this partly in order that the use of literary evidence may appear more legitimate, more central and more accessible. In crude terms, the imaginative writer can be read as a fellow-historian, who shares the commitment to putting some pattern on the chaos of human existence, and to presenting that pattern in a meaningful and persuasive manner. None of this argument should be taken as implying that literature's chief value is as historical evidence, but neither should its primary artistic character be regarded as exhausting its meaning or importance. In practice, questions of 'evidence' and 'art' are inseparable, and the challenging of such generally accepted oppositions must be an important element in any agenda for a more broadly conceived approach to cultural analysis. Such considerations are likely to worry literary scholars rather than historians, few of whom use literary evidence. Those who do normally regard it as supplementary or secondary source material, a matter merely of colour or corroboration. A wider view of the potential of such evidence has been advanced by Oliver MacDonagh in his paper to this conference. The novel, he believes, 'vivifies, personalises and renders concrete what the historian already holds'. Furthermore, it 'suggests fresh ranges of historical investigation', and may contain 'the seeds of many doctoral dissertations and fresh or revisionary books'.[17] This is admirable, so far as it goes, but I would suggest that literary evidence can have a more profound value than that of enabling the historian to make 'a leap of the imagination', as David Hempton argues, also in this volume. His paper is a particularly fine proof of MacDonagh's two propositions, and constantly tests recent historical research by the evidence of the novels he uses.[18] MacDonagh's own analysis of *Sanditon*, however, tends to go even further, and uses a literary fragment to define in a new way the essence of an elusive period, thus demonstrating the potential of imaginative writing as *primary* rather than supplementary evidence. The logic of this is particularly clear in intellectual and cultural history, but literature can also be a central source for a vast range of social and political analysis. There seems to be no reason why literary texts cannot be used successfully as primary source material for all aspects of the most difficult, yet most fundamental feature to understand about any age or society, the ways in which it perceived and interpreted reality. These texts offer the testimony of those who were particularly concerned with such perceptions and interpretations. Like other forms of historical evidence, literature has to be treated with caution and sensitivity, its particular language and conventions understood, its bias and motivation taken into account, its limitations accepted. What I am advocating is that modern historians should study literary texts in the same detailed and systematic way as literary scholars, using such established literary critical techniques as may be useful, and even developing some new ones, perhaps, suited to their different purposes. Nor would they find modern literary theories entirely strange, as many of them correspond to guiding principles which have evolved on a more practical if less coherent level in historical research, such as the ideological nature of interpretation or the importance of the implied reader in the composition of texts.

There have, of course, been notable exceptions to the general failure of historians to take proper account of literary evidence and literary techniques, such as the work of Christopher Hill, particularly in *Milton and the English Revolution*. Most dramatic and experimental of all, perhaps, is the work of Le Roy Ladourie, whose *Carnival in Romans* used some literary as well as anthropological models in analysing the symbolism of popular festivals in pre-industrial society. More recently his exhaustive and imaginative dissection of a short eighteenth-century literary text from Languedoc, with its basis in folklore, used an even wider range of literary approaches, from structuralism, linguistics and semiotics. This remarkable study of literary evidence as a primary source, published in English as *Love, death and money in the Pays d'Oc*[19] both delineated particular literary and folk genres in an entirely new way, and established complex connections between fictional and real worlds. Lauro Martines has applied some of the same techniques to a study of the high culture of a social elite in his *Society and History in English Renaissance Verse*.[20] This book also attempts what Le Roy Ladourie avoided, a theoretical discussion of problems and approaches — a rare assessment of modern literary theories by a working historian. As such, it is a sustained and enthusiastic polemic, which may attempt too much in too short a space, but is a valuable contribution to what should become a major debate. The work of historians has also much to offer literary studies and in more areas than simply the illumination of contexts. A strong appeal for the restoration of the historical dimension to literary analysis has been a heartening feature of some recent literary criticism, notably by Marxist critics, like Frederic Jameson and Terry Eagleton.[21] The latter ends his stimulating *Literary Theory, an introduction,* with a plea for the abolition of artificial academic barriers, and the setting up instead of new departments of cultural studies. Martines has the same idea in his proposal of a new research area of 'social literary analysis', based on the proposition — 'unite historical and literary analysis and the result is bound to be a new vision'.[22] It is an exciting prospect, and the response of historians and literary critics to the challenges involved will be crucial for the future development of both forms of cultural analysis.

*   *   *   *   *

The above theoretical discussion may seem remote in some respects from the conference papers which follow, although it is largely prompted by reflection on them, and they illustrate many of the possibilities and problems discussed. Rather than theory, they offer a range of practical approaches to the historical dimensions of particular literary sources, mainly by historians, but also by some literary scholars, all of whom were also asked to reflect a little on the problems and potential of the literary sources used. The discussions after individual papers, and the two general sessions on the conference theme, also dealt with the theoretical questions raised, and important contributions were made by the general session chairmen, Nicholas Canny and Roy Foster, and from the floor by Pat Coughlan, Kevin Barry and Luke Gibbons in particular. The offerings of the historians (including that of the editor) may betray an unfortunate innocence of literary theory, but they illustrate, hopefully, the value of even modified traditional historical approaches to a wide range of literary material — as well as indicating the possibilities inherent in the future loss of such innocence! Much was learned from the contributions of the literary scholars involved including their interventions in the discussions, and a marked feature of the conference was the ease with which those from several different areas of cultural studies communicated. It is hoped that each of the case studies offered here will be a useful contribution to its own area of specialisation, and that the volume as a whole will both stimulate interest in literary sources among historians and encourage a more general debate on the many important connections between literature and history.

NOTES AND REFERENCES

1. In D. La Capra and G.L. Kaplan (eds), *Modern European intellectual history. Reappraisals and new perspectives* (Ithaca and London, 1982) a group of leading American historians discuss the current state of their discipline, with particular reference to the impact of continental theorists, including the *Annales* group.
2. R.C. Richardson, 'The identity and purpose of the journal' in *Literature and History*, Vol. ii, No. 1 (Spring 1985), pp 3-11.
3. R. Barthes, 'Historical discourse' in M. Lane (ed.), *Structuralism: a reader* (London, 1970), pp 145-55.
4. P. Ricoeur, 'The narrative function' in J.B. Thompson (ed.), *Hermeneutics and the human sciences. Essays on language, action and interpretation* (Cambridge, 1981), pp 274-96.
5. See Leo Braudy, *Narrative form in history and fiction: Hume, Fielding and Gibbon* (Princeton, 1970).
6. Jane Austen, *Northanger Abbey* (Penguin ed., 1972), p. 123.
7. J. Marriott, *English History in English Fiction* (London, 1940), pp 6-7.
8. T. Eagleton, *Literary Theory. An introduction* (Oxford, 1983), p. 20.
9. Barthes, op. cit.
10. H. White, *Tropics of discourse. Essays in cultural criticism* (Baltimore and London, 1978), Chapter III. See also, 'The question of narrative in contemporary historical theory', in *History and Theory: studies in the philosophy of history*, Vol. XXIII (1984), pp 1-33.
11. Hans-Georg Gadamer, 'The problem of historical consciousness', in P. Rabinow and W.M. Sullivan (eds), *Interpretative social science, A reader* (Berkeley, Los Angeles and London, 1970), pp 134-5. For an analysis of the implications of a key debate in hemeneutics for history, see M. Jay, 'Should intellectual history take a linguistic turn? Reflections on the Habermas-Gadamer debate', in Capra and Kaplan (eds), *Modern European intellectual history*, pp 86-110.
12. H. White, 'The question of narrative', p. 30; P. Ricoeur, 'The narrative function', pp 274, 293-4, 295-6.
13. H. White, *Tropics of discourse*, p. 94.
14. U. Eco, 'Rhetoric and idelogy in Sue's *Les Mystères de Paris*', in *The role of the reader. Explorations in the semiotics of texts* (Indiana, 1979), pp 125-43.
15. M.M. Bakhtin, *The dialogic imagination: four essays* (ed. M. Holquist) (Austin, 1981).
16. See, especially, Wolfgang Iser, *The implied reader* (Baltimore, 1974); *The act of reading* (London, 1978); D. La Capra, 'Rethinking intellectual history and reading texts' in La Capra and Kaplan (eds), *Modern European intellectual history*, pp 47-85.
17. See below, p. 130.
18. See below, p. 193.
19. C. Hill, *Milton and the English Revolution* (New York, 1979); E. Le Roy Ladourie, *Carnival in Romans* (New York, 1979); *Love, death and money in the Pays d'Oc* (Harmondsworth, 1984).
20. L. Martines, *Society and history in English renaissance verse* (Oxford, 1985).
21. F. Jameson, *The political unconscious. Narrative as a socially symbolic act* (London, 1981); T. Eagleton, *Literary theory, an introduction* (Oxford, 1983).
22. Martines, op. cit., p. 99.

The Irish hagiographer: resources, aims, results

CHARLES DOHERTY

In the seventeenth century Leribert Rosweyde (1569-1629) prepared the groundwork for what was to become the *Acta Sanctorum*.[1] On his death his work was taken up by Jean Bolland, who together with Godefroid Henschenius, set out to edit the 'lives' of all known saints of the church calendar. They began with the first of January. This month's saints appeared in volume I in 1643. The month of February followed in 1658.[2] The small groups of scholars who continued this work throughout the following centuries became known, eventually, as the *Société des Bollandistes* named after Jean Bolland, and they have attempted to complete the task. The most recent volume to appear ends on the 10th of November. It was published in 1925. This category of material must make up the single largest body of evidence for medieval life and thought. Froude, in an essay in 1852, commented on this enormous undertaking, and saw in the 'lives' a fund of lore which could be subjected to the same critical treatment which philosophers had already applied to classical mythology. He says: 'It is no more than a fraction of that singular mythology which for so many ages delighted the Christian world, which is still held in external reverence among the Romanists, and of which the modern historians, provoked by its feeble supernaturalism, and by the entire absence of critical ability among its writers to distinguish between fact and fable, have hitherto failed to speak a reasonable word'.[3] For the reasons given by Froude many scholars have dismissed this body of evidence. One cannot blame them for, at first sight, hagiography does not appear to lend itself to the same historical approach which scholars would normally use when confronted with more familiar documents.[4]

Of course, all of this is changing. In a recent collection of essays[5] there is appended an *Annotated bibliography*. This amounts to 108 pages, and provides a very comprehensive list of works on many aspects of the subject. This impressive collection (containing 1309 items) is divided into eighteen sections. Saints' 'lives' as literary works of art is not one of them.[6] This, perhaps, is not surprising. Although a few 'lives' are fine literary works, the vast bulk of them cannot be described in this way. Indeed as literary products they are sometimes crude in the extreme. For this reason hagiography as a genre can only be understood and explored within its own limitations.

Robert Hertz, whose essay appears first in the book which I have referred to above was a pupil of Emile Durkheim, and he was one of the first to use a structuralist approach in his study of the cult of St Besse.[7] A similar use of anthropological models has been used with most interesting results by Evelyne Patlagean.[8] Approached in this way the 'life' of a saint is a paradigm — a paradigm which may change according to circumstances. It operates outside historical time, and it has been this aspect, in particular, which has caused some scholars in the past to feel so disoriented that they have simply dismissed the 'lives' as having no value for the historian. However, since 'hagiography provides a timeless account of the passage of men beyond the human condition'[9] the unconscious record within the paradigm is a goldmine for the historian of social conditions, values, and mental horizons of the people of the Middle Ages.

In Ireland we have a very large body of hagiographical documents.[10] Some of them have scarcely been read, and only a small number have been critically analyzed.[11] Hagiographical writing begins here in the late sixth century, although our first texts date to the seventh. These seventh-century documents are distinguished, and each of them in its own way deserves to be described as a literary work. Much of this material came into being as a result of the development of the cults of the major saints — Brigid, Patrick, and Colum Cille. It happens at a time of physical elaboration of the cult centres, and elevation of the relics of the cult figures. Hagiographical writing is seldom undertaken for its own sake; it normally makes an appearance at a point of change. From the very beginning the 'lives' of the Irish saints are complex statements containing conscious, and, at the same time, unconscious data about the writer, his time, and his environment. The problem is to decode this information.

With our seventh-century documents we are particularly fortunate in that we know the names of the authors and their approximate, and relative dates, although scholars are far from being in agreement.[12] With the remainder of Irish hagiography we enter the unknown. When we make a comparison between the seventh-century material in terms of literary quality and what comes after we again have a contrast. As Bieler has shown[13] the 'life' of Patrick by Muirchú is a highly dramatic work, cleverly contrived, making powerful use of classical and biblical themes. Picard has likewise demonstrated the linguistic and literary command of Adamnán [14] and he has recently suggested that what, at first sight, appears to be a haphazard collection of notes by Tírechán has a definite structure and model behind it. [15] McCone in his work on the 'lives' of Brigit has suggested that the 'life' attributed to Ailerán, and dated to the mid-seventh century, although no longer extant in its original form, had a fine Latin style. [16] In a few 'lives' which are later than the seventh century there are occasional hints that the original may have been written in a reasonable Latin.

When one examines the contents of the 'lives' for historical information about the saint it can soon be seen that such evidence is thin. One exception to this is the 'life' of Colum Cille by Adamnán. Adamnán, as a young boy in Iona, would have met old men who would have been contemporaries of the saint. He cites older members of the community as sources for a variety of topics. It is because of this that we get a feeling for the personality of the saint in Adamnán's text. It is not so for other 'lives' of the seventh century. Here we are presented with shadows. By the mid-seventh century it was now at least 250 years since the introduction of christianity. The writer had little information on the fifth or even the sixth century. The documents that had survived from the missionary period were few. Tírechán, that assiduous researcher, used documents, inscriptions, crosses, tombs (both pagan and christian), placenames, oral tradition, fragments of prayers or liturgy, dyptychs, and whatever other memorials he could find. By the mid-seventh century there had also been much political change. Churches patronized by powerful dynasties of the fifth and sixth centuries declined with their protectors. The hagiography of the period is the propaganda of the survivors — their justification for having absorbed the property, and having acquired control over the rights and jurisdictions, of others; and of course it also reflects their pretensions and claims.

As we have seen, the hagiography of the seventh century is varied and, by contemporary standards, is of good quality. The material of the eighth and subsequent centuries follows a paradigm which is uniform. Within this framework motifs borrowed from the bible or other 'lives', or from secular sagas, occur with a boring regularity. The basic ingredients of the paradigm are the miraculous events surrounding the conception, and birth of the saint, accompanied by other-worldly signs of his future sanctity. This corresponds to the conception of the hero in secular saga — the *compert*. Then follows his boyhood deeds (*macgnímartha*) in which the power latent within him becomes evident in his capacity to produce miracles. Next is his voyage through life — his adult adventures (*echtrai*) when he founds churches and makes friendship with other saints. This is the body of the 'life' and it is here that most information is conveyed concerning the churches owned or claimed by the paruchia or monastic federation, and the relationships that exist between the saint's paruchia and those of his neighbours. The final section of the paradigm is the death of the saint (*bás*).

Almost all of these 'lives', as we now have them, are to be found in manuscripts of the post-Norman period. Without detailed examination they may be assigned to the period between the tenth and the twelfth centuries. Some, because of references to the reform of the Church, may be tentatively assigned to the twelfth century in their present form. It is clear, however, that the texts, as we now have them, are highly stratified, rather like an archaeological excavation. The original 'acta' have grown as the result of copying and rewriting over the centuries. The end result is often a text which contains many accretions of legends and motifs introduced with a particular purpose, at a particular time, in the history of the text. The work of separating the various layers is similar to the work carried out by biblical scholars on the various books of the bible.

I would now like to look at the 'lives' of St Aidan or, as he was more popularly known, St Maedóg (Mo-Áed-óc), founder of the monastery of Ferns in Co. Wexford and also patron saint of the church of Drumlane in Co. Cavan and Rossinver in Co. Leitrim. 'Lives' of this saint are in both Latin and Irish. The Latin 'lives' are in British Library, Cotton MS. Vespasian A xiv, f.96v-f.104v — a manuscript dating to c. 1200[17] Plummer edited this 'life' in his *Vitae Sanctorum Hiberniae*.[18] It occurs also in the fourteenth-century *Codex Salmanticensis* and has been edited most recently by W.W. Heist.[19] There is a copy in Primate Marsh's Library in Dublin, MS. V. 3.4 beginning f.41c, dating to c. 1400,[20] and two copies in the Rawlinson collection in Oxford.[21] A further copy is in the Franciscan Convent Library, Dublin. It is a copy of Rawl. B 505. The 'life' in the Salmanticensis collection, those in the Rawlinson collection and in the Franciscan Library are basically the same. There are two important variants — that in the Cotton manuscript, which is also the most 'primitive' (V), and that in Marsh's Library (M). It is basically these two texts that I would like to examine.

It is fairly clear that V was taken from an Irish original. M was developed from a text like V but contains none of the peculiarities of V. It is longer than V but this is mostly due to a more literary approach than the addition of material. From internal evidence it can be shown that M is a further historical development of V. In M, 'Things likely to cause difficulty or scandal are toned down or omitted, and style and matter are more homogeneous than in S'.[22] We may look at the version in the Cotton manuscript V first.

The earliest historical stratum in the 'life' is the record of the saint's birth-place and the people from whom he descended. Often a saint of humble tribal origins is given a more respectable pedigree in the course of time, but in this case there seems to have been no interference. His father was Sétna of the Uí Moccu Uais (a branch of the Airgialla) and his mother was of the Uí Amalgaid (a tribal-name now fosalized in the barony of Tirawley in Co. Mayo). His birth-place was the island or crannóg of Inis Brechmaige in Mag Slécht in Co. Cavan. As is often the case in the 'lives' it is just such incidental material which contains information to be found nowhere else. There is no other record of the Uí Moccu Uais having been in this area of Co. Cavan. After a sojourn in Wales, like many other Irish saints, he returns to Leinster where he eventually stays.

It will simply not be possible to go into all the details of this 'life' here so I will examine only the major points. When one reads through V one is struck by what seems to be a glaring inconsistency. In V §34 Maedóg meets his successor and desires to go to Heaven: *Set Dominus eum diutius in carne manere multorum causa voluit.* This is our first hint that the compiler of the 'life' had more material at hand, which he wished to include, and the death of the saint in one of the sources he was using causes him a momentary embarrassment. Further on in V §43 an individual called Sárán kills Brandub, king of the Leinstermen, but a few paragraphs later on in V §54 Brandub is alive and in such a perfect state of health that he defeats the forces of the North. It is clear that this 'life' was put together without much regard for these obvious inconsistencies. This very lack of style makes it a more valuable source. As can be seen in the more literary version, M, these inconsistencies are smoothed somewhat. The episode where Maedóg wishes to go to heaven is separated from the story in which he meets his successor and is inserted as a separate paragraph after the killing of Brandub. This rounds if off rather better, especially since mention of Brandub is omitted from the episode towards the end where the Leinstermen do battle with the Northerners.

In V §24 mention is made of *Cluain Mar.* In M §24 this causes embarrassment since the author is at pains to point out the *proper* name of the place, *Cluain Mor Dícholla Gairbh (qui Dicholla erat sanctus abbas ipsius loci sub cura patris Maedhog).* Now there are two places called Cluain Mór. One, Cluain Mór Maedóg in the barony of Rathvilly, Co. Carlow, and another, Cluain Mór Dícholla Gairbh, Clonmore, four miles south-west of Enniscorthy, Co. Wexford. The latter through history is little more than a name. Cluain Mór Maedóg, on the other hand, was a large monastery appearing occasionally in the annals, and it was famous for its cemetery. In the *Martyrology of Tallaght,* which dates to c. 800 we find mention of *Maedoc hua Dunlaing i Cluain Mor.* In the genealogies this saint's pedigree is found among the North Leinster dynasty of the Uí Dúnlainge, and one of the points given for the location of his family is the river Tolka, north of Dublin. Here we are faced with two saints of the same name — one a Leinsterman whose festival is recorded at April 11 in the martyrologies, and the other from Cavan in the kingdom of Bréifne whose feast day is January 31. From the appearance of Cluain Mór in V, and the embarrassment it causes in M, and in particular the episode common to both 'lives' in which the saint wishes to go to heaven but God tells him that his time has not yet come, we must be faced with two traditions, and possibly two 'lives' conflated, with Maedóg of Ferns emerging the victor. The annals are not particularly helpful on this matter. The entry of the death of Maedóg in the Annals of Ulster is an interpolation by a later hand. This does not mean that the entry in *A.U.* sa. 624-625 is wrong, but it is not contemporary. *Chronicum Scotorum* has the death of Maedóg recorded twice at 625 and 656, as does the *Annals of Tigernach,* at 625 and 659. This may contain annalistic evidence of the orbits of two saints but it cannot be proved. The folklore of south Leinster preserves a tradition that Maedóg had a 'wild' brother who built a rival church on the other side of the river Bann.[23] This may be a folk memory of the other Maedóg but it cannot prove anything by itself.

Why should the 'acta' of these two saints be combined? In order to answer this question we must look at the politics, ecclesiastical and secular, in south Leinster during the pre-Norman period. Information on the monastery of Ferns only becomes contemporary with the record of the death of Dachua Luachra in 654. It is not until the second quarter of the following century that we begin to see the rise in importance of the monastery in the secular politics of the local Uí Chennselaigh dynasty. During the lifetime of the saint the Uí Chennselaigh, under their king Brandub, who died in 605, had been at their most powerful. Brandub had been king of the province and had defended it against the encroachments of the Uí Néill in the midlands.[24] Following his reign they had had to take second place to the Uí Dúnlainge, centred on Kildare in north Leinster, and it was not until the eleventh century (with a possible brief exception) that they again dominated the province. During this period they consolidated their position in south Leinster — the various segments of the dynasty taking over the lands of the politically unsuccessful and politically irrelevant communities in the area. From the early eighth century onwards their position was secure. For a brief period under their king, Áed mac Colgan, 734-738, they were sufficiently powerful to dominate Leinster. It is significant that it was at precisely this time that they gained control of the monastery of Ferns. This can be paralleled in the previous century, for as soon as the Uí Dúnlainge first emerged as the dominant force in north Leinster they immediately gained control of Kildare. It was at this point that Bresal, brother of Áed, became abbot of Ferns. He died in *A.U.* sa. 749. The segment of the dynasty to which he belonged was the Síl Cormaic who by now controlled the area from the coast of Wexford across to the river Barrow in Co. Carlow. It is clear that Ferns was growing in wealth, no doubt under the patronage of this dynasty. This is still in evidence in the remains of the stone high-crosses on the site. By analogy with what was happening on other sites throughout the country we may say that the monastery by now as a large and populous ceremonial centre at the core of a network of estates, and the focal point of a redistributive system. It was rich in lands, animals, and people. No segment of a dynasty interested in controlling the kingship could be successful without gaining access to such wealth.

Our first indication that this is the case is in *A.U.* sa. 769 when a battle took place at Ferns between the Síl Cormaic and their rivals in south Wexford, the Síl Maeluidir (a name fossilized in the barony of Shelmaliere). This represented a victory, albeit short-lived, for the Síl Maeluidir in their bid to control the kingship of south Leinster. By *A.U.* sa. 783 they tried again, and on this occasion a *bellum* a 'war' took place in the monastery between the abbot and the steward. The abbot here was a Síl Cormaic appointment while the steward belonged to the Síl Maeluidir. By 809 the Síl Maeluidir had gained the kingship of south Leinster but the monastery still lay within the control of the Síl Cormaic. Things came to a head in 817 when the Síl Maeluidir, leading the forces of the monastery of Taghmon, mounted a major attack against the *familia* of Ferns. In this *bellum* 400 people were killed. This episode dispels any illusions we may have about the 'golden age' of the Irish church or about monasteries as islands of peace and retreat. Shortly after this 'war' took place the Vikings put an end to the ambitions of the Síl Maeluidir. Situated on the south coasts of Wexford, in control of Tech Munnu (Taghmon), they felt the full force of the Norse attacks in this area. The Síl Cormaic survived.

During the course of the ninth century the dynasty split up into two further segments — the Síl nÉlathaigh (fossilized in the barony of Shillelagh in south Co. Wicklow), and the Síl nOnchon (the ancestors of the

MacMurchada family). It was the Síl nOnchon who were, eventually, to overshadow the others. Their arrival on the scene may be heralded by an abbot of Ferns called Diarmait who it is tempting to suggest was a member of this dynasty. He died in 870 (*A.F.M.* sa. 868). Conditions during the ninth and tenth centuries were unsettled. The Norse provided a stimulus to the transformation that had been taking place in society, and hastened political changes. Ferns had been attacked by the Norse in 835[25] and again in 839,[26] and it may be that this may account for what appears to have been a break in the succession to the abbacy in the early ninth century. In common with other churches of the late ninth and tenth centuries we begin to find abbots of Ferns who are in control of several churches at the same time. Lachtnán mac Mochthigern abbot of Ferns was bishop of Kildare and died in *A.U.* 875. A Fergill, recorded only in the *A.F.M.*, as abbot of Ferns sa. 880 and as abbot of Cluain Mór Maedóg sa. 887 seems to be a single person who is a double office holder. A Lachtnán who died in 905 may have been a member of the Síl Maeluidir (LL 317 ac29);[27] his son Fionnachta died in sa. 957 and is given the title of *airchinnech*.

By the late eighth century Síl Cormaic power had shifted westwards and their power center was now Ráith Etain (Rathedan) in the barony of Idrone in Co. Carlow. Áedh mac Duibhghiolla, Uí Chennselaigh king of Uí Dróna who died in 911 was buried at Ferns, according to a poem preserved in the *A.F.M.* sa. 906. It is clear that the monastery still claimed the Síl Cormaic and their descendants as its patrons. The poem makes the claim that the ancestral king, Brandub, was buried there also. The relationship between church and dynasty remained close. The first reference to a *comarba* of the monastery occurs in the title given to Laidhgnén, *comarba* of Ferns and Tallaght, who died in 939.[28] This title means 'heir' of the saint, and was normally given to the person who resided in the mother house as head of the monastic federation. It also had more secular overtones. The descendants of this man virtually monopolized the abbacy during the tenth and eleventh centuries.

Throughout the tenth century the power of the Síl nOnchon had been growing despite the opposition of the Síl nÉlathaigh. These segments in the tenth century were following the same pattern of expansion and consolidation of their forebears, and were doing so at their expense. Towards the end of the tenth century the Síl nOnchon house itself showed signs of internal tension. Áed mac Echtigern *tánaise* of Uí Chennselaigh was killed in 1003 (*A.U.* sa. 1002) in the oratory of Ferns by the king of Uí Chennselaigh, Donnchad (Mael-na-mBó). He was clearly regarded as a serious threat to the ruling king. Áed's brother, Coirpre, died in 974 (*A.F.M.*

sa. 972) as *comarba* of Cluain Mór Maedóg. This site would seem to have been the power-base of the rival faction. This becomes quite clear in the next generation when in 1040 (*A.F.M.* sa. 1040) Diarmait mac Mael-na-mBó plundered the churches of his rivals including Cluain Mór Maedóg. This king was ruthless. Not merely did he establish himself securely within south Leinster, but he was the first of the Uí Chennselaigh kings to dominate the province of Leinster (with the possible exception which I have mentioned above) since the reign of Brandub who died in 605. The domination established by this king was to last until the coming of the Normans in the twelfth century.

At this point we may return to our 'lives'. We have some external evidence which helps to provide a rough dating for the V text. Kathleen Hughes has shown that the manuscript, Vespasian A xiv, containing the V text was copied at Gloucester c. 1200 from material gathered at Llanbadarn Fawr in the 1130s.[29] Rhigyfarch, who wrote a 'life' of St David possibly as early as 1081, used the 'lives' of Maedóg and Brendan in his compilation.[30] Rhyigyfarch, son of Sulien, 'the wise', belonged to the ecclesiastical family of Llanbadarn Fawr, so it is natural that the 'life' of Maedóg which he used should be bound with the other material compiled at this monastery. His father, Sulien, later bishop of St Davids had studied in Ireland about 1059-1072[31] and it is likely that on his return to Wales he brought the 'life' of Maedóg with him. The V text may have been translated from an Irish original into Latin especially for this purpose.

From the above we may suggest that a text of V (possibly in Irish) was extant in Ireland sometime before 1072. In this text the 'Brandub' episode is prominent. As I have suggested above, the 'life' is a rather unskilful conflation of the 'acta' or the 'lives' of two Maedógs. This conflation may have been in Irish, from Irish originals. This Irish text has been lost and is represented by the Latin translation of V. I think that we can place this conflated version in the reign of Diarmait mac Mael-na-mBó who was king of Leinster from 1042 to 1072.

In the eleventh century there was a renewed interest, or rather a quickening of interest in native literature. One product of this period may help to throw further light on the 'life', and this is the Bórumha saga. In origin this was a tribute due to the king of Tara from the Leinstermen. Mac Eoin has shown that the tradition is first found in early poetry and genealogies. This is given unity and propaganda value in the work of Orthanach ua Caellama who died in 839. The outline of the story as it is found at its fullest development is represented by the work of Flann mac Maelmaedóg, *airchinnech* of Glenn Uissen (in Uí Bairrche), who died in 979. The final stage in the eleventh century is the work of a redactor who gives the material a pro-Laigin slant and introduces the Leinster saints, Moling, Maedóg, and bishop Áedán of Glendalough into the story. From a study of placenames and the prominence given to Moling, Tech Moling in Co. Kildare is almost certainly the place of origin of the final version of the tale.[32]

The Bórumha saga, then, has borrowed from hagiographical themes and tales current in the Leinster monasteries of the time. In its final form it has a strong hagiographical flavour about it. The traditions about Brandub in the 'life' seem to represent an independent tradition, which does not show borrowings from the saga. The later version of the 'life', which can be shown to be twelfth-century, M §24, shows that the author is aware of the saga. The most interesting point is the fact that the Maedóg of the saga is Maedóg ua Dúnlaing. He is the saint of Cluain Mór Maedóg *not* the Maedóg of Ferns. There may have been a 'life' of Maedóg of Cluain Mór in which the Brandub material played a large part. Even if there was not an actual life, it does show that in the eleventh century the traditions concerning Maedóg of Cluain Mór were strong enough to retain the identity of their hero in the face of the more powerful foundation at Ferns. On the whole it tends to place the conflation of the 'acta' of the two saints nearer to the time of the final edition of the saga in the eleventh century. The propaganda value of this saga would have been of greatest use to Diarmait mac Mael-na-mBó. I think that it was probably compiled during his reign. Mac Eoin's suggestion that it is Leinster's answer to the Táin is good in the light of the historical background.

In the eleventh century the ambitions of Ferns, Tech Moling, the hereditary ecclesiastical family controlling Ferns — the Uí Laidhgneáin, and Diarmait mac Mael-na-mBó, meet in Conchobhar Ua Laidhgneáin, *airchinnech* of Ferns and Tech Moling who died in *A.F.M.* sa. 1062 and Ughaire, of the same name and office died in *A.U.* sa. 1085. Whether or not it was an Ua Laidhgneáin who compiled this material, it was such a combination of forces which gave birth to the saga and the V text.

There is a final point which may allow us to tie down the creation of the V text a little closer. In V §33 the first of the three requests granted to Maedóg by God is *Quicunque de genere Laginensium sederit in sede illius, non erit secum in celo.* Since all officers of Ferns who can be identified with reasonable certainty were Leinstermen this does not make much sense. However, there was a break in the monopoly of comarbship held by the Ua Laidgneáin family after the death of Conchobhar in 1043 whom I have mentioned above. He had not been given the title of *comarba* merely *airchinnech* that is the head of a dependent church — not the mother church.

A bishop of Ferns, Diarmaid Ua Rodacháin, died in *A.F.M.* 1050. But more important is the death notice of one Conaing Ua Faircheallaigh, *airchinneach Droma Lethain, comharba Maedhócc la Connachtaibh occus Laighniu* in *A.F.M.* 1059. It is clear that the headship of the federation has shifted to Ua Ruairc's territory of Bréifne. The Uí Faircheallaigh were the hereditary family at Drumlane and the chief ecclesiastical family in Bréifne throughout the middle ages. This is their first appearance on the stage and it represents an enormous challenge to the Leinster portion of the paruchia. Given the propaganda value of the 'life' for Diarmait mac Mael-na-mBó, it may not be going too far to suggest that the text of V as we now have it, was put together between the accession of Diarmait to the kingship of Leinster in 1042 and the death of Conaing Ua Fairchellaigh in 1059.

The writing of the V text may have been a response to the new developments within the paruchia, but as we have seen it also reflected more immediate interests. Diarmait's opposition to the power base of his rivals, Cluain Mór Maedóg, is paralleled in the hagiography. The conflation of the 'acta' of the two saints surely represents the attempt to prevent the cult at Clonmore from being used as propaganda by the rival segment of the dynasty. Ferns continued to be the main church in south Leinster.

There are very many aspects which could be the subject of comment in this 'life' particularly when a political background can be established. However I have not had the time to develop these. Some of them would strengthen the case which I have already made. The main point of this exercise is to clearly establish that this literary genre, far from being the outpourings of an over-credulous medieval mentality, is within its own terms of reference, a sophisticated means of communication which is of the utmost value to the historian, not merely for its capacity to throw further light upon secular and ecclesiastical propaganda but on an area which has scarcely been touched upon as yet — the exploration of the mind of medieval man, as Froude, writing in 1852, may have been the first to realize.

NOTES AND REFERENCES

1.   He stated his ideas and plans in his *Fasti sanctorum quorum Vitae in belgicis bibliothecis manuscriptae* published in Antwerp in 1607. His chief work, the *Vitae Patrum*, was described as '. . .véritablement la pierre fondamentale des *Acta Sanctorum*' by H. Delehaye, S.J. in *L'oeuvre des Bollandistes à travers trois siècles 1615-1915* (2nd ed., Bruxelles, 1959), p. 17.

2. Delahaye, *L'oeuvre des Bollandistes*, pp 22-8; R. Aigrain, *L'Hagiographie, ses sources, ses méthodes, son histoire* (Paris, 1953), pp 329-34.

3. J.A. Froude, *Short studies on great subjects* (London, 1906; reissue, 1964), p. 122.

4. See the comments of E. Patlagean in Stephen Wilson (ed.), *Saints and their cults: studies in religious sociology, folklore and history* (Cambridge, 1983), pp 103-4.

5. Wilson, *Saints and their cults.*

6. It must be said that in Wilson, *Saints and their cults*, pp 382-88, there are over eighty references, some of which deal with this aspect of the subject.

7. Ibid., pp 55-100; J. Maitre, 'La sociologie de catholicisme chez Czarnowski, Halbwachs, Hertz et Van Gennep' in *Archives de Sociologie des Religions*, 21 (1966), pp 55-68.

8. Wilson, *Saints and their cults*, pp 101-21.

9. Ibid., p. 111.

10. The main collections of 'lives' are to be found in Charles Plummer (ed.), *Vitae sanctorum Hiberniae* (2 vols, Oxford, 1910); *Bethada náem nÉrenn; Lives of Irish Saints* . . . (2 vols, Oxford, 1922, reprint, 1968); Whitley Stokes (ed.), *Lives of Saints from the Book of Lismore* (Oxford, 1890); W.W. Heist (ed.), *Vitae Sanctorum Hiberniae ex codice olim Salmanticensi nunc Bruxellensi* (Bruxelles, 1965); Ludwig Bieler (ed.), *Four Latin Lives of St Patrick,* Scriptores Latini Hiberniae vol viii (Dublin, Institute for Advanced Studies, 1971); *The Patrician Texts in the Book of Armagh,* Scriptores Latini Hiberniae vol x (Dublin, Institute for Advanced Studies, 1979). References to other 'lives' and hagiographical material may be found in Charles Plummer, *Miscellanea Hagiographica Hibernica* (Bruxelles, 1925, reprint 1984); James F. Kenney, *The sources for the early history of Ireland: an introduction and guide, vol. i: ecclesiastical* (New York, 1929, reprint 1966); Michael Lapidge and Richard Sharpe, *A Bibliography of Celtic Latin literature 400-1200,* Royal Irish Academy Dictionary of Medieval Latin from Celtic Sources, Ancillary publications 1 (Dublin, 1985), pp 101-30. For two recent surveys of Irish hagiographical documents see Maire Herbert, 'Beathaí na naomh', *Léachtaí Cholm Cille* (Maynooth), viii (1977), pp 5-18; and Kim McCone, 'An introduction to Early Irish Saints' Lives', *The Maynooth Review*, 11 (1984), pp 26-59.

11. Most work has been carried out on the 'lives' of the major saints, Patrick, Brigit and Colm Cille.

12. L. Bieler, 'The Celtic hagiographer', *Studia Patristica*, 5 (1959), pp 243-65; McCone, op. cit.

13. L. Bieler, 'Muirchu's Life of St Patrick as a work of literature', *Medium Aevum*, 43 (1974), pp 219-33.

14. J.-M. Picard, 'The Schaffhausen Adomnán — a unique witness to Hiberno-Latin', *Peritia*, 1 (1982), pp 216-49.

15. Lecture give to the M. Phil. Seminar in University College Dublin, March 1985. Article to appear in *Peritia,* vol. 4.

16. K. McCone, 'Brigit in the seventh century: a saint with three lives?', *Peritia*, 1 (1982), pp 124-5.

17. K. Hughes, 'British Museum MS. Cotton *Vespasian A.xiv* ('Vitae Sanctorum Wallensium'): its purpose and provenance', in N.K. Chadwick, K. Hughes, C. Brooke and K. Jackson (eds), *Studies in the Early British Church* (Cambridge, 1958), pp 183-200; C. Brooke, 'St Peter of Gloucester and St Cadoc of Llancarfan', in N.K. Chadwick (ed.), *Celt and Saxon, Studies in the Early British Border* (Cambridge, 1963), pp 183-99.

18. C. Plummer, *Vitae SS Hib.*; vol. ii (1910), pp 295-311.

19. W.W. Heist (ed.), *Vitae Sanctorum Hiberniae ex codice olim Salmanticensi nunc Bruxellensi* (1965), pp 234-47.
20. Also edited by Plummer, *Vitae SS Hib.,* ii (1910), pp 141-63.
21. Rawlinson B 485 f.154d dating to c. 1350 or 1200-1250, and Rawlinson B 505 f.180c dating to c. 1300-50. The text in Rawl. B 505 is a copy of that in Rawl. B 584. See Plummer, *Vitae SS Hib.,* i (1910), pp ix-xxiii.
22. C. Plummer, *Vitae SS Hib.,* i (1910), p. xxii.
23. Patrick Kennedy, *Legendary fictions of the Irish Celts* (London and New York, 2nd ed., 1891), pp 302 f.
24. For the political background in Leinster see F.J. Byrne, *Irish Kings and High-kings* (London, 1973), pp 130-64.
25. *A.F.M.* sa. 834.
26. *A.F.M.* sa. 838.
27. M.A. O'Brien, *Corpus genealogiarum Hiberniae,* vol. 1 (Dublin Institute for Advanced Studies, 1962), p. 349.
28. *A.F.M.* sa. 937.
29. Hughes, in N. Chadwick, *Studies in the Early British Church,* pp 183-200.
30. Ibid., p. 190.
31. C. O'Rahilly, *Ireland and Wales* (London, 1924).
32. G. Mac Eoin, 'The mysterious death of Loeghaire mac Néill', *Studia Hibernica,* 8 (1968), pp 22-48.

Legend as Critic

DONNCHADH Ó CORRÁIN

Sed ego qui scripsi hanc historiam aut uerius fabulam quibusdam fidem in hac historia aut fabula non accomodo. Quaedam enim ibi sunt praestrigia demonum, quaedam autem figmenta poetica, quaedam similia uero, quaedam non, quaedam ad delectationem stultorum.

Twelfth-century scribe of Táin Bó Cúalnge, LL 104b.

We imagine that we remember things as they were, while in fact all we carry into the future are fragments which reconstruct a wholly illusory past.

John Banville, Birchwood (London, 1973), chap. 1.

The term legend in the title is meant to name a kind of discourse in narrative form which seems, to me at least, to stand in an intermediate position between myths (the greater and more remote — in a sense, primary — narratives which purport to emplot cosmologies, recount theomachies, provide the aetiology of human character, and the like) and 'ordinary' or common-or-garden fictions, close to the reader's own time and experience (perhaps one should say mentality) that make no pretence at 'philosophical depth' or 'wisdom' and, consciously at least, have nothing much to say about 'public affairs', 'the historical process', or similarly weighty matters. These distinctions (if they may be so called, for I make no claim that they are inherent in the narratives themselves), are working demarcations rather than categories, and may be useful props in attempting to present some reflections, of a kind historians tend to be preoccupied with, on certain kinds of narratives in early Irish literature. At the least, they may be useful to the extent of allowing one to set up some kinds of opposition between myth, legend, and 'ordinary' fiction.

These legends, essentially narratives produced by the early Irish mandarin caste, must be denied the name myth, if myth is the fabulated origin of the ultimate things, because christianity in the form of an economically highly developed and intellectually richly articulated ecclesiastical culture, provided the all-embracing mythology of society and one that — as I hope to show — mediated and subsumed the pagan past.

Neither are these legends 'ordinary' fictions, as described above, for they deal in kings and kingship, the legitimation and the norms of political power, the origins of institutions, the nature of law, the function of the scholarly caste, the role of the hero within settled society and without, the relationship of the (often very largely folkloristic) otherworld to christian society, the bond of lord and vassal, and similar group, public, and political matters. Besides, their authors and shapers are learned, very self-conscious as a caste, and capable of a high degree of reflection on their role and their products.[1]

Again, they cannot be called 'historical texts'. Old-fashioned scholarship, on its own terms, denies them historicity: they do not report what happened, and to the degree to which they do report it, they do not do so in an appropriate way; hence their 'mythologizing' and 'legend-building' is formally opposed to history.[2] But other scholarly fashions also exclude them. Hayden White's dictum:

I will consider the historical text as what it most manifestly is — that is to say, a verbal structure in the form of narrative prose discourse that purports to be a model or icon of past structures and processes in the interest of explaining what they were by representing them[3]

does not, I think, save them for 'history'. They are 'narrative prose discourses', they do use 'models or icons of past structures and processes', but what they purport to be (or to do) is quite another matter. One cannot assert that they confine themselves to explaining the past in one way or another, or even that they purport to explain the past at all. Some, as we shall see, appear to be a commentary on the present while others are models for action in future time while framing their arguments in terms of the past.

The case for keeping the term legend is somewhat strengthened by the early Irish term for this kind of literature, *légend, léigenn,* a derivative of latin *legendum,* the primary meaning of which is written literature and literate scholarship. The principal medieval exponent of the type of literature we are discussing is the *fer légind,* often rendered 'lector' and translated into Latin by the learned John Colgan in the seventeenth century as *scholasticus.*

The legends are often described as belonging to 'tradition' or being the product of 'tradition', and since that term will be used here, it is only right that I should offer some explanation of the value I attach to it.

Communities, it seems, define their present identity and political awareness by choosing their past, for the constituents of the past and the past itself are not 'found' or 'uncovered', but constructed. From a very wide range of symbols, the members of a community choose a past which, once chosen, is to them a single and ineluctable reality, an absolutely valid historical interpretation. Yet they choose their past from many possible pasts and the choice itself is conditional in that it is constantly reaffirmed (and reaffirmation must imply its opposite), adjusted, or radically revised to meet the conscious and unconscious needs of the community as a living organism. The choice is not necessarily nor usually a homogeneous one nor is it constructed of non-conflicting constituents. Some groups within the community at varying levels and for various reasons of group solidarity, geographical contiguity, segementary identity and the like, interpret the group's past in their own way and thus choose a somewhat different identity which can (and does) issue in conflict. Conflict management in a given community — the achievement of a subjectively tolerable level of social and political consensus — is the management of cultural politics, the control of the past. The handiest term to name the cumulative reality of the making of such choices, the methods by which they are carried on, the materials of 'memory' from which they are continuously made, and their consequences is tradition. However, tradition, though it points to ways, is not the dead hand of the dead nor is it a pre-determining code (like a biological one) which cannot be changed (at least consciously and in conscionable time) but a series of sets of *possible* options which allow the community to interpret and re-interpret its past and thus choose its present in terms compatible with its own internal rhythm of continuity and change. If tradition is understood in this way (and not as mindless repetitions of a static model of the past, which seems to be the view of the majority of Celticists), then the legends are traditional.

Reference has been made above to the materials of 'memory' from which the past is chosen and it may be useful to look a little more closely at it here. Memory of the past alone makes criticism of the present possible. In absolute terms, the kind of memory — whether Rankean state-of-the-archives reports, Wordsworthian 'emotion recollected in tranquillity', the achievements of twentieth-century historiography, or the traditional legends of medieval Irish mandarin managers of the past — is not the fundamental pre-condition, for any or all of these can bring about the necessary conjunction of past and present. However, the quality of the memory and the manner of its management by its keepers and its reception by its consumers and users, determine its effects. In general, the more extensive, varied and subtle the 'record' of the past (the imagined past, if you prefer), the more complexified by rhetorical discourse, symbolic realization, logical analysis and self-conscious (though not necessarily logical) reflection, the greater the potential range of criticism of one's society and of one's present in it, and the more varied the means of communicating it. The converse also holds good. That potential may or may not be realised: it is enabled or disabled by other factors, and the most important of these has to do with the identity and purpose of those who have control of the past. In the present case, who chooses the early Irish past, who 'keeps the memory', and controls its expression?

The keepers of the past were a very self-aware, highly educated mandarin caste. Whatever hereditary oral-learned classes that may have survived from the pagan past (and this inheritance has, in my view, been greatly overstated) had been christianised at an early date — in any event, long before the surviving texts were written — and had merged with the clerical literati who brought with them much of the learning and culture of christian late antiquity, not only in the matter of content but of form. The channels of communication were kept open with the Latin West and somewhat later works, such as Isidore's *Etymologiae*, reached Ireland quickly and were avidly read and assimilated.[4] The ecclesiastical scholars, grammarians (of Latin and Irish), poets, canonists, 'secular' lawyers and historians formed a single mandarin caste whose writings, in Latin and in the vernacular are the products of a single, if latitudinarian, ecclesiastical culture. The members of this caste modelled themselves consciously on the tribe of Levi and saw their position in society as being similar to the priestly/levitical caste in the Old Testament. In fact, this is a very perceptive reading of Old-Testament history in combination with a high level of self-awareness in regard to their own society and the function of their own caste within it: the model works. As the Latin and vernacular law tracts show, this caste of hereditary (sometimes quasi-hereditary) scholars quite self-consciously held themselves in high esteem and filled roles of very considerable political and social importance. As early as the seventh century, they reduced the Irish past to a system, fitted Ireland's pre-history into the story of the nations as told in the Old Testament and in the works of the ancients, and traced the origin of the Irish in an unbroken line of ascent to Noah and to Adam. With the passage of time, the text grew more elaborate and in the eleventh- and twelfth-century version, 'In Lebor Gabála', won universal acceptance. The learned tradition became the anchor in time and space of a vast web of kinship, expressed in most elaborate genealogical tracts, linking the Irish kings and nobility to one another, to their ancestors, and ultimately to world history, to the patriarchs and Adam. Here, literature, in the sense of extended narratives, lies close to genealogy in its origin, for while pedigree may be enough to prove the race, aetiological narrative is needed to legitimate the dynasty, to emplot statements of right, claims of precedence, assertions of destiny or divine right, and the like. The mandarin caste itself, quite apart from being ecclesiastical in culture, was recruited from the discard segments of royal and aristocratic kindreds and shared, therefore, many of the values of noble society.[5] Hence its latitudinarianism and artistic tolerance, amply evidenced in the literary *corpus* and the subtle treatment of the pagan past in legal as well as literary texts. Hence, too, the profoundly aristocratic system of values in Irish traditional legends, whether hagiographical or 'secular', where only the saint and the scholar (or their conventional literary equivalent, the druid) are on the same footing as the king and the aristocratic hero.

The texts we possess, whether of law, saga, dynastic legend or genealogy, are the work-books of these mandarin specialists. We are, so to speak, looking over their shoulders and this has its own dangers, for we see their raw materials without their explanatory discourses — the lecturer's notes are not lecture.

Take, for example, the following problem. The received framework of Irish history and pre-history was, as we have seen, elaborated in 'In Lebor Gabála' and related legends. These texts linked the Irish with sacred history and brought them into contact with Mosaic Egypt. Side by side with this general historical explanation, however, are explanations of particular phenomena. I instance two.

The Irish lawyers, in the seventh century and later, were well aware that much of their legal material was borrowed though not slavishly from the Pentateuch, and there evidently was much debate in Irish learned circles as to the nature of the law in use in pre-christian Ireland and the relationship between inherited and borrowed elements in Irish law. Non-narrative discussions in the Latin and vernacular laws indicate that these questions were posed at a sophisticated level. The following tale, which, as it stands, is no later than the eleventh or early twelfth century, occurs as one of the introductions to the law tracts:

The first author that ever was in Ireland was Aimirgin Glúingeal the poet. He was a foster-son of Caí Caínbrethach, one of the 72 disciples of the school of Fénius Farsaid. It was that Caí who learned the Law of Moses before he came from the east and he gave judgements according to the Law [of Moses], and thus that matter is related. When Fénius sent his 72 disciples to learn the many languages throughout the world, it was Caí who went to Egypt, though he was a Hebrew by origin, and he learned the Egyptian language. He told Pharaoh about the dispersal of the school throughout the world and it was with Caí that the messengers came from Pharaoh asking Fénius to come to him. And the reward he gave them was that Scot, daughter of Pharaoh, was given as wife to Nél son of Fénius. Hence the Irish are called Scotti. When the school and their teacher had come to Pharaoh they learned Egyptian with Caí. This is the time when the great signs were wrought in Egypt i.e. the plague *et ailia quae in lege scripta sunt et cetera*. When Fénius and all the scholars saw the great judgements which were performed *per seruos Dei* they went to learn with them for they considered that it was through superior knowledge and application that the Israelites outdid the Egyptian druids and performed the many signs. When the Israelites went in flight, Caí went with Moses. The school fled in terror of the signs already mentioned, did not go on the hosting with Pharaoh, and for fear of Pharaoh and his reproach on his return, Fénius put to sea. Caí remained in the company of Moses at this time and he was with him while crossing the desert and he parted from them [the Israelites] after he had learned the Law of Moses. He did not go to the Promised Land but to Greece and he lived in Thrace. . . Caí came with the fleet which came from Thrace to meet his own people and he showed them his achievement since they parted viz., the Law of God for men and His judgements. After that Caí was judge for the whole fleet.[6]

Another and somewhat earlier version of this legend occurs in conjunction with an account of an ordeal which appears to be a transposition into imagined pagan terms (since the events are placed in the pagan past) of the famous ordeal described in Numbers 5:11-28 by which a woman clears herself of the suspicion of adultery:

That is a proof which they used at that time to distinguish between truth and falsehood, namely, Waiting at an altar, that is, to go nine times round the altars and afterwards to drink water over which a wizard's incantation had been uttered. Now if he [the accused] were guilty the sign of his sin was manifest upon him but if he were innocent it [the water] would do him no harm. Now Caí Caínbrethach — the pupil of Fénius Farsaid, the twelfth or the seventy-second disciple of the school which Fenius dispersed from Greece in order to learn the many languages throughout the countries of the world, — it was that Caí who brought this ordeal from the land of Israel. He came to the Chosen People (*Tuath Dé*) and he learned the Law of Moses, and it was he that delivered judgements in the school after it had been gathered from every side and it was he that ordained the 'Breth Caí'. It was the same Caí moreover who first ordained in Ireland the law of the four tracks [= Cetharshlecht Athgabála], for only two of the school came to Ireland: Aimirgin Glúngeal the poet and Caí the judge. And Caí remained in Ireland until he had outlived nine generations, in consequence of the righteousness of his judgements, for the judgements which he used to deliver were judgements of the law of Moses, and therefore the judgements of the Law [of Moses] are very abundant in Irish law (*fénechas*). These were judgements of the Law which served Cormac.[7]

A very much earlier and briefer account of Caí occurs in Cormac's Glossary and in the law tracts:

Aliter, quod uerius est: Cai Cainbrethach, dalta Feniusa, iss e in deiscibul rosiacht Maccu Israheil fri fogloim n-ebra, 7 is he ba brithem la longus Mac Miled. 7 is aire asberar Cai Cainbrethach de, fobith it bretha recta nobeired, 7 is aire it imda issin berla 'Another version, which is the truer one: Caí Caínbrethach, the pupil of Fénius, he is the disciple who went to the Sons of Israel to learn Hebrew, and he was the judge with the fleet of the Sons of Míl [the ancestors of the Irish]. And the reason why he is called Caí Caínbrethach [C. of the good judgements] is that he gave judgements of the [Mosaic] law and that is why they are abundant in Irish law'.[8]

This traditional legend is part of the extensive development of interpretative materials concerning the origin and nature of law and can be understood in a number of ways. It is a defence of the Irish legal system as a whole in different times and circumstances and a justification of the practice of law, especially by clerics, but it is much more. It projects the Irish legal tradition backwards in time to venerable antiquity, to what was conceived to be the very beginning of Irish history, and it provides a framework within which to justify legal rules and practices which self-evidently did not derive from the authoritative source of law: revelation, and the interpretation of revelation by the Fathers and other christian authorities. These texts are witnesses to a lengthy concern (within an unbroken literary tradition stretching over many centuries) with the problem of the nature of inherited native law and its relationship with natural law and the Mosaic law. The problem is approached consciously and in clearly defined terms, the interpretation is expressed in the form of a dramatic narrative. The tales cited above and the famous story of the encounter of St Patrick, king Loegaire and the poet-jurist Dubthach moccu Lugair and the resolution of the conflict between christianity and pre-christian law[9] are examples of the genre.

I doubt whether the scholars who wrote and re-wrote these narratives believed them to be literally true, that is, believed them to be accounts of a sequence of events which actually took place in the real world. I imagine rather that these tales are discourse in symbolic form within a well-practised genre familiar to the intended readership or audience. Like the New-Testament parables and the figurative meaning of all of Scripture within some exegetical modes, which we can take to have been well known to the mandarin caste, they are narrative devices by which abstact ideas are conveyed and may be understood on a number of different levels, varying with the degree of understanding and intention the reader or hearer brings to the text. The narratives in Genesis are the best-known stories in Scripture, the whole pre-historical construct (from which the whole web of genealogy hangs) is already spliced to some of the most dramatic events described in these narratives: does it not make good pedagogical sense to expound the complex (and current) problem of the relationships between legal systems in the same terms? The clever may read it as a symbolic representation of an abstract problem and its solution, the dunce may cling to the story as explanation and mnemonic. The level of authorial consciousness and the precise relationship of their scholarly creators to the tales are no doubt complex — as complex as that of the modern historian to his interpretative hypotheses?

A very similar narrative is used to explain the origins of the Irish language in a remarkable text of the Old-Irish period, *Auricept na n-éces*:

The authors of the Irish say that the reason for the invention of the Irish language was a strange and unlawful deed that took place in the world, i.e. the construction of Nimrod's Tower [Gen. 11:1-9].

Who invented this language and in what place was it invented and at what time was it invented? Answer. Fénius Farsaid invented it at Nimrod's Tower ten years after the dispersal from the Tower; and those who went from the Tower to settle in their territories were men of common language, not of common kin, as for instance Caí Caínbrethach, one of the 72 students of the school. He was of the Hebrews, and he was sent to Egypt. And Fénius himself remained at the Tower and lived there until the school asked him to extract for them out of the many languages a language that only they, or somebody who learned it from them, might speak. It is there that the language was extracted from the many languages, and it was assigned to one of them and the language is called by his name. And Goídelc [Irish] is so called from Goídel mac Angin mic Glúnfhind mic Láimfhind mic Agnumain of the Greeks . . . this language was there given its rules: what was best, fullest and most beautiful was extracted for Irish . . .[10]

Much the same kind of epistemological question arises here and both traditional legends evidently derive from the same intellectual milieu. It seems to me that the modern scholar, in silently imposing his own categorization of genre, is likely to misinterpret the texts and malign their authors. One could make the argument that the medieval scholar, using modes of discourse different from his modern successors, makes a series of important comments on the conflict of law and his perception of his own vernacular — in other words, he uses traditional legend (and its resonances and associations for his hearer) to make critical comments on the nature of law and language.

The mandarin managers of the past are their best when they engage in polysemic discourse on the nature of kingship, its possession and legitimation. Among the texts dealing with the Uí Néill occurs the following aetiology of the supremacy of the descendants of Niall amongst those dynasties who claimed his siblings as their dynastic ancestors and eponyms — Uí Briúin, Uí Fiachrach and others.

Eochu Mugmedón was king of Ireland. His wife, Mongfind daughter of Fidach bore him four sons: Brian, Fiachra, Ailill and Fergus. He had a fifth son, Niall, son of Cairenn Chasdub, king of the Saxons. Before Niall's birth, Mongfind treated his mother harshly. She bore Niall in the field and none would come near mother and child for fear of Mongfind who was a great witch. (i) Tórna Éces, the poet/druid took the little Niall to his breast and his future was revealed to the poet who foretold in verse that Niall would be a great warrior, that he would be king of Ireland for 27 years and that all the kings of Ireland would descend from him. Tórna fostered him in secrecy until he was old enough to be king and came with him to Tara. He clad his mother in purple clothes and the men of Ireland chose him as king to succeed his father. (ii) Mongfind said angrily to Eochu: "Adjudge between you sons as to which of them will succeed you". The king said that Síthchenn, the druid/smith, should do so. He sets fire to a forge in which the sons are. Niall emerged with the anvil and its block: "Niall vanquishes", said the smith. Brian emerged with the sledgehammer: "Brian is your warrior", said the smith. Fiachra came with a pail of beer and the bellows: "Fiachra has your beauty and your gifts", said the smith. Ailill came with the weapon-chest: "Ailill to avenge you", said the druid. Fergus came with the firewood: "Fergus the withered", said the smith, and there was no good of his seed but one. Mongfind was furious because of this judgement and she has the smith supply them with arms. (iii) The smith gave the best arms to Niall and the rest to the others: "Now hunt and try your arms". They went hunting and they went astray. They kindled a fire and roasted some of the quarry and ate. Now they were thirsty from eating. "Let some one go for water", they said. "I will go", said Fergus. He found a horrible old woman guarding the well. She was black from head to foot, half-bald with a grey bristly mane, long green teeth, covered in pustules etc. etc. She was guarding the well and would allow him to take the water on condition he kissed her. He refused. So also did Brian. Fiachra came and asked for water. "A kiss for it", said she. "I would give a few kisses for it", said he. "You will visit Tara", said she [and that came true for two of his issue took the kingship of Ireland, Dathí and Ailill Molt and none of the issue of the others did]. Fiachra returned without water. Then came Niall whom she asked for a kiss. "I will lie with you as well as kiss you", said he and he threw himself upon her and kissed her. When he looked upon her she was the most beautiful woman in the world, white as the melting snow, with plump and queenly arms and long fingers, pearly teeth and lips red as rowan berries. "I am the sovereignty", said she, "go to your brothers and take water with you and the sovereignty will be yours and your children's forever save only two of the children of Fiachra, Dathí and Ailill Molt and one king out of Munster, Brian Bórama. You have seen me loathsome, bestial, and horrible at first: and then — beautiful. So also is the sovereignty for it is seldom gained without battles and conflicts but everyone finds it beautiful and goodly afterwards. (iv) However, do not give your brothers water until they grant their seniority to you." They granted him their seniority and he bound them by oath never to oppose himself or his descendants. They return to Tara and Niall narrates their doings. "Why is it not Brian the senior who tells these tales?", said Mongfind. "Because we have conceded seniority to Niall", said they, "for the water". "Ye have conceded it forever", said Sithchenn the smith, "for henceforth his children will always have the dominion and the sovereignty of Ireland".[11]

This is an extremely complex piece of narrative exposition which can be understood on different levels, some of which will correspond directly to the objects of modern academic disciplines. Quite evidently, structural social anthropologists could see the text globally as normative, as a cautionary commentary on the problem of sibling rivalry among royals in a patrilineal polygynous society and the potential evils of maternal influence and rivalry. That interpretation is very likely to be correct but it does not exhaust the meaning of the text. Historians of magic and popular belief might be impressed by serious references to witches and divination and by the appearance of the pagan goddess of sovereignty in a clerical royalist text which, as it stands, is no older than the eleventh century. They might conclude that the belief-systems of the mandarin caste (or their royal masters?) were partly christian and partly pagan or — more likely, given the simplicity of many historians of this kind — lightly christianized paganism. That interpretation is very likely to be wrong. The Irish mandarins, as copious evidence shows, never intellectually despised nor historically rejected their pagan past. In fact, they treasured its memory, idealized its conventions in the sagas (and did so with such success that the use of their testimony as evidence for pagan practices is a perilous undertaking) and saw it as another human world in past time, different but not essentially opposed to theirs, rather as the Old Testament relates to the New. Its people, on some occasions at least, could be the object of God's saving grace. Here the witches and the divination are dramatic narrative devices (tropes if you prefer), which carry a highly encoded commentary on the nature and legitimacy of political power and the pre-ordained privileges of the royal dynasty. It can, indeed, be read as a statement on the ambiguity of the moral role of kingship as an institution of the natural order and an office achieved by violence, as the goddess herself is made to observe. And yet we have not touched on the particular (as distinct from the general) meaning of this text, this individual assemblage and particularization of certain narrative constitutents which are to be found as discrete elements or differently assembled motifs elsewhere. For that, we must examine the text in its own context of dynasty, time and place. This will require some detailed historical exposition, largely of dynastic politics.

The main elements of the plot are clear: of the five sons of Eochu — Brion, Fiachra, Ailill, Fergus and Niall — the last is destined to succeed his father and found a lineage which will provide the kings of Ireland. The others, despite the machinations of their mother, are excluded. The tale, which establishes the pecking order between the Uí Néill and those who claimed to be their cousins — Uí Briúin, Uí Fiachrach, Uí Ailella and Uí Fergusa — is placed in what modern historians know to be pre-historic time, and what their medieval forebears knew to be 'long ago'. Niall's destiny is articulated in four separate incidents, cast in a linear chronological form, as the hero passes from childhood to young manhood, and the cumulative effect is impressive: (1) Tórna Éces reveals it on seeing the infant; (2) Sitchenn, the druid/smith divines it by burning a forge over the sons and interpreting the significance of the weapons with which each youth emerged; (3) the narrative motif of the 'Loathly Lady', a common allegory of kingship, is then used to re-affirm Niall's destiny; [12] and finally, (4) on the advice of the hag-goddess, he has his brothers formally concede him precedence. On internal evidence, the tale is Uí Néill dynastic propaganda of the eleventh century, though some elements which make it up are as old perhaps as the eighth century.

A related text which occurs side by side with the first in two manuscripts, 'Aided Crimthainn', may be used as a co-text of the first and helps to establish the probable dynastic context. Following on the first, it sets out the aetiology of the superiority of Uí Briúin within Connacht — and here one notes that the action of the royals' mother, her divinatory dream, is successful and the social anthropologist would perhaps point out that the influence of the mother on the siblings who are her offspring is not fraught with such serious potential for conflict within the royal dynasty. The plot is as follows:

Eochu was married to Mongfind daughter of Fidach who bore him four sons: Brian, Fiachra, Ailill and Fergus. She dreamt a dream of them thus: that they passed into the shape of four hounds — Brian took the form of a lion, Fiachra that of a greyhound, Ailill that of a beagle, and Fergus that of a cur. And they were tearing and fighting each other. Every second time the greyhound beat the lion but eventually the lion triumphed over the other three and they surrendered to him timidly and obediently. Mongfind related this dream to Síthchenn the druid. "Truly", said he, "Brian, and his race after him, will be a greedy and wrathful lion and a virulent weapon against the angers of every other one. Fiachra, and his race after him, will be a hound of battle and rapine. These two will attack each other and the kingship will be divided among their children. However, the race of Brian will prevail over all the rest and they alone will have the sovereignty. Ailill will be a hunter seeking territories and gaining an abode for his brothers. As for Fergus, his descendants will be only a miserable peasant of his seed and his descendants will scarcely be known at all." [13]

This text is an explanation of the pecking order among the royal races of Connacht, that is, the existing historical situation and the known historical record are realized in a traditional narrative, which is both explanation and commentary, in terms of the aristocratic and military values of twelfth-century Ireland (and in terms, too, of the mandarin literary vocabulary of praise-poetry and the clichés of contemporary verse histories). Next, the text concedes overall sovereignty to the descendants of Niall in a general way. However, the precise current political point of the text becomes evident only towards the end when it engages in tendentious and brutally explicity political claims against the southern neighbours of Uí Briúin. Thomond, it declares, belongs as of right to Connacht for the province of Connacht extends from Bundrowes in the north to Limerick in the south; the land on which the men of Thomond are settled to-day is the cause of contention, warfare 'and of every mutual destruction that was wrought between them'; this is the land which Lugaid Menn son of Óengus Tírech ('the Landed') seized by force and because of that it is known as 'the Rough Swordland of Lugaid of the Red Hand'; it and Ossory are the two territories which the Munstermen have seized by force.

The nature of these claims becomes evident when we turn to the kingdom of Dál Cais (Uí Briain). The statement that Connacht extends from Limerick to Bundrowes leaves no room for that kingdom. Further, the Uí Briain claimed that their ancestor, Lugaid Menn, had conquered Thomond in remote antiquity, they stressed that he had taken it by heroic force and conflict, and they claimed that no king in Ireland but the king of Dál Cais had any rights over it. [14]

This text belongs to the reign of the greatest warrior-king in twelfth-century Ireland, Tairdelbach Ua Conchobair, king of Connacht (1106-56) and claimant to the kingship of Ireland (his dynasty was Uí Briúin), and very probably it belongs to the period from 1114 to 1130 when he was busily destroying the power-base of Uí Briain, the dynasty that had dominated

Irish politics for most of the previous century and forced even the Uí Néill framers of traditional legend to admit their ancestor, Brian Bóruma. Here, the Uí Briain dynastic claims are deleted and their right to the heartland of their own kingdom of Thomond is rejected, and it is evident from the precision of the rejection, that the Uí Briain 'charter', a traditional legend which had been in service for two centuries or more, was carefully considered and the rejection framed accordingly.

It is possible that these two texts, taken together, form part of the dossier of claims of Tairdelbach Ua Conchobair, part of the work-book of his mandarin interpreters of the past, who cast their work in the form of traditional legend, but within the wider context of the traditional legends of the Uí Néill, whose siblings the Uí Briúin were considered to be in the overall genealogical schema and in the narratives. There is, however, an apparent contradiction: the second expresses his claims eloquently, but the first appears to boost the Uí Néill at the expense of Uí Briúin. A relatively satisfactory interpretation of this apparent contradiction is possible on a number of levels. In the first place, the kingdoms of the Uí Néill were by now much reduced and Ua Conchobair could concede the shadow when he had the substance. More important, the Uí Néill had been the dominant dynasty in Ireland for many centuries and had attracted to themselves the traditional legends of royal sovereignty: in order to be credible and in order not to do violence to that world of the imagination which accompanies, answers to, and justifies the real world of politics, that association had to be gently unhitched. As the literature shows, that process was complete and the contradictions resolved by about the year 1190. In a poem belonging to that period the matter of both texts is skilfully wedded.[15] The poet declares that 'the era of the Uí Néill is over as the Sovereignty herself ordained'. He then proceeds to rehearse the encounter with the hag-goddess; once again, only Niall copulates with her and she reveals the future of his lineage, but now with one striking limitation — when fifty of his descendants have reigned the kingship will return 'to the foremost of Brian's generous offspring'. The political world and the world of traditional legend are now at one, and the trimming of the past to fit the present is done with consummate skill.

That twelfth-century repertory of aristocratic and chivalrous tales, *Acallam na senórach*, throws a good deal of light on the methods of the mandarins. The warrior Finn, who is regarded as a contemporary of Cormac mac Airt, is now, like a number of the ancestors of leading dynasties, represented as having knowledge of the true faith:

"Maith, a anam, a Chailte", ar Patraic, "ar chreideabairse do rig nime 7 talman no an fetubair a beith ann etir?" Frecraidh Cailte sin: "rofitir in flaithfeinnid", ar

Caílte, "or ba drai 7 ba faidh 7 ba flaith, 7 do thuicemarne uile cu raibhi Dia ann . . ." "Well indeed, Caílte", said Patrick, did you believe in the king of heaven and earth or did you know that he existed at all?" Caílte answers that: "the royal warrior knew", said Caílte, "because he was a druid, a prophet and a lord, and we all understood that God existed".[16]

Later, an even bolder claim is made for the success of Patrick's mission: that the king of the *síd* submitted to Patrick and believed.

7 ni cian do badur ann co facadur in n-aenoclach da n-indsaigid 7 leine do thsroll rig ria chnes, inar maethsroill tairsi 7 brat corcra corrtharach uime, 7 delg oir issin brut ossa bruinne 7 claidem orduirnd ina laim, 7 cathbarr oir ima chenn, 7 iss e do boi ann .i. Donn mac Midhir, 7 tuc a chenn a n-ucht Patraic, 7 tuc comus Tuaithe De Danann do, 7 ro slechtsat uile do Patraic. Conid ann do chreidset Tuatha De Danann do Patraicc "and they were not long there when they saw a single warrior coming towards them, a shirt of royal satin next his skin, a tunic of smooth satin over it, and a purple fringed cloak about him, a golden brooch in his cloak over his breast, a gold-hilted sword in his hand and a golden helmet on his head. Donn son of Midir it was, and he laid his head in Patrick's breast and he gave him power over the Tuatha Dé Danann, and they all submitted to Patrick. It was then that the Tuatha Dé Danann believed in Patrick's teaching.[17]

Acallam na senórach is a lengthy text cast in the form of a dialogue between St Patrick (who represents the world of christian and clerical values, though in a sophisticated and tolerant way) and Caílte (who represents the world of past martial prowess and pagan virtue). In a sense, these are surface distinctions, for it is possible to interpret the whole text as an imaginative realization in narrative of a normative doctrine of knightly chivalry that answers to the ideals and aspirations, if not the realities, of twelfth-century Irish aristocratic society. In many ways, Irish society resembled, in structure and values, the contemporary societies in western Europe, and there are predictable similarities in the literatures of these societies. On another level, the texts from the *Acallam* cited above, betray an anxious preoccupation of the makers of traditional legend: their world, of reality and imagination, was under attack. When Domnall Ua hÉnna († 1098), the old-style bishop of Killaloe, wrote to Lanfranc, archbishop of Canterbury, on certain theological problems, he also solicited the archbishop's opinion on certain literary matters. The archbishop's philistine reply survives:

Quaestiones saecularium literarum nobis solvendas misistis: sed episcopale propositum non decet operam dare hujusmodi studiis. Olim quidem juvenilem aetatem in his detrivimus; sed accedentes ad pastoralem curam, abrenunciandum eis decrevimus.[18]

In the face of reformers of this kind (and they were to gain the upperhand in the twelfth century), the clerical mandarins, who effortlessly had mediated the worlds of past and present, came under intellectual pressure. The *Acallam* is a rich record of their ambivalent position and response: they present St Patrick, the highest traditional ecclesiastical authority in the land, as approving enthusiastically of the cultivation of a literature which speaks lovingly and nostalgically of the pagan past (the imagined past of generations of composers of traditional legends). In the narratives cited above, the mandarins make a further concession: they mediate the conventional oppositions in that literary world, make Finn, the archetypical pagan warrior, a precocious deist (if not christian), and have the king of the Otherworld and his folk, submit to St Patrick and become true believers. In the world of traditional legend, the past is 'understood' and history becomes intelligible by being constantly re-created — not simply as paradigm of the present, but as a complex and subtle critical and imaginative commentary on life. In the colder climate of late twelfth-century Ireland this kind of commentary seems to have become more difficult. *Sed ego qui scripsi hanc historiam aut uerius fabulam* . . .

NOTES AND REFERENCES

1. 'Uraicecht na riar', in D.A. Binchy (ed.), *Corpus iuris Hibernici* (Dublin, 1978), pp 2336-41 [an edition by Dr Liam Breatnach is to be published by the Dublin Institute for Advanced Studies]; Liam Breatnach, 'The caldron of poesy', in *Ériu*, xxxii (1981), pp 45-93; xxxv (1984), pp 189-91; Seán Mac Airt 'Filidecht and coimgne' in *Ériu*, xviii (1958), pp 139-52. For their reflections on law and its origins and evidence of their legal culture, see D. Ó Corráin, Liam Breatnach and Aidan Breen, 'The laws of the Irish', in *Peritia*, iii (1984), pp 382-438; Kim McCone, 'Dán agus tallann', in P. Ó Fiannachta (ed.), *Léann na cléire*, Léachtaí Cholm Cille xv (Maynooth, 1986), pp 9-53.
2. See the criticisms in Hayden White, 'The question of narrative in contemporary historical theory', in *History and Theory*, xxiii (1984), pp 1-33; see further the germane observations in regard to Irish studies in Francis John Byrne, 'Senchas: the nature of Gaelic historical tradition', in J.G. Barry (ed.), *Historical Studies*, ix (Belfast, 1974), pp 137-59.
3. Hayden White, *Metahistory. The historical imagination in nineteenth-century Europe* (Baltimore and London, 1973), p. 7.
4. J.N. Hillgarth, 'Ireland and Spain in the seventh century', in *Peritia*, iii (1984), pp 1-16 (a most valuable survey of recent literature).
5. D. Ó Corráin, 'Irish origin legends and genealogy: recurrent aetiologies' in Tore Nyberg et al. (ed.), *History and heroic tale: a symposium* (Odense, 1985), pp 51-96; id., 'Nationality and kingship in pre-Norman Ireland' in T.W. Moody (ed.), *Nationality and the pursuit of national independence* (Belfast, 1978), pp 14-19; id., 'The early Irish churches: some aspects of organisation' in D. Ó Corráin (ed.), *Irish antiquity* (Cork, 1981), pp 328-31.

6. Binchy, *Corpus,* pp 1653-54 = *Anc. laws Ire.* i 20-22.

7. Whitley Stokes (ed.), 'Irish ordeals, Cormac's adventure in the Land of Promise and the decision as to Cormac's sword' in *Irische Texte,* 3. Ser. 1. Heft (Leipzig, 1891), pp 192-93. The Cormac in question here is Cormac mac Airt, the paragon of Irish kingship, who is elsewhere represented as being made privy, in pagan times, to revelation and refusing to be buried with his pagan ancestors at Brug na Bóinne (R.I. Best and O.J. Bergin (ed.), *Lebor na hUidre* (Dublin, 1929), pp 127-33).

8. Kuno Meyer (ed.), 'Sanas Cormaic: an Old-Irish glossary', in O.J. Bergin, R.I. Best, Kuno Meyer and J.G. O'Keeffe (ed.), *Anecdota from Irish manuscripts,* iv (Halle a.S., 1912), p. 14; Binchy, *Corpus,* p. 1311.

9. Binchy, *Corpus,* pp 339, 877, 1650; McCone, 'Dán agus tallann', pp 32-42.

10. George Calder (ed.), *Auricept na n-éces: the scholar's primer* (Edinburgh, 1917), pp 6-9, 174; Anders Ahlqvist, *The early Irish linguist: an edition of the canonical part of Auricept na n-éces,* Commentationes Humanarum Litterarum 73 (Helsinki, 1982), pp 47-48. In the interest of simplicity, my translation (though based on Dr Ahlqvist's text and translation and much indebted to his) is very much freer.

11. Whitley Stokes, 'On the death of Crimthann son of Fidach, and the adventures of the sons of Eochaid Muigmedon' in *Rev. Celt,* xxiv (1903), pp 191-203; Standish O'Grady (ed.), *Silva gadelica* (2 vols, London, 1892), i 326-30. An early version of section (ii) is edited by Kuno Meyer, *Z.C.P.,* viii (1912), pp 304-5, and dated by Gerard Murphy to the eighth century (*Saga and myth in ancient Ireland* (Dublin, 1961), pp 48-49).

12. The Loathly Lady has attracted considerable scholarly attention: R.A. Breatnach, 'The lady and the king: a theme of Irish literature' in *Studies* (Dublin), xlii (1953), pp 321-36; James Carney, *Studies in Irish literature and history* (Dublin, 1955), pp 334-35; P. Mac Cana, 'Aspects of the theme of king and goddess in Irish literature', in *Etudes Celt.,* vii (1955-57), pp 76-104; 8 (1958), pp 59-65.

13. Stokes, loc. cit., pp 175-89; O'Grady, loc. cit., pp 330-36.

14. M.A. O'Brien, *Corpus genealogiarum Hiberniae* (Dublin, 1962), p. 207.

15. Brian Ó Cuív (ed.), 'A poem composed for Cathal Croibhdhearg Ó Conchobhair', in *Ériu,* xxiv (1983), pp 157-74.

16. Whitley Stokes (ed.), 'Acallam na senórach', *Irische Texte,* 4. Ser. 1. Heft (Leipzig, 1900), p. 41; for a re-iteration of this claim, ibid., p. 148.

17. Ibid., p. 147.

18. James Ussher (ed.), *Veterum epistolarum Hibernicarum sylloge* (Dublin, 1632), ep. XXVIII, repr. in Elrington Ball (ed.), *The whole works of James Ussher* iv (Dublin, 1847), p. 497.

Winner and Waster and the
Mid-Fourteenth-Century Economy

JOHN SCATTERGOOD

I

'No wise historian neglects the literature of the age he sets out to study. At the least it will tell him what matters interested the people of that time, what virtues they admired and what evils they denounced: at the best it will describe for him their towns, countryside, means of travel, houses, furniture, dress, food and drink, education and entertainment, and illustrate and discuss the problems that most vexed their minds.' Thus J.J. Bagley on the subject of fourteenth-century verse.[1] And there is no reason to disagree with any of this, except to make the point that some types of literature are more useful to the historian than others and that arguably the most useful of all is that which addresses itself in a direct fashion to contemporary issues.

It is ostensibly a natural enough thing to write about political and social problems, and a number of poems from the Anglo-Saxon period survive which celebrate victory in battles, or occasionally lament defeat. From the twelfth century onwards poems in Latin and Anglo-Norman were being written about contemporary English affairs, though by the fifteenth century poems in these languages were becoming few.[2] The earliest surviving political poem in Middle English is a brief *sirvente,* in carole form, exulting in the discomfiture of Richard, Earl of Cornwall, and celebrating the victory of Simon de Montfort and the barons over the king's party at the Battle of Lewes in 1264.[3] And in the fourteenth and fifteenth centuries, as the native language gained in status, the number of poems on contemporary political issues increased rapidly. Poems were written on most major events, and types of poems which were distinctively political began to emerge. Apart from poems celebrating victories in battle, and the *sirvente* against defeated enemies there appeared among others the 'evils of the age' poem complaining of general contemporary decadence, the *planh* or lament for a dead king or prominent nobleman, the venality satire, and the political prophecy. Something of a tradition of political verse grew up as

39

poets began to imitate, and sometimes steal from, earlier poems, but other genres of poetry were always likely to be ransacked by a poet seeking ideas or effects.[4]

Political verse, however, always differed to some extent from other types of verse: it was, for example, more susceptible to loss because the relevance of a poem tended to disappear along with the contemporary events which gave rise to it.[5] Political verse also more than any other kind, had a value in the formation of opinion: it was therefore commissioned assiduously by the rich and powerful; but, conversely, its production was also discouraged by the establishment, if it was likely to be unfavourable in posture. Certain types of political verse were forbidden by law: an act of 1402 was passed which forbade the composition and dissemination of prophecies, and rulers down to Elizabeth I found it expedient to frame or re-enact similar legislation; in the fifteenth century the posting of 'bills' on doors, walls, and gates had become so common and dangerous that a proclamation was issued forbidding it.[6] Men were executed for writing political verse: in 1456 John Holton was executed 'per scriptarum billarum' touching the person of Henry VI;[7] and in 1484 Wyllyam Collyngbourne was 'put to the most cruel deth at the Tower Hylle' for writing a couplet deriding Richard III and his supporters and for posting it up on the doors of St Paul's Cathedral, London.[8] Political verse was dangerous, and, not surprisingly, much of it is anonymous.

Winner and Waster is an anonymous poem of 503 alliterative long lines: the end of it is lost, though there are probably not many lines missing. It is the final surviving item of British Library Additional MS 31042, a miscellany compiled in the middle of the fifteenth century, probably between 1430 and 1440, by Robert Thornton, a country gentleman from East Newton near Pickering (Yorkshire),[9] who also owned another collection of verse, Lincoln Cathedral Library MS 91.[10] The title it bears in the manuscript is more descriptive of the debate form of the poem than its contents: 'Here begynes a tretys and god schorte refreyte bytwixe Wynnere and Wastoure'.[11]

But its earliest editor, Sir Israel Gollancz, had no doubt about the specific occasion and contemporary importance of the poem. He adduced a variety of evidence based on what he took to be allusions in the poem and concluded: 'The cumulative value of all this evidence clearly points to the winter of 1352-3 as the date of composition, for the poet is evidently writing concerning events which are just happening, or are fresh in his memory. His poem is in fact a topical pamphlet in alliterative verse on the social and economic problems of the hour, as vivid as present day discussions on like problems.'[12] This view has been accepted by most subsequent scholars, and even developed: J.M. Steadman sifted and reordered some of Gollancz's evidence but came to similar conclusions and went so far as to suggest that the significance of the poem disappears unless it is considered in the context of 1352-53;[13] and D.V. Moran, more precisely, argued that the parliament of January 1352 was the occasion for it.[14] Not everybody has taken this line, however: J.R. Hulbert correctly pointed out that though a *terminus a quo* could be established on the basis of internal allusions, no comparable *terminus ad quem* was possible, and he argued that any date between 1351 and 1366 would be possible;[15] and more recently Elizabeth Salter has subjected the evidence for dating to a sceptical review and concludes, '. . . any line-by-line correlation of the poem with the verifiable data of historical record tends to give a picture of some complexity, and we may with reason begin to suspect that the purpose of the poet was less exact than the literal and contemporary reporting of the political, economic and social conditions of any given year. It follows that we should be unwise to accept any longer, a categorical dating for the composition of *Wynnere and Wastoure* . . .'[16] In view of arguments such as this, it is not surprising that a number of more recent scholars have concentrated less on the political and historical aspects of the poem and more on its formal literary qualities: as T.H. Bestul puts it, '. . . clearly *Wynnere and Wastoure* is much more than a topical tract . . .'[17] and proceeds to an analysis mainly of its conventions and generic relations.

The arguments about the date of *Winner and Waster* have had, in my view, an unfortunate polarizing effect on responses to the poem. It has been treated either precisely as historical source material, or it has been assessed more generally in literary terms, but rarely as both. A limited and limiting twentieth-century view, which effectively denied artistic status to anything which could remotely be described as politically oriented or socially engaged has impinged on it. In the Middle Ages, though, no such opinion obtained. Contemporary politics constituted a valid subject for poetry, and poems on historical events were regarded as accurate records and were sometimes used by chroniclers as source material or were incorporated as a whole into chronicles. It will not do, however, to treat poetry in the same way as other kinds of discourse or other sorts of record. Poets have their own distinctive procedures which need to be understood in order that the sorts of statement being made may be appreciated. It is my view that *Winner and Waster* is about the mid-fourteenth-century economy, that it relates particularly to the years 1352-53, and that it focusses on Edward III. But equally it has to be recognized that the kinds of statement made about these matters are distinctively poetic ones, and have to be understood in literary terms.

II

Though *Winner and Waster* is anonymous the author discloses enough about his purposes for his attitude towards his poem and his stance in relation to his material to be clear. He does this by means of a complaint against the contemporary fashion he discerns among patrons for ignoring serious writers and rewarding trivial entertainers:

> Whylome were lordes in londe that loved in thaire hertis
> To here makers of myrthes that matirs couthe fynde.
> And now es no frenchipe in fere bot fayntnesse of hert,
> Wyse wordes withinn that wroghte were never,
> Ne redde in no romance that ever renke herde.
> Bot now a childe appon chere withowtten chyn-wedys,
> That never wroghte thurgh witt three wordes togedire,
> Fro he can jangle als a jaye and japes telle,
> He schall be levede and lovede and lett of a while
> Wele more than the man that made it hymselven. (19-28).

Such a complaint, of course, is not unique: there are many examples in classical and late antique literature. And medieval poets frequently complain that their serious efforts are ill-recognized while the trivial productions of lower-grade entertainers are largely rewarded: John de Hanville laments that the 'histrio suspectus' is unjustifiably preferred to better men; Chrétien de Troyes points out that those who make a living telling stories before kings and nobles were accustomed to 'Depecier et corronpre' their material; Jean Froissart, presenting his *Chroniques* to Philippa of Hainault, wife of Edward III, criticizes 'jouliours et enchantours' who have corrupted 'par les chancons et rimes controuvées la juste et vraie histoire'; and there are further examples in Wace, Jean de Conde and elsewhere.[18] Closest to the author of *Winner and Waster* perhaps is the Chandos Herald who, in his *Prologue* to his *Vie et Gestes du Prince Noir,* draws a similar contrast between the past and the present. Once upon a time, he says

> . . . ceux qui faisoient beaux ditys
> Estoient tenu par aucteur
> Ou par ascune amenceueur . . .

[. . . those who made fine poems were regarded as authors or at least as recorders . . .]

These men were rewarded and honoured. But now,

> . . . homme tiendroit plus grant acompte
> D'un Jangelour ou d'un fauxe menteur
> D'un Jogelour ou d'un Bourdeour . . .[19]

[. . . one would take greater account of a chatterer or a false liar or a juggler or a jester . . .]

Such men, with their grimaces and contortions which provoke laughter, are more readily attended to than those who write well. The author of *Winner and Waster* in all likelihood probably did not use any of these examples as a source. But by associating himself with this tradition of complaint he is declaring his seriousness. And though he adopts a minstrel posture by calling for refreshment at the end of Fitts I and II — 'Full freschely and faste, for here a fitt endes' (217 and 367) — he was no doubt aware that distinctions could be made between 'mynstralles' who made 'murthes' and obtained reward 'giltless' and those 'japeres and jangeleres' who 'feynen hem fantasies, and fooles hem maketh' condemned by Langland on the basis of a Pauline text from Ephesians v 4.[20] The author of *Winner and Waster* adopts the stance of an oral poet of the old fashioned sort, but he assures his audience that he is not concerned with trivial matters.

The poem he offers is also announced as serious: its opening makes it plain that it is at least partly a complaint against the times in a prophetic mode. Originally the generalized 'abuses of the age' poem was a separate type:[21] it originated in the 'duodecim abusiones', attributed in manuscripts of the ninth, tenth and eleventh centuries to Cyprian, Augustine and Origen, though much of its popularity derives from its use in the 'sexta tabula' of the widely known *Speculum Christiani* and particularly from its appearance in the *Gesta Romanorum*, where the abuses form the basis of the 'sayings of the four philosophers'. In this story, a king whose land has been struck by various disasters asks the four wisest men in his kingdom for an explanation. In pithy, gnomic sayings of a generalized sort each gives three reasons, which differ from version to version, but which have in common the fact that they attribute their country's failings to moral degeneracy and wickedness. Many late medieval writers saw the possibility of using this story with a particular application to English politics and were ready to explain the problems of the realm in terms of divergence from traditional moral values. The author of *Winner and Waster* begins his poem with the traditional long historical perspective about the fall of Troy and the foundation of 'Bretayne' (1-2), and then moves into material which is purely from the 'abuses of the age' tradition:

> For nowe alle es witt and wyles that we with delyn,
> Wyse wordes and slee, and icheon wryeth othere . . . (5-6)

and a little later, 'And now es no frenchipe in fere bot fayntnesse of hert'
(21). These concerns appear in the English version of *The Sayings of the
Four Philosophers* (1311): 'ffor wit is qued, þe lond is wrecful' (66), 'ffor
frend is fo, þe lond is loueles' (44).[22] They also appear frequently elsewhere
in complaints of the 'abuses of the age' sort.

There is little variation in the mood and tone of these poems but much in-
genuity was expended on their forms. The traditional material sometimes
appears in 'punctuation' poems (which present a perfect state of things or
an imperfect one depending on how they are punctuated) and in poems
with 'destroying' refrains (in which typically the body of a stanza sets forth
a description of a perfect state of things but the refrain overturns this by
alluding ironically to something impossible such as the stability of fashions
of women, or the straightness of a ram's horn, or the forward movement of
a crab).[23] But a favourite device was to incorporate 'abuses of the age'
material into prophecies. That the author of *Winner and Waster* wishes to
do this is clear from the following lines:

> Forthi sayde was a sawe of Solomon the wyse —
> It hyeghte hard appone honde, hope I no nother —
> When wawes waxen schall wilde, and walles bene doun,
> And hares appon herthe-stones schall hurcle in hire fourme,
> And eke boyes of no blode, with boste and with pryde
> Schall wedde ladyes in londe, and lede tham at will,
> Thene dredfull domesdays it draweth neghe aftir. (10-16)

Solomon was not only regarded in the Middle Ages as a sage and a
repository of ancient wisdom but also as a magician, necromancer and
prophet.[24] What is more, the 'sawes of Salomon' are occasionally invoked
in political contexts.[25] Wisdom tended to accumulate around his name (as
with Merlin and Bede) and the enigmatic sayings attributed to him here can
be paralleled in prophecies attributed to others. *Thomas of Erceldoune's
Prophecy,* from British Library MS Harley 2253,[26] contains the lines:

> When hares kendles o þe herston;
> When wyt & wille werres togedere;
>
> . . . .
> When laddes weddeþ louedis. . .(4-5, 15)

In addition, *Waldhaue's Prophecy* has:

> When a lad with a Ladie shal goe ouer the fields
> Then shal be wasted there cheife landes . . .[27]

The occurrence of these *impossibilia* (such as hares upon hearthstones) and disruptions of accepted social norms (lads marrying ladies) are usually, in prophecies, taken as presaging disaster for a country: these are the 'selcouthes' and 'ferlies', the wondrous events and marvels, of which this type of poem characteristically speaks.[28] The author of *Winner and Waster,* however, moves the emphasis from a vague future to a firm present: he repeatedly insists that these 'selcouthes' (3) are evident 'nowe' (3,4,7) and that 'dredfull domesdaye' approaches fast. By the sixteenth century, when Shakespeare amongst others made fun of them,[29] prophecies had become somewhat *déclassé,* but in the fourteenth century they were taken seriously.[30] Whether this author believed in the closeness of doomsday in any literal sense is difficult to say, but since he repeats that anyone who 'sadly will see and the sothe telle' will affirm that it 'es neghe here' (17-18), he clearly wishes to emphasize as strongly as he can that England is facing a crisis.

The Prologue to *Winner and Waster,* therefore, testifies to the seriousness of the poet's conception of his role and to the potential disastrousness of the political situation in England. But something is also suggested about the nature of his concern: both the complaint against the times and the prophecy deal usually, as here, in enigmatic generalities not in precise solutions, and this implies that the poet sees his poem as providing admonishment and warning rather than policy. His concern is to raise issues not to provide answers.

And certain other aspects of the rest of the poem's formal organization support and develop this view. In the opening of Fitt I the poet offers his audience 'a tale that me betyde ones' and alludes to the fictive occasion of the poem: 'Als I wente in the weste wandrynge myn one' (31-32). This, in brief, is the typical opening of the *chanson d'aventure,* originally a French genre, but one which had become, by the mid-fourteenth century, thoroughly assimilated into English poetry. Characteristically, the narrator, walking or musing alone, often in some named place or district at some particular season, comes unexpectedly upon something which reveals previously unsuspected knowledge.[31] English *chansons d'aventure* are written on all sorts of subjects — religious, secular and political — but the wisdom they communicate is essentially poetic and unofficial: as Anne Middleton puts it, 'A poem in this mode does not present authoritative truth to cognition, but represents such a transaction "in game"; its definitive features are that its speaker has no authority, and that the "truth" of its discourse is purely contingent.'[32] This typical 'wandrynge' narrator is so overcome by the beauty of a paradisal landscape through which he travels that he falls asleep and has a dream which forms the substance of the poem. 'I was swythe in a sweven sweped belyve' (46). It is hard to be sure about the precise significance of Middle English dream terminology, and the narrator is not helpful about the significance or otherwise of his dream, but it appears to conform most closely to that which Macrobius called a *somnium* — the enigmatic dream which 'conceals with strange shapes and veils with ambiguity the true meaning of the information being offered, and requires an interpretation for its understanding.'[33] As A.C. Spearing says, 'the precise terms used by Macrobius about the *somnium* are of special interest in implying that such dreams are "natural" equivalents to the artifice of allegory, and thereby explaining why allegorical fictions so often come to be set in dreams.'[34] The allegorical fiction of this poem is set in the form of a debate, but significantly it is an inconclusive or 'horizontal' debate: neither disputant concedes defeat, and the enigmatic, sidestepping judgment of the king is not of the sort to grant victory one way or the other.

III

The debate between the allegorical personifications, when it eventually begins, turns on the subject of wealth and its proper use. This was a question which had ethical and political dimensions, as well as the obvious practical ones, and had been treated earlier from a variety of viewpoints, several of which are important in relation to *Winner and Waster,* for the poet's approach is not a simple one.

The most influential treatment of this subject in Western thought comes in Aristotle's *Nicomachean Ethics* where the virtue of liberality is defined as being an avoidance on the one hand of prodigality and on the other of meanness: 'Coming to the giving and acquiring of money we find that the mean is "liberality", the excess "prodigality", the deficiency "meanness". But here we meet a complication. The prodigal man and the mean man fall short in opposite ways. The prodigal exceeds in giving and falls short in getting money, whereas the mean man exceeds in getting and falls short in giving it away.'[35] This philosophical concept — that virtue is a mean between two undesirable extremes — was a widely influential one, particularly among the Stoics, and these ideas on the use of wealth reappear with great frequency in Horace, Cicero, Seneca and others.[36] They were taken over by Albertus Magnus in his *Ethica,* and by his more famous pupil Thomas Aquinas in the section of the *Summa Theologica* which analyses virtue and vice. In the section on liberality, Aquinas demonstrates that it is a virtue and that it has to do with money before going on to define and discuss covetousness and prodigality which he considered were opposed both to liberality and to each other: '. . . the opposition between prodigality and covetousness is one of excess and deficiency; either of which destroys the mean of virtue.'[37] These ideas on the use of wealth became standard and reappear throughout the Middle Ages, particularly in penitential treatises on the capital sins: Chaucer's Parson asserts that 'largesse' is a remedy for avarice, but adds that 'men oughten eschue foollargesse, that men clepen wast';[38] and in *Jacob's Well* beneath the ooze of covetousness and the 'the gravel of wast' is 'largenesse' or almsgiving.[39] These ideas also appeared frequently in poetry particularly in works of the 'psychomachia' type using personification allegory: in a battle between virtues and vices in Alanus de Insulis *Anticlaudianus* 'avaritia' is conquered by a personified 'largitas',[40] and in John of Hanville's *Architrenius* there is a long description of a battle 'inter largos et avaros'.[41] Dante has the avaricious and the prodigals clashing in the same circle of Hell:

> Percoteansi incontro; e poscia pur li
> si rivolgea ciascun, voltando a retro,
> gridand: "Perche tieni?" e "Perche burli?"

[They clashed together when they met and then at that point each turned about and rolled his weight back again, shouting: "Why hoard?" and "Why squander?"]

Their faults are described later in a balanced reductive phrase as, 'Mal dare e mal tener'[42] [ill-giving and ill-keeping].

That these ethical ideas have political relevance is clear and they are frequently used in works of the 'mirror of princes' type. In the *Policraticus,* John of Salisbury says: 'Although prodigality is palpably at fault, I think that there should be no place for avarice. No vice is worse and none more execrable, especially in those who are at the head of states or who hold any public office.'[43] The transmission of these ideas into political literature was largely due to their inclusion in the *De Regimine Principum* of Aegidius Romanus and in the pseudo-Aristotelian *Secreta Secretorum*, both of which were widely translated into the vernaculars. *Li Livres du Gouvernement des Rois,* a fourteenth-century French version of Aegidius, for example, has a long passage on the subject: 'il covient avoir une vertu meeine entre avarice et fole largesce, et cele vertu est apelee largesce et liberalite, et aussi comme force de courage oste poour de l'omme et atempre sa hardiesce, tout aussi largesce oste l'avarice de l'omme et atempre la fole largesce, et est ceste vertu en user droiturelment des richeces'.[44]

[It is necessary to have a mean virtue between avarice and prodigality and this virtue is called largesse and liberality, and just as strength of heart takes away fear in a man and tempers his boldness, in quite the same way largesse takes away avarice and tempers prodigality and this virtue resides in using riches properly.] A Middle-English version of the *Secreta Secretorum* makes much the same point, but more coercively: '. . . he that dispendith the goodis of his Rewme out of ordir and discrecioun, and yevith such as be not worthi, ne have no nede therto, that kyng distroyeth his peple and the comoun good of the Rewme, and is not worthi forto regne, for he is fool large. The name of skarste is unconvenient to a kyng, and yville bicometh to his royalle maieste. Than if a kyng wolle regne worshipfully, it bihovyth neyther to have that on ne that othir of two vices, skarste ne fool large.'[45] And, of course, these principles were applied in specific cases. Walter Map has a long section of his *De Nugis Curialium* on the difficulties he experiences in controlling his household: an economical steward is accused by some of 'avaricia', and others take 'Absit omnis parcitas' as their watchward and ruin him with extravagance. And the king, he says, has a much more difficult task in controlling a much larger household. Later in the book he praises Henry I for his sensible attitude towards the use of wealth: 'The same prince, though he so held the mean between miser and prodigal, that he could not be nearer a prodigal without falling into the vice, was always blessed with all affluence, and flourished in the prosperous condition of men and affairs thorughout his realm.' But there is criticism too: Walter uses his praise of Henry I as a basis for reproving Alfonso VI of Spain for his miserliness concerning the building of the Abbey Church at Cluny.[46]

Edward III appears to have been attacked on several occasions in these terms. Simon Islip's *De Speculo Regis Edwardi III* is a polemical attack on the king's abuse of his rights of purveyance. Edward III is accused of being an 'avarus' because of his constant demands for money and goods from his people and at the same time as a 'prodigus' because of his extravagant household, his over-generous and unnecessary presents, and his unpaid debts. In a memorable phrase, heavily influenced by the 'mirror for princes' type of work, he is described as a 'depopulator rei publice et destructor regni et regiminis'.[47] Much the same phraseology is used on the same subject about Edward III in John of Erghome's *Prophecy of John of Bridlington:* 'rex sic faciendo destruit populum et thesaurum suum'. Here it is maintained that Edward III would always be in need of money because he was both warlike (and wars are expensive) and avaricious: 'The third condition pursuing him continually is a shortage of money, because at all times of his life he will either need money and wealth because of his wars, or because of his avarice; even when he will cease from wars he will be very greedy for wealth, and at times more for wealth than honour, which is contrary to the way of a noble man . . .'[48] The author of *Winner and Waster* does not mention Edward III by name, but the king with the 'Berybroun . . . berde', the 'kirtill and mantill . . . brouderde with fewlys' sitting in the highly elaborate 'cabane' (83-91) irresistably suggests him through a number of allusions: the quartered arms of England and France,

> Two with flowres of Fraunce, before and behynde,
> And two out of Ynglonde with sex grym bestes,
> Thre lebardes on lofte, and thre on lowe undir . . . (78-80)

appear to be those assumed by Edward III in 1340; the order of the Garter, whose motto in English appears at line 68, 'Hethyng have the hathell that any harme thynkes', was instituted by Edward III in 1348; and the 'Ynglysse besantes full brighte, betyn of golde' (61) which decorate the 'cabane' probably refer to the reissue of gold coinage by Edward III in 1351. Whether the young man 'that faylede hym never' who he had made a knight and whose amorials contained 'Thre wynges . . . wroghte in the kynde' (102-103, 117) is to be identified with Edward, the Black Prince is less certain: though this is the traditional identification, it has recently been proposed that one of the Wingfield family may be meant.[49] But what is not in doubt is the poet's wish to associate the matter of the dispute with Edward III. Both disputants know the king well:

> Wele know we the kyng; he clothes us bothe,
> And hase us fosterde and fedde this fyve and twenty wyntere.
> (205-206)

Indeed, they perhaps wear his livery if 'clothes' is that specific.[50] He, in his part, recognizes them and accepts them as members of his household:

> The kynge henttis by the handes, and hetys tham to ryse,
> And sayde, welcomes, heres, as hyne of oure house bothen.
> (211-212)

Whatever else he means the poet intends to implicate Edward III closely in the debate.

In the fiction of this poem Edward III's first problem is the practical one of keeping the peace, for the two armies of Winner and Waster are intent on physical conflict: 'if thay strike one stroke, stynt thay ne thynken' (195). This is solved by getting them to argue rather than fight ('are any wrake falle' 198) and by a promise that he will act as a judge in their dispute: 'If I schall deme yow this day, dothe me to here' (220). And the issues that he hears about are both ethical and political. The two disputants characterize themselves and each other as the traditional misusers of wealth: Winner is the 'avarus' who exceeds in acquisition and is deficient in giving, Waster is the 'prodigus' who exceeds in spending but is deficient in getting. As Winner puts it: 'I gadir, I glene, and he lattys goo sone' (231). But a political dimension appears too for the poet makes the spokesmen of the armies representative of important social groupings. Winner is an acquisitive merchant, who has 'wyde howses full of wolle sakkes', crammed with goods and money:

> The bemes benden at the rofe, siche bakone there hynges,
> Stuffed are sterlynges under stelen bowndes . . . (250-252)

Waster is a prodigal landowner living in the unfavourable circumstances after the Black Death: he has the accoutrements of his position still, 'heghe howses and howndes full kene', but his estate is ruined,

> His londes liggen alle ley, his lomes aren solde,
> Dowun bene his dowfehowses, drye bene his poles . . .
> (234-237)

But neither army is restricted to members of these social groups: Winner's army contains various foreigners, lawyers, and churchmen, particularly friars (138-187);[51] Waster's has 'bowmen many' (194). And, as the debate develops, it is not confined to differences between merchants and landowners. Other issues of contemporary relevance are raised, such as the untrustworthiness of executors (302-305, 441-444) or the extravagance of fashions (408-414). The poem resists a simple response: it addresses a number of subjects though it appears to have a precise political focus.

IV

To establish the precise context of *Winner and Waster* is not easy. It is usually impossible to date Middle English texts precisely, but in this case there is a certain amount of evidence on which to base a hypothesis.

The English arms quartered with those of France (78-80), the Garter motto (68), and the gold coinage (61), already mentioned, mean that the poem may have been written after 1340, 1348 and 1351. But it appears from other evidence to be a little more recent. The mention that the king had looked after Winner and Waster for 'fyve and twenty wyntere' (206) must, if the number is meant to be precise, refer to the twenty-fifth year of Edward III's reign, that is 1351-52. The year 1352 is also the date of the promulgation of the Statute of Treason: this is the English 'usage', in the opinon of most scholars, on the basis of which the king forbids the armies, on pain of loss of life and property, 'to lede rowte in his rewme' and 'thynke/Pertly . . . his pese to disturbe' and to 'be so bolde with banere for to ryde/withinn the kyngdome riche' (124-135).[52] This legislation, and indeed much of the legislation enacted in these years, was largely the work of Chief Justice Sir William Shareshull,[53] who is cursed along with other lawyers and wisemen by Waster in lines 317-318:

> That alle schent were those schalkes, and Scharsull it wiste
> That saide I prikked with powere his pese to distourbe.

This was taken by J.M. Steadman and Jesse M. Anderson to refer to an uprising in Chester in 1353 (the only one in the west of England between 1349 and 1365) provoked by the proclamation of an eyre for Chester and Flint at which Shareshull and Justice Roger Hillary were to preside.[54] And, in addition, it has been pointed out that lines 275-276 with their allusions to 'the colde wyntter and the kene with gleterand frostes' and 'dropeles drye in the dede monethe' refer to the drought and the harsh weather which, according to contemporary chroniclers, lasted from December 1352 to March 1353.[55] None of this evidence is entirely conclusive, and most of it has been questioned from time to time, but taken as a whole the case for dating the poem 1352-53 is a strong one, though the poet recalls earlier events too.

Winner and Waster is concerned with issues which are relevant to England and to Edward III, and if the poem has a precise focus it is to be found in the parliamentary business for the years 1352-53, particularly that of the parliament of January 1352. This was opened by Shareshull with a speech about the disorderly state of the country: 'Primerement, Pur ceo qe nostre Seigneur le Roi ad entenduz qe la Pees de son Roialme n'est pas bien garde come estre deveroit, & qe les destourbours de la Pees & meintenours des quereles & des riotes faites en pais grevont trop a son poeple, sanz ceo qu due punissement est fait de eux . . .'.[56] [Firstly, because our Lord the King has heard that the peace of his realm is not as well kept as it ought to be, and that the disturbers of the peace and the maintainers of quarrels and riots made in the land injure his people too much without due punishment being made to them . . .]. And it may well be that the line 'That prikkede with powere his pese to disturbe' (318) is an echo of this. But the main problem at this parliament was finance: on the one side, money had to be raised to enable Edward III to continue the war with France; but on the other there were various agrarian and commercial hardships which had to be alleviated. The major providers of finance for Edward III's wars were the mercantile classes. As G. Unwin points out, 'the King during the first period of the French War attempted to form an Estate of Merchants, by whose aid he might levy taxes without recourse to Parliament and at the same time secure loans in advance of the taxes'. This group had an important role in the parliaments of 1352-1354, even to the extent of becoming 'a dangerous rival to the House of Commons'.[57] In 1352 the Commons were reluctant to grant money for the wars because they were 'molt empovery si bien par la pestilence mortiele que nadgairs avient en a terre, comme par entre soviers taxes, taillages & plusour autre cheances que les ont survenuz'.[58] [much impoverished just as much by the deadly pestilence which lately came to the earth as by taxes, tallages, and various other mishaps which have befallen them.] They petitioned the king on behalf of the merchants that the subsidy on wool should cease and that there should be some relief from export duties, and some relief was obtained. Gardiner Stillwell[59] admits that there is no direct reference to taxes in the poem, but Winner does seem angry about supplying money for the military classes, especially in lines such as: 'I pryke and I prynne and he the purse opynes' (232). Certainly, later in the poem Edward III makes it plain that he will need the support of Winner when he resumes the war with France:

> And wayte to me, thou Wynnere, if thou wilt wele chefe,
> When I wende appon werre my wyes to lede. (496-497)

The financing of the war with France was certainly a major issue at this parliament, but it was not the only one. As D.V. Moran has pointed out, '. . . the petitions presented to Edward III by the commons included complaints against forestalling, unauthorized bearing of arms, the devious practices of foreign merchants (particularly the Lombards), and the abuses of the clergy, both for the exorbitant tithes they collected and the number of foreigners among them . . .'[60] And all these grievances are mentioned in the poem.

If *Winner and Waster* is to be dated 1352-53, therefore, it can be said that the debate Edward III listens to reflects some of the complexity of the contemporary situation. The judgment that he makes on the central problem — the proper use of wealth — has puzzled and irritated various commentators on the poem, and does indeed rather avoid the issue: the solution proposed is not really a solution. And this may seem odd, for the traditional teaching on the subject provides a number of answers. The poet could, most obviously, have had the king invoke the concept of liberality — the mean of virtue between the opposing vices. Or he could have had both the avaricious and the prodigal roundly condemned in ethical and political terms. Or he could have attempted to distinguish between the relative sinfulness of the two in Aquinas's manner: 'Prodigality considered in itself is a less grievous sin than covetousness, and this for three reasons. First, because covetousness differs more from the opposite virtue . . . Secondly, because the prodigal man is of use to the many to whom he gives, while the covetous man is of use to no one, not even to himself . . . Thirdly, because prodigality is easily cured . . .'[61] This last solution may reasonably have had some appeal for the poet because prodigals (and landowners) were traditionally supporters of minstrels.[62] But none of these solutions is used. The king regards both Winner and Waster with affection: he 'lovely lokes on the ledis twayne' (456). Then he sends each to where he is best loved: Winner is sent abroad to 'The Pope of Rome' where he will be looked after by cardinals (460-465); but Waster remains in England, in Cheapside 'Ther moste waste es of wale' (473-474). He seeks to keep them apart, presumably to avoid the potential violence with which the poem started, but he reserves the right to call Winner back to England if he is needed:

> Bot loke, lede, be thi lyfe, when I lettres sende,
> That thou hy the to me home on horse or fote (466-467)

at which point Waster will be dismissed: 'when I knowe thou will come he shall cayre uttire' (467). The king makes no attempt to reconcile the two, or to change them: he tells each literally to go his own way. The implication is that the situation is contained but not altered. The well-balanced economy needs the accumulation of capital and also the free flow of wealth, those who acquire and those who spend. The nearest the poet comes to enunciating this is when he has Waster say, 'Who so wele schal wyn, a wastour moste he fynde' (390), or when the king says to Waster, 'The more thou wastis thi wele, the better the Wynner lykes' (495). This recognizes the interdependence of the two economic tendencies, but only a very pragmatic and low-key level.

The authors of Middle-English political verse display a wide range of attitudes and ideas: they rejoice over battles won and lament defeats; they praise their political friends and deride their enemies; they complain about unpopular ministers, unjust taxes, and social grievances. The response to events is usually direct, unequivocal, and partisan. Even in a highly sophisticated and deeply pondered poem such as *The Libelle of Englysshe Polycye* of 1436 the elaborate analysis of England's foreign alliances, overseas trade, and navy serves as the background for a defensive national policy: 'Kepe than the see abought in speciall'.[63] *Winner and Waster* has similarly been regarded as partisan. T.H. Bestul says, 'Although any interpretation of *Wynnere and Wastoure* must be provisional because the text of the poem is incomplete, it seems reasonable to suppose that the poet has written a satire directed at the extravagance and greed of Edward III.'[64] That other poems like *De Speculo Regis Edwardi III* and *The Prophecies of John of Bridlington* attack him is clear, but *Winner and Waster* does not seem to me to do so. The poet's attitude towards him is approving to the highest degree: he is one of 'the lovelyeste ledis' under the sun (88-89). That the king who is referred to in the poem is Edward III and that the main subject of the debate is the proper use of wealth do not seem to me to be matters for dispute, and it seems highly likely to me that the political context of the poem is the problem of war finance in 1352-53. But all the strategies of the poem, if my analysis is right, seem designed to produce inconclusiveness. No doubt the poet wished *Winner and Waster* to come to the attention of Edward III, but he intends to warn and admonish rather than criticize or suggest a policy.

NOTES AND REFERENCES

1. J.J. Bagley, *Historical Interpretation* (Harmondsworth, 1965), p. 131.
2. For collections of political verse in Latin and Anglo-Norman see Thomas Wright (ed.), *Political Songs of England* (Camden Society, 1839), and *Political Poems and Songs,* 2 vols (Rolls Series 14, 1859-1861); see also Isabel S.T. Aspin (ed.), *Anglo-Norman Political Songs,* (Anglo-Norman Text Society 9, 1953).
3. See Wright, op. cit., pp 68-71.
4. For thirteenth- and fourteenth-century verses see A.K. Moore, *The Secular Lyric in Middle English* (University of Kentucky Press, 1951), pp 76-100, and for later verses V.J. Scattergood, *Politics and Poetry in the Fifteenth Century* (London, 1971).
5. See R.M. Wilson, *The Lost Literature of Medieval England* (London, 1953), pp 193-214, and Scattergood, op. cit., pp 22-26.
6. For the forbidding of prophecies see Rupert Taylor, *The Political Prophecy in England* (New York, 1911), pp 104-07; for the proclamation against 'bills' see Thomas Rymer, *Foedera* (1727), XI, p. 268.
7. See H.T. Riley (ed.), *Registrum Abbatiae Johannis Whethamstede* (Rolls Series 28, 1972), I, pp 247-48.
8. See Robert Fabyan in H. Ellis (ed.), *The New Chronicles of England and France* (1911), p. 672.
9. See *The Thornton Manuscript*, introduction by D.S. Brewer and A.E.B. Owen (London, 1975); and for an exhaustive description Karen Stern, 'The London "Thornton" Miscellany, a New Description of BM Add. MS 31042', *Scriptorium*, 30 (1976), pp 26-37, 201-18.

10. See G.R. Keiser, 'Lincoln Cathedral MS 91: the Life and Milieu of the Scribe', *Studies in Bibliography,* 32 (1979), pp 159-65.

11. The earliest edition of the poem was by Sir Israel Gollancz, *A Good Short Debate between Winner and Waster* (Oxford University Press, 1921), reissued by D.S. Brewer 1974. Gollancz emended his text a great deal, however, and I have preferred to use the slightly modernized edition of Thorlac Turville-Petre in *Medieval Literature: Chaucer and the Alliterative Tradition* (The New Pelican Guide to English Literature, ed. Boris Ford, I, Part I, Harmondsworth, 1982), pp 396-415. The most reliable and authoritative edition, unfortunately unpublished, is by Karen Stern, 'A Critical Edition of Winner and Waster' (London University M.A. thesis, 1972). I am much indebted to Mrs Stern's work.

12. Gollancz, op. cit., introduction.

13. 'The Date of Winnere and Wastoure', *Modern Philology,* 19 (1921), pp 211-19.

14. 'Wynnere and Wastoure: an Extended Footnote', *Neuphilologische Mitteilungen,* 73 (1972), pp 683-85.

15. 'The Problems of Authorship and the Date of *Wynnere and Wastoure*', *Modern Philology,* 18 (1920), pp 31-40.

16. 'The Timeliness of *Wynnere and Wastoure*', Medium *Aevum,* 47 (1978), pp 40-65.

17. *Satire and Allegory in Wynnere and Wastoure* (University of Nebraska Press, 1974), p. 3. Though I do not finally agree with Bestul's estimate of the poem, I am much indebted to his sensible and informative book.

18. For an account of this kind of complaint see E.R. Curtius, *European Literature and the Latin Middle Ages,* trans. W.R. Trask (London, 1953), pp 468-73 and Elizabeth Salter, *Fourteenth Century English Poetry: Context and Readings,* (Oxford, 1983), pp 92-94 where full references are given. See also Bestul, op. cit., pp 58-59.

19. ed. M.K. Pope and E.G. Lodge (Oxford, 1910), lines 1-30.

20. A.V.C. Schmidt (ed.), *The Vision of Piers the Ploughman* (London, 1978), B Prologue 33-39.

21. For an account of this type of poem see Scattergood, op. cit., pp 299-306, and Bestul, op. cit., pp 55-58.

22. For the text see Robbins, *Historical Poems,* No. 54.

23. For this type of poem see Scattergood, op. cit., pp 301-04.

24. See particularly R.J. Menner, *The Poetical Dialogues of Solomon and Saturn* (London, 1941), pp 21 ff. See also M.Y. Offord (ed.), *The Parlement of the Thre Ages* (Early English Text Society, Original Series 246, 1959), lines 599-604.

25. See Robbins, *Historical Poems,* No. 95, line 44.

26. For the text see Robbins, *Historical Poems,* No. 8.

27. For the text see D. Laing (ed.), *Collection of Ancient Scottish Prophecies in Alliterative Verse* (Bannantyne Club, Edinburgh, 1833), p. 39.

28. See Bestul, op. cit., pp 60-61.

29. See Hotspur on Glendower's prophecies in I Henry IV, III, i, pp 148-55.

30. See Morton W. Bloomfield, *Piers Plowman as a Fourteenth Century Apocalypse* (Rutgers University Press, 1961), and for a more general view Bernard McGinn, *Visions of the End: Apocalyptic Traditions in the Middle Ages* (Columbia University Press, 1979).

31. For a survey of the tradition see Helen E. Sandison, *The Chanson d'Aventure in Middle English,* Bryn Mawr Monographs XII (Pennsylvania, 1913).

32.   'The Audience and Public of *Piers Plowman*', in David A. Lawton (ed.), *Middle English Alliterative Poetry and its Literary Background* (Cambridge, 1982), p. 114.

33.   See W.H. Stahl, *Macrobius: Commentary on the Dream of Scipio* (Columbia University Press, 1952), pp 84-91.

34.   See A.C. Spearing, *Medieval Dream Poetry* (Cambridge University Press, 1976), p. 10.

35.   *The Ethics of Aristotle*, translated by J.A.K. Thomson (Harmondsworth, 1955), pp 68-69 (2.7.4).

36.   On the history of ideas about liberality, covetousness and prodigality see especially Bestul, op. cit., pp 5-14 where full references are given.

37.   *The Summa Theologica of St Thomas Aquinas*, literally translated by Fathers of the English Dominican Province, 2nd ed. (London, 1935), II, ii, qq. 117-119. The quotation is from Question 119, Second Article.

38.   The Canterbury Tales, X, 813-814 in F.N. Robinson (ed.), *The Complete Works of Geoffrey Chaucer,* 2nd ed. (Oxford, 1957).

39.   Arthur Brandeis (ed.), Early English Text Society, Original Series, 115, 1900, p. 309.

40.   *Anticlaudianus,* 9.8. in J.P. Migne, *Patrologia Latina,* 210, pp 573-74.

41.   For the *Architrenius,* see Thomas Wright, *The Anglo-Latin Satirical Poets and Epigrammatists of the Twelfth Century* (London, 1872), I, pp 240-392. The battle is described on pp 321-24.

42.   *The Divine Comedy of Dante Alighieri,* ed. and trans. John D. Sinclair (Oxford University Press, 1961), pp 98-100 (*Inferno,* VII, 28-30, 58).

43.   Quoted from the translation by Joseph B. Pike, *Frivolities of Courtiers and Footprints of Philosophers* (University of Minnesota Press, 1938), p. 307 (*Politraticus,* VII, iv, pp 241 ff.).

44.   ed. Samuel Paul Molenaer (New York, 1899), p. 60.

45.   See Robert Steele (ed.), *Three Prose Versions of the Secreta Secretorum,* English Text Society, Extra Series 74, pp 7-8. This is from the BL MS Royal 18 A viii version.

46.   See *Walter Map, De Nugis Curialium: Courtiers' Trifles,* ed. and trans. by M.R. James, rev. by C.N.L. Brooke and R.A.B. Mynors (Oxford, 1983), pp 438-39 (Dist. 5, cap. 5). For the account of Walter's own household see pp 12-25 (Dist. 1, cap. 10).

47.   ed. Joseph Moisant (Paris, 1891), pp 140-41.

48.   See Thomas Wright, *Political Poems and Songs,* pp 172, 139 (my translation).

49.   See the interesting case made by Elizabeth Salter, 'The Timeliness of *Winner and Waster*'.

50.   See Hans Kurath, et al. (eds), *Middle English Dictionary* (Ann Arbor, 1956) —, s.v. *clothen* v. 3b, *clothing* ger. 2b.

51.   According to J.A. Yunck, the poet '. . . places the usual subjects of venality-satire in the camp of Wynnere, the representation of avarice' in *The Lineage of Lady Meed* (University of Notre Dame Press, 1963), p. 269.

52.   See J.G. Bellamy, *The Law of Treason in England in the Later Middle Ages* (Cambridge, 1970), especially pp 59-101 for the Statute of 1352, and pp 102-37 for its scope.

53.   For this man see Bertha Haven Putnam, *The Place in Legal History of Sir William Shareshull* (Cambridge, 1950). For his relation to *Winner and Waster* see especially pp 146-47.

54.   See particularly Jesse May Anderson, 'A Note on the Date of *Winnere and Wastere',* *Modern Language Notes,* 43 (1928), pp 47-49.

55.   See J.M. Steadman, op. cit for the evidence from contemporary chronicles.

56.   *Rotuli Parliamentorum,* II, 236-37.

57. See the essay on 'The Estate of Merchants, 1336-1365' in G. Unwin (ed.), *Finance and Trade Under Edward III* (Manchester, 1918), especially pp 241, 232.
58. *Rotuli Parliamentorum,* II, 237.
59. '*Wynnere and Wastoure* and the Hundred Years War', *English Literary History,* 8 (1941), pp 241-47.
60. Moran, p. 623.
61. Aquinas, II, ii, Question 119, Article 3.
62. See, for example, Chaucer's *Canterbury Tales,* X, p. 114. For a recent reading of the poem which suggests that the poet has greater sympathy for the position of Waster, see Nicholas Jacobs, 'The Typology of Debate and the Interpretation of *Wynnere and Wastoure*', *Review of English Studies,* New Series, XXXVI (1985), pp 481-500.
63. ed. Sir George Warner (Oxford, 1926), line 1092. For an account of this poem see Scattergood, op. cit., pp 91-95.
64. Best, op. cit., p. 80.

Bardic Poetry as a Historical Source

KATHARINE SIMMS

For the historian research into Gaelic Ireland has always been hampered by the failure of Irish chieftains to keep administrative records of the chancery and exchequer type, forcing us to rely heavily on less precise sources such as annalistic compilations, sagas, genealogical tracts and of course incidental references in ecclesiastical and Anglo-Norman records. By contrast bardic poems normally received their first performance in the presence of the patron who paid for them.[1] Any genuine eulogy is thus strictly contemporary with the chief or noble it celebrates, and occasionally a poem may be explicitly or implicitly dated to a particular year. For instance the majestic lament for Brian Ó Néill, *Aoidhe mo chroidhe ceann Briain,* gives the date of the battle in which he was killed as 1260 by three separate modes of computation in verses 57-9, but then goes on to name other chieftains as dying not long after this event whose obits occur in the annals under the year 1261, suggesting that by the time the poem was composed an interval of some twelve months had elapsed since the death of Ó Néill himself.[2] In the nature of things most elegies can be similarly placed within a year or two by the help of annalistic obits, and a minority of other poems, especially those celebrating inaugurations, can be given a fairly precise date.

Moreover they are a class of document peculiarly difficult to forge. The name of the patron himself, his father and grandfather, wife and maternal relatives, his place of residence and the territory he rules are repeatedly woven into the verse structure, so that any substitution would risk distorting the rime scheme. The elaborate metrical requirements of *dán díreach* were normally only achieved by trained professionals[3] providing an authenticity of form more difficult to simulate than the diplomatics of the papal chancery. It was widely recognised that no-one but the man named in a eulogy, or his nearest and dearest in the case of an elegy,[4] had any interest in paying for such a composition. A comic tale in the *Leabhar Branach* ridicules a Dublin merchant who expected Ó Conchubhair Sligigh to pay twenty pounds for a bardic poem over a hundred years old, which was not

58

addresed to his father, his grandfather or any of his relatives.[5] Those forgeries which have come to light, as the poems on the Grace family of Kilkenny,[6] tend to be concocted for sentimental reasons in the post-bardic age for antiquarians with aristocratic pretensions wishing to demonstrate the illustrious position held by their ancestors. Since they could not at this late date call on the services of a professional bard, sub-standard metre provides a preliminary warning in such cases.

There is indeed one group of poems about which no expert has been able to say with certainty whether they are forgeries or not. These are the compositions attributed to Muireadhach Albanach Ó Dálaigh, a master-poet of the early thirteenth century, whose adventures the Four Masters record under the year 1213 in a prose narrative with many clearly legendary features, referring to three of the poems in question and citing one by its first line.[7] The poems are addressed to the most prominent chiefs of Muireadhach's day in Ireland and Scotland, and contain enough incidental references to the poet's own career to reconstruct a series of incidents similar to, but not identical with, the implausible story of the Four Masters. It would be easy to dismiss the group as the verse accompaniments to a romance, like the Battle of Clontarf cycle,[8] or the lamentations of Gormlaith for Niall Glúndubh.[9] The main argument for taking the poems as genuine compositions of the early thirteenth century is simply their superlative quality, which few authors could be expected to attain, together with a less easily definable freshness and lyricism such as Nicholas Williams among others has seen as typifying the early period.[10] Extracts from them are quoted as models of composition in the bards' grammatical tracts[11] and there is an apparent reference to an anthology of Muireadhach Albanach's poems as early as the fifteenth century.[12] It is certainly conceivable that a top-ranking bard of about the fourteenth century could have composed this series of poems to accompany a lost prose narrative as a work of art, and to glorify the name of the thirteenth-century poet, rather than the miscellaneous political figures to whom the poems are addressed. Because of this possibility, out of the five poems listed in the Royal Irish Academy's catalogue as addressed to Donnchadh Cairbreach Ó Briain, king of Thomond († 1242), the three attributed to Muireadhach Albanach must be regarded with some reserve, and not used as a source for biographical details of the king in question.[13] On the other hand, since the verse was undoubtedly composed by *some* master-poet of the high middle ages, it can be confidently drawn on for some more general concepts about the relationship between king and poet etc. The high literary standard of these works puts them in a class by themselves, but even in this doubtful case there is no question of a calculated forgery for the more usual motives of financial gain or political propaganda.

At one level then the typical bardic poem, composed by a single author to be recited in the presence of a particular patron on some special occasion, has the immediacy and individual touch of a letter or diary in other cultures. Some poets play on this person-to-person confrontation to lend an air of urgency and excitement to their verse:

Keep your face before me, Aodh . . . Stir not East nor West till I aim for your face. Wait for the shower of praise . . . shift not a foot sideways from me, lest an arrow miss its mark.[14]

Other poems are pleading or coquettish in tone, in keeping with the conventional role of the poet as the patron's lover.[15]

Yet the odes were for public performance rather than private communication, and having begun by emphasizing their authenticity, their contemporary nature and their individual message, at the risk of seeming perverse I must now add that their real value lies in their insincerity, even their falsity, if one wants to call it that. The fact that every bardic eulogy was delivered in expectation of a substantial reward meant inevitably that the sentiments it contained were either directly requested by the patron,[16] or the poet confidently expected them to be welcome hearing. The historian is thus not dependent on the idiosyncratic views of a single man of art, however gifted. He learns the standpoint of the politically powerful patron, and to a lesser extent current public opinion, which might or might not coincide with the bard's private bias.

A poet who consistently supported one political stance, that of peaceful cooperation between the Uí Dhomhnaill of Tír Conaill and the rulers of Tír Eoghain, was Giolla Brighde MacConmidhe.[17] The MacConmidhe family were a branch of the Cineál Eoghain who occupied lands about the modern Baronscourt, Co. Tyrone, near the border of Tír Conaill, so that when the Ó Domhnaill chief raided his Cineál Eoghain rivals, Giolla Brighde's own property suffered, as he gently implies in one poem:

Though he took many cows from us, it would not be right for us to begrudge it him; the kingship of the soft chief of Búill is the cement of our country.[18]

In the course of his lifetime Giolla Brighde served as chief poet to Domhnall Mór Ó Domhnaill, Brian Ó Néill and Domhnall Óg Ó Domhnaill. In such circumstances one might expect the pacific tone of his poetry to reflect the bard's own wishes, and indeed two centuries later another poet of this family, Brian Ruadh MacConmidhe, hints as much when he addressed Neachtain Ó Domhnaill († 1452) with these words:

> I am equally related to the sons [of Niall of the Nine Hostages] Conall and famous Eoghan.
> Though the family be split into two branches,
> It is not for me to take sides.
>
> Giolla Brighde, closely connected with us,
> used to confirm what I have said.
> It was the same case for him as for me,
> This is the race who held him dear.[19]

Yet however advantageous a peaceful alliance of the two kingdoms might have been to Giolla Brighde's private interests, it would have been impossible for him to urge this in his poems, if it had not already formed part of his patrons' plans. In 1208 the Four Masters tell us 'a peace . . . was concluded between O'Neill and O'Donnell, who entered into an alliance to assist each other against such of the English or Irish as should oppose them'. The *Annals of Ulster* place a somewhat different interpretation on this alliance when they state that in 1211 it was Aodh Ó Néill, king of Tír Eoghain, who mustered the forces of Cineál Conaill, Cineál Eoghain and Oirghialla to oppose the Anglo-Normans near Belleek.[20] After the death of this Aodh in 1230, his son and heir Domhnall Ó Néill was opposed and eventually killed in 1234 by a distant kinsman, Domhnall MacLochlainn, who had already embarked on hostilities against Domhnall Mór Ó Domhnaill, Aodh's former ally.[21] From a poem of Giolla Bridhe MacConmidhe we learn that Domhnall Mór fostered his infant daugher, Gormlaith, with a 'Domhnall in the East' as 'the key of the lock of the Irish' which would have 'closed the doors of war'.[22] However this foster-child died young, and in 1241 her brother Maoilsheachlainn Ó Domhnaill, the new king of Tír Conaill, used his forces to defeat MacLochlainn and place Brian Ó Néill in the kingship of Tír Eoghain.[23] Thus Giolla Brighde's constant harking back to a tradition in which overlordship of these two kingdoms or of all Ireland is said to alternate between the rulers of Cineál Conaill and Cineál Eoghain[24] can be seen as directly reflecting the events of his own lifetime. It was an allusion more obviously complimentary to the historically less powerful Ó Domhnaill chiefs and is not found in his two poems for Ó Néill.[25]

His fifteenth-century descendant, Brian Ruadh MacConmidhe, was similarly placed, having served as chief poet to Ó Néill from an early age,[26] and witnessed a period of close political ties between Tír Conaill and Tír

Eoghain; at first dominated by Niall Garbh II Ó Domhnaill († 1439),[27] and then by Éinrí Ó Néill. In 1442 Neachtain Ó Domhnaill was forced to submit to Éinrí and hand over his castle on the River Finn to be garrisoned by Éinrí's troops.[28] In these circumstances a more eminent bard than Brian Ruadh, Tadhg Óg Ó hUiginn, recommended friendship with Ó Néill for the future:

Let the hero of Áth Liag think of what land is held by the Goill [Anglo-Irish] of Banba's Field; that should annoy him more than the power of Eoghan's race, for that race of Niall is of his own flesh and blood.

May graceful Neachtain, Toirdhealbhach's son, understand the wisdom of my advice — seeing that the Goill are near to him too — not to attack Niall's strong folk.[29]

The Uí Uiginn were based in the modern Co. Sligo and so had no strong personal reasons for mediating between Ó Domhnaill and Ó Néill. Since Neachtain was thus exhorted by two different poets to tolerate the Uí Néill it is a reasonable conclusion that Brian Ruadh MacConmidhe was not primarily moved by family considerations, nor was Tadhg Óg Ó hUiginn offering gratuitous advice, but that both bards were reflecting Ó Domhnaill's own desire for some heroic justification which would explain his prudent reluctance to attack Ó Néill.

Indeed it is something of a tribute to the good sense of Irish chieftains that there are at least as many bardic odes extant which urge them *not* to take up arms, for one reason or another, as there are positive exhortations to battle. The same Tadhg Óg who advised Neachtain to refrain from resisting the Uí Néill in order to concentrate on the English enemy told Éinrí Ó Néill not to attack the English until all Ulster was subdued.[30] Once again there is a poem by Brian Ruadh MacConmidhe, Éinrí's own *ollamh*, conveying the same message.[31] Tomás Óg MagUidhir, an abject vassal of Ó Néill, was represented as eagerly seeking supreme power, but hindered by his subjects' reluctance to leave their delightful homeland of Fermanagh:

We must not go to the Dún of Eamhain and thus rouse up war with Í Néill; nor to Dún Geanainn either; securer are our own lands.[32]

In the late sixteenth century Tadhg Dall Ó hUiginn exhorted the unsuccessful Conn Ó Domhnaill to abandon his rights over Donegal and Sligo in favour of the mythical highkingship of Tara,[33] while a poem by the celebrated Eochaidh Ó hEoghusa begged Aodh MagUidhir to cease campaigning for the sake of the poets, since his warlike lifestyle prevented him from holding the banquets which gave them employment.[34]

Such poems are only 'false' or insincere in so far as their message has been presented as a piece of spontaneous advice, even as a petition from the poet, whereas the political background to the various cases suggests they are rather attempts to clothe the naked and often unpalatable facts with heroic words and striking imagery. From another point of view they are far truer than they pretend to be, since they reflect an existing situation, not merely something the poet would have liked to take place.

Given that a bard composed for payment, the only unwelcome or unexpected demands he might voice were normally requests for his personal benefit, to obtain a new saddle-horse,[35] or support in a law-suit,[36] or immunity in time of war.[37] Occasionally he may have been employed as a mouth-piece or ambassador, in which case the man he addressed was not the patron who had paid him. Tadhg Dall Ó hUiginn was an unsuccessful emissary of this kind. In *Molfaid Conallaigh clann Táil* he complains:

my kinsfolk, my own friends, oblige me to go and seek protection and surety from the stern, powerful kindred of Dálach.

Despite all they had lavished upon me, this I have to say of the tribe of Conall, they had no mind to undertake my protection; unhappy the condition of the friends.[38]

He is careful to emphasize that he has not personally been plundered by Ó Domhnaill's followers, and if, as seems likely, the original poem of intercession which had been ignored was *Dia do bheatha, a mheic Mhaghnuis*, the 'kinsfolk' and 'friends' in question were not merely his own Ó hUiginn relatives, but the whole kingdom of North Connacht, which Ó Domhnaill was then threatening to invade!

Since it is thine, thou smooth and soft of skin, thou wouldst not ravage Connacht, O blameless hand; the babe was begot by thee.

Thou hast spared Conn's Croghan, thou hast protected the haven of ancient, clear-streamed Sligo against Conall's line, in spite of the impatient men of Ulster.

Didst thou follow the counsel of the rest, Telton would be in a blaze, and Croghan dismantled; listen not to their entreaties.[39]

Another possible example of the poet as intercessor is *Dimghach do Chonall Clann Dálaigh* which urges Niall Garbh II Ó Domhnaill not to insist on passing his kingship on to his own sons. Towards the end of Niall's reign there was a war between his brother Neachtain and Niall's son, Toirdhealbhach. Since this bardic address also contains the unpleasing information that there is widespread dissatisfaction among Niall's subjects at the heaviness of his taxation,[40] it seems reasonable to speculate that it was commissioned by Neachtain, rather than Niall himself.

So far the poems looked at have reflected contemporary events faithfully enough, but of course merely to say that a bardic ode represented the considered policy of the patron rather than the whim of the poet is no guarantee of its literal truth. The commonest lie was to use the title *rí* or 'king' in addressing a patron who was not in fact the head of his family. This cannot be dismissed as idle flattery, because a nobleman who countenanced his bard addressing him as 'king' must be in a position to defy the resentment of the reigning chief. A particularly well-documented case is that of the Uí Néill of Clann Aodha Bhuidhe in the mid-fifteenth century. When the chief, Brian Ballach Ó Néill, died in 1425 he left four sons of whom Muircheartach Ruadh was the senior, described as 'captain of his nation' by Primate John Swayne in 1427.[41] Yet seven complete bardic poems and a fragment bear eloquent testimony to the ambition of the youngest brother, Aodh Buidhe II.[42] The fragment praises both Muircheartach Ruadh and Aodh Buidhe as 'Ulster's well of hospitality', but adds that the poetic order receives greater honour from Aodh Buidhe.[43] *Ní haois fhoirfidheas a Aedh* is a long ode on the legal principle that an elder kinsman must give place to a younger if the latter is better qualified,[44] and the point is hammered home in other poems: 'Whom has your dynasty produced comparable to you?'[45] — 'The princes of Leath Cuinn who would fain rival him — he is as far beyond them in the greatness of his ways as the moon is beyond the stars'.[46] Again and again royal titles are showered on Aodh, though in complimentary rather than legalistic terms: 'A King of the true royal blood',[47] 'King of the Hill of Howth',[48] 'King of the Irish host',[49] 'King of the fort of Tara'.[50] In 1443 Aodh Buidhe took steps to translate these dreams into practical reality when he seized large herds of cattle from his elder brother, Muircheartach Ruadh, and forced him to yield submission as the price of their return.[51] In the event Aodh was never to be inaugurated as chief, however. He was killed prematurely in 1444 while attempting to enforce his overlordship of a neighbouring chief, Art MagAonghusa.[52] Two of the three elegies on him which survive testify to the almost comical dismay of the poets, anticipating a cold reception from Aodh's relatives in revenge for the favouritism they had earlier shown him.[53] One poem mentions that Aodh had issued a *gairm sgoile,* a general invitation to the learned classes of Ireland, similar to the two famous feasts held by his mother-in-law Mairghréag Ní Chearbhaill in 1433.[54] Repeatedly the common motif of quixotic generosity towards the bardic order occurs with unusual emphasis in relation to Aodh Buidhe:

Let no king of Conn's race
practice hospitality at his side.
An impulse, however splendid, from another man
is petty beside Aodh.[55]

After all he gave at the coming of the poets
not many cattle belong to his curly hair,
the generous man does not usually possess wealth,
Aodh's profit is [having] everyone subject to his will.[56]

All in all the evidence suggests that Aodh Buidhe II made a calculated use of poets, and paid heavily for their services, in a propaganda campaign to undermine the position of his elder brother and chief.

Bestowing royal titles on a patron without naming the kingdom he was supposed to rule[57] was one device by which the bards endeavoured not to abandon altogether their theoretical role as custodians of the truth.[58] There were other ways of conveying a false impression which yet came short of an outright lie. Young Feidhlim Fionn Ó Conchobhair Ruaidh was hailed as a king on his way to the inauguration ceremony c. 1464-8, at a period when he was in fact surrounded by enemies, and faced with a lifelong struggle to achieve formal recognition of his authority.[59] In 1387 Niall Óg Ó Néill, who wished to be accepted as King of Ulster rather than merely King of Tír Eoghain, went to the trouble and expense of erecting a house for the entertainment of poets within the old hill-fort of Eamhain Macha and was duly hailed by the bards as successor to Conchobhar mac Neasa and Cúchulainn, in spite of the element of genealogical confusion this involved.[60] A more fantastic compliment was paid to Art MacMurchadha Caomhánach by Eoghan MacCraith, who used the genuine tradition of gold-mines in the Wicklow hills to support his audacious claim that gold was ubiquitous in MacMurchadha's own court:

Gold for poems is given
by the heroes of Mogh's hill;
they get gold in tribute;
their alms are gold coins.

Bright gold is on their chess-board,
wrought gold on their helmets,
gold-work on the shining bridles
of the steeds of Laighin's green-lanced host.

"Laighnigh of the gold"
is no false name for them at banquet;
at carouse no hero
quaffs drink but from gold.[61]

The fact that its author was nicknamed *an t-Órthóir*, 'the Gilder' (a man who painted gold-leaf over wood, leather or base metal objects) strongly suggests that even his contemporaries found this poem absurd. It violated the admonitions to every properly-qualified *file* attributed to the legendary master-poet, Dubhthach mac hUí Lugair:

Let him not be a vessel of old proverbs for reward or friendship, for a man with proper training(?) will not cite old judgements: let him not be bashful or timid(?) in the presence of a great family; unless he is thus distinguished he does not deserve his fee.[62]

The last clause in this piece reminds us that Irish nobles were paying not solely for the message the bardic verse contained, still less for its aesthetic value, but in large measure they were buying prestige. One way of achieving this was to lavish rewards on the privileged orders indiscriminately, as proof of one's extravagant generosity and respect for their calling. The wife of a fourteenth-century MagShamhradháin won praise for such a policy:

MagUidhir's stately daughter . . . has (often) rewarded even a faulty poem — an approach to the hearts of scholars in training! . . .

Nualaith is never niggardly in rewarding poems (even) when a poet presumes too far; her anger will not fall on a poet-band, however many come with their harps.[63]

Undoubtedly, however, the greatest prestige was conferred by the best poems, and patrons were alive to this consideration. It was said of the chief Maghnus MagShamhradháin († 1303) that he sought out poets of reputed talent to purchase their eulogies in advance, sight unseen.[64] The Mac-Domhnaill Lords of the Isles repeatedly issued unsuccessful invitations designed to lure the most skilful Irish bards of their day over to Scotland.[65] In an interesting address to Fiacha mac Aodha Uí Bhroin his own *ollamh*, Fearghal MacEochadha, complains about his master's indiscriminate patronage of poets from other parts of Ireland and lays down three conditions for prestigious verse. In the first place, its praise must be founded on truth — praise that is 'false' because excessive or unearned is not praise at all. Secondly the poet who voices it should be of noble blood, and thirdly he should be a fully-trained and skilled practitioner. The incompetent verse of a half-trained student is a source of mockery rather than prestige and should be valued as copper beside the golden compositions of a first-class bard.[66]

With Fearghal's pronouncements in mind it is of some interest to note that among Aodh Buidhe Ó Néill's eulogists the most sycophantic were

Amhlaoigh Ó hEachaidhéin, of a local East Ulster family, and Aodh's own *ollamh*, Donnchadh Mac an Chnáidhe, a surname otherwise quite unrecorded. Aodh's only surviving eulogy by a poet with a nationwide reputation came from the Leinster visitor, Dubhthach MacEochadha, who was careful to avoid any extravagant claims, referring to Aodh merely as *mac ríogh*, 'a king's son'.[67]

It was generally recognised that bards of the first rank seldom composed for minor chieftains, although it is less clear whether this was merely a result of the prohibitive expense involved, or whether master-poets were deliberately selective in order to maintain the convention that their praise conferred prestige. Certainly inferior poetry came at a cheaper price. Mag Shamhradháin was assured:

Only princes who store up wealth and devote no time to their pleasures find a greater charm in the band which goes around with wretched *abhráns* and in misshapen crooked faulty poetry (*an camdhán fiar fíorlochtach*).

Their prizes, namely the getting of food by means of their doggerel(?), are their very nature; there is a great demand for their wares, they seek not gold or kine.[68]

Classic poems addressed to politically unimportant figures almost invariably occur in special circumstances. Tuathal Ó Máille, a chief from West Connacht, extended his horizons beyond his family inheritance by taking mercenary service in Ulster. On some occasion he quarrelled with a master-poet, who stabbed and seriously wounded him. Instead of claiming *éaraic* (the legal payment for bloodshed) Ó Máille asked for a eulogy, and the poet congratulates him on his choice:

You did not claim a pledge for your wound, you ignored the (loss of) the best blood; here to requite you for it is a melodious poem, you deserved from me the price of your healing . . .

You have procured the fame of the men of Umhall. . . if I were to pray for the grace of God upon your family, I owe it owing to your clemency to me.[69]

The boast was justified. Not only is the poem itself a magnificent specimen of bardic art, but it is the *only* poem to an Ó Máille now extant. No doubt these chieftains were eulogised by other poets from time to time, but not in 'immortal' verse, of the kind that was generally admired and copied by the bardic schools rather than depending for survival on the chance preservation of a family poem-book.[70]

Similarly only one poem to an Ó hAnnluain has been preserved from the whole medieval period. Giolla-Pádraig Ó hAnnluain († 1243) had been satirised by a lesser member of the MacConmidhe family, and his anger was such that the *ollamh* Giolla Brighde MacConmidhe agreed to compose a eulogy in reparation. Once again Giolla Brighde congratulates the victim on his good fortune:

I will make a poem for his soft cheek that will lessen Giolla Pádraig's hurt . . . Did he but know it, long is the achievement of him who satirized Ó hAnnluain.[71]

And once again the boast came true. The self-confidence shown by these master-poets was founded not only on conscious artistry but, as Fearghal MacEochadha had implied, on social rank, 'nobility of blood'. The title *ollamh* often meant leadership of a hereditarily learned landowning family rather than mere court office.[72] The Uí Dhálaigh had even been territorial sub-chiefs of Corca Raidhe[73] in the twelfth century; and in the early fourteenth their family head, Aonghus Ruadh, was not only a skilled bard in his own right, but great-grandson of the celebrated Donnchadh Mór Ó Dálaigh.[74] His apology for satirising the Westmeath chieftain Ruaidhri Ó Maolmhuaidh was almost offhand:

Why should I go to the Plain of Midhe among my folk if thou art going to oppose me? . . . O young Prince of Almha, O joyous-faced hero who never shirkest fight, if thou art angry with Í Dhálaigh I will, owing to that anger, stay with Brian's fair-haired race . . .[75]

Apparently Ó Maolmhuaidh proved irreconcilable, and Aonghus Ruadh fulfilled his threat of emigrating to Ó Briain's lordhsip, where he became ancestor to Ó Dálaigh Corcumruadh.[76]

There were two significant limitations to the independence of a great poet. In the first place, he was not in a position to pressurize powerful paramount chiefs with impunity. The MacConmidhe poets occupied an estate in west Tír Eoghain whose long association with their family is suggested by its title *Fearann an Reacaire,* 'the Reciter's land'.[77] The fifteenth-century Conchobhar Ruadh MacConmidhe called his possessions 'charter-land', signifying hereditary ownership rather than tenancy. As a newly-appointed *ollamh* he had served as intermediary, persuading the rebellious Brian Óg Ó Néill to submit to his chief, and guaranteeing his safe-conduct to and from the Great Ó Néill. When Ó Néill and his sons severed Brian Óg's hand and foot in flagrant breach of MacConmidhe's safe-conduct, the poet satirized his employers. He was promptly banished and his lands annexed by Ó Néill's son. Eighteen years later he was still an exile in Connacht, pleading to have his estates and office restored.[78] The notorious Aonghus Ruadh Ó Dálaigh, who satirized almost every noble

family in Ireland at the end of the sixteenth century, did not dare to insult
the Uí Dhomhnaill:

> Should I satirize the Clann Dálaigh
> The race of Adam would not be a shelter to me;
> The Clann Dálaigh would be a shelter to me,
> Were I to satirize the race of old Adam.[79]

The other limitation on a poet's influence was simply his lack of interest
in political questions which did not affect him personally. In the well-
known words of Goffraidh Fionn Ó Dálaigh:

In the foreigners' poems we promise that the Irish shall be driven from Ireland; in
the Irishmen's poems we promise that the foreigners shall be routed across the
sea,[80]

Ostensibly spontaneous outbursts of patriotism can nearly always be traced to the influence of some patron, as in the case of the political poem
Fúbún fúibh, a shluagh Gaoidheal, where the poet condemns all the nobles
of Ireland for their craven acceptance of Henry VIII's policy of Surrender
and Regrant, but makes a favourable exception of Ó Cearbhaill 'to whom',
he says, 'I am bounden by oaths'; who was presumably therefore his own
territorial chief or employer.[81]

One preoccupation of this paper has been to emphasize the importance
of distinguishing between insincerity and untruth, a vital consideration for
the study of professional poets. Professor Carney has drawn attention to
the contrast between the apparent emotions and the underlying message in
the poems of Eochaidh Ó hEoghusa, for example his passionately affec-
tionate refusal to join his employer at the siege of Kinsale,[82] comparable
with the savage incitements to refrain from fighting discussed earlier.[83] In
each case the euphemisms, metaphors and eulogistic epithets are only the
sugar coating designed to make the medicine of the inner meaning more acceptable, not only to the patron himself, but to the audience of friends and
followers before whom the first public performance of such a poem took
place. There was also a wider audience to take into account. A poem that
was considered sensational either in form or content was not merely spread
and immortalized by the bardic schools, as when we hear that a composition of the fourteenth-century Geoffraidh Fionn Ó Dálaigh was recited to a
sixteenth-century Mag Uidhir for its literary worth,[84] but if the contents
were politically controversial rumour swiftly carried a report to those ears
most likely to be offended. Giolla Brighde MacConmidhe had cause to
lament the 'fast-travelling news' (*sgéal siobhlach*) that he had been inciting

the Cineál Eoghain to attack Ó Domhnaill, a spiteful tale carried by Ó Domhnaill's groom, he claimed.[85] Deliberate satires were particularly likely to be reported at second or third hand, since from understandable prudence it seems they were seldom recited in the victim's presence. The fact that the poets when apologizing to an offended patron tended simultaneously to deny that the insult had been uttered and to reinterpret its purport[86] suggests that they hoped the patron had heard only a garbled summary of the controversial work, but they feared he might acquire the full text. These indications that recently composed poems were discussed by people not in a position to recite them word for word brings out the importance of the contents rather than the form to the non-learned audience in later medieval Ireland.

For the latter-day historian also the contents of bardic poetry must be the prime consideration. Detailed comparison of the compositions of eminent bards with those of the more obscure indicates that literary excellence involved dextrous use of complex metres such as *rannaigheacht* and *droighneach,* ornamentation with *breacadh* (optional superfluous rimes), puns and figures of speech, and the inclusion of learned or entertaining apologues to illustrate the main argument. However from a strictly utilitarian point of view the presence of such features in abundance is only of interest to the historian as suggesting that the poem was an expensive one, and consequently that the patron was either wealthy and influential, or ambitious to become so. The Mag Shamhradháin chiefs of Teallach Eachach and the Gabhal Raghnallach branch of the Ó Broin family were both minor dynasties, but the fourteenth-century Mag Shamhradháin poem-book and the sixteenth-century *Leabhar Branach* each contain some works by major bards[87] as well as pieces from local practitioners; and in each case their compilation coincides with a peak period in the political influence of the family concerned.[88]

It has long been recognised that small nuggets of factual information can be mined from bardic poems. They often supplement the patrilinear genealogies with the names of a patron's wife and his maternal relatives. It was a traditional function of the king's *ollamh* to keep a reckoning of his master's military exploits and victories,[89] and the bare names of the battlefields can be accompanied by circumstantial details. Another set piece was eulogizing a patron's house, particularly when newly-built, sometimes with prayers for its future security, and a description of its interior.[90] Elegies on a dead king occasionally describe the manner of his death.[91]

However it has been the purpose of this paper to suggest that every professional eulogy or elegy can also be analysed to yield the bard's intended message, an undertaking that requires not so much special training as a certain amount of diligence. Only after reading a number of such poems does it become easy to recognise recurring motifs, praise of personal appearance, fertility during the just king's reign, liberality to poets, prowess in war and so forth, and penetrate through them to the comparatively few verses with a distinctive purport. Once the impression the bard intended to convey has been brought into focus, the question still remains, did this correspond to an existing state of affairs or voice a political ambition? Every possible source of independent information on the patron has to be brought into play — annals, genealogies, state papers or ecclesiastical records — before this can be answered, if at all. What is a safe bet, a probability of ten to one, is that the policy expressed by the poem was accepted by the patron himself at the time of composition. Only the rare occasions where the poet speaks as the mouth-piece of another patron, or has a personal interest at stake, form the exceptions.

By no means all surviving bardic poems are composed for patrons, whether as eulogies or elegies. Preliminary work I have done on a comprehensive survey of the extant corpus indicates that out of a total of some 1,800 to 2,000 poems, just over half are addressed to earthly patrons, with a further 20% cast in the same mould, but directed heavenwards, invoking God and the saints. The remaining 28% or so comprise *dánta grádha* (Elizabethan and Jacobean poems on courtly love), bardic contentions, including the celebrated *Iomarbháidh na bhFileadh* of the early seventeenth century, and miscellaneous pieces, which might deal with the death of a lapdog, an old brown cloak, or the pleasures of reading.

Rather more than 60% of the poems have already been published, two-thirds of them with English translations, and the total number of edited texts is being increased daily. Since about half date to the late sixteenth century and after, they deserve more attention from modern historians than has been the case until recently.[92] The fact that so many have been published as single items in numerous disparate journals, concerned with Celtic studies, local history or ecclesiastical interests, poses something of a chore for research students trying to track them down, but adds to the excitement of a successful capture. For as I can testify from personal experience, the study of bardic poetry for its historical content, originally undertaken to serve the interests of a wider field of research, can become an end in itself. After the first fifty or a hundred poems a fascination, an addiction even, develops.

NOTES AND REFERENCES

1. E. Knott, *Irish Classical Poetry* (Dublin 1960), pp 57-8; H.F. Hore, 'Irish Bardism in 1561' in *U.J.A.* 1st series vi (1858), p. 167.
2. N.J.A. Williams, *The Poems of Giolla Brighde Mac Con Midhe* (Dublin 1980), pp 152, 319, 320.
3. One of the few amateurs to achieve strict *dan díreach* was the late sixteenth-century William Nugent; see G. Murphy, 'Poems of Exile by Uilliam Nuinseann' in *Éigse* vi (1948-52), pp 9-10. The talented Earl Gerald the Rimer was restricted to the simpler *óglachas* mode; see G. MacNiocaill, 'Duanaire Gearóid Iarla' in *Studia Hibernica* iii (1963), pp 8-9.
4. J. O'Donovan, 'Fearghal Og Mac an Bhaird's poem on the Battle of Dun' in *Miscellany of the Celtic Society* (Dublin 1849), pp 410-11.
5. S. MacAirt (ed.), *Leabhar Branach* (Dublin 1944), p. 215.
6. C. Ó Lochlainn, 'Literary Forgeries in Irish' in *Éigse* ii (1940), pp 123-36; A.P. MacGréagóir, 'Cionnus do ceapadh Marbhna Oiliféir Grás agus dhá dhán eile', *ibid.*, pp 267-73; T.F. O'Rahilly, 'Literary Forgeries in Irish' in *The Irish Book Lover* xxvii (1941), pp 273-5. I have discussed another probable forgery, *MacCairtean triath na n-each seang* in an appendix to my Ph. D. thesis 'Gaelic lordships in Ulster in the later middle ages' (T.C.D. 1976), pp 807-10.
7. B. Ó Cuív, 'Eachtra Mhuireadhaigh Í Dhálaigh' in *Studia Hib.* i (1961), pp 56-69.
8. C. Ó Lochlainn, 'Poets on the Battle of Clontarf I' in *Éigse* iii (1941-2), pp 208-18.
9. O. Bergin, *Irish Bardic Poetry* (Dublin 1970), pp 202-15.
10. Williams, *Poems of Giolla Brighde*, p. 1.
11. Bergin, *Irish Bardic Poetry*, pp 93, 101.
12. G. Murphy, 'Two Irish poems written from the Mediterranean in the thirteenth century' in *Éigse* vii (1953), P. 74.
13. A fourth poem, otherwise anonymous, is ludicrously attributed in one late manuscript to the sixteenth-century Muiris mac Dáibhí Dhuibh; see N. Williams (ed.), *Dánta Mhuiris Mhic Dháibhí Dhuibh Mhic Gearailt* (Dublin 1979), pp 21-2. Osborn Bergin (*Irish Bardic Poetry*, p. 192) was disposed to attribute it to Muireadhach Albanach, presumably because the author implies he is a pilgrim; but the final verse in compliment to the obscure figure of Maol Ruanaidh, the king's carver, suggests this poem is genuinely contemporary, whoever the author, and Giolla Brighde Albanach, undisputed composer of the fifth poem to Donnchadh Cairbreach, had gone on pilgrimage to the Holy Land (see Murphy, as above note 12, p. 71).
14. Con*n*uimh rom t'aigh*idh* a Aodh . . . Ná cuir cor dhíot siar na soir . a Aodh go n-aimsin t'aigh*idh* . fuire ris an bfras molta . . . Na sgib uaim troigh*idh* trasna . . . go nach tig soighid seochad' — R.I.A. MS no. 490 (23/N/15), p. 161. (My translation.)
15. J. Carney, *The Irish Bardic Poet* (Dublin 1967), pp 12-13, 37-8.
16. E. Knott, *The Bardic Poems of Tadhg Dall Ó hUiginn* (London 1922, 1926), poem no. 8, verses 15, 36.
17. Williams, *Poems of Giolla Brighde*, no. 1 verses 6-17; no. 2 verses 3-5, 9; no. 3 verses 6, 24, 27; no. 8 verse 28; no. 9 verses 37-8; no. 10 verse 17.
18. *Ibid.*, p. 93.
19.   'Comghar dam duth*chas* na cloinne
                             Conull is Eog*an* fhuair bl*ad*
                             ge beith an clann na da cinedh
                             rann ar leith ni dlig*ed* dam

Gilla Bridhde gar becc duinne
do derb*ad* a ndubh*air*t me
as inand scél do 7 damhsa
ag so an frem lerb annsa é'
J. Fraser and J.G. O'Keeffe, 'Poems on the O'Donnells' in *Irish Texts*, ii, ed. J. Fraser,
P. Grosjean and J.G. O'Keeffe (London 1931), p. 41. (My translation.) In another
poem to Neachtain, Brian Ruadh makes a similar reference to Giolla Bridhde more
briefly — *ibid.*, p. 39.

20. In 1226 Ó Domhnaill yielded a son as hostage to Aodh Ó Néill (*Ann. Conn.*).
21. *A.U.*
22. Williams, *Poems of Giolla Brighde*, p. 23.
23. *A.U.*; Williams, *Poems of Giolla Brighde*, pp 34-7.
24. See W.M. Hennessy and D.H. Kelly (eds.), *The Book of Fenagh* (Dublin 1875), pp 358-64.
25. Williams, *Poems of Giolla Brighde*, nos. xiii and xvi.
26. D. Greene (ed.), *Duanaire Mhéig Uidhir* (Dublin 1972), pp 218-21.
27. K. Simms, 'Niall Garbh II O Donnell' in the *Donegal Annual* (1977), pp 7-21.
28. *A.U.*
29. L. McKenna (ed.), *Aithdioghluim Dána* ii (Dublin 1940), p. 57.
30. K. Simms, ' "The King's Friend": O'Neill, the Crown and the Earldom of Ulster', in *England and Ireland in the later Middle Ages*, ed. J.F. Lydon (Dublin 1981), p. 228; McKenna, *Aithdioghluim Dána*, no. 17 verses 19-21.
31. Simms, ' "The King's Friend" ', p. 227.
32. K. Simms, 'The Medieval Kingdom of Lough Erne' in the *Clogher Record* (1977), p. 134; McKenna, *Aithdioghluim Dána*, ii, p. 67.
33. Knott, *Poems of Tadhg Dall*, no. 1, verses 44, 50, 51.
34. L. MacCionaith, *Dioghluim Dána* (Dublin 1938), p. 237.
35. L. McKenna (ed.), *The Book of Magauran* (Dublin 1947), nos. vi and vii.
36. Knott, *Poems of Tadhg Dall*, no. 22.
37. P. Walsh (ed.), *Beatha Aodha Ruaidh* i (Dublin 1948), pp 208-11.
38. Knott, *Poems of Tadhg Dall* ii, p. 14.
39. *Ibid.*, p. 12.
40. Simms, 'Niall Garbh II O'Donnell', pp 17-18.
41. P.R.O.N.I. Registrum Iohannis Swayne, Lib. iii, fo. 133r. (T.C.D. MS 557/4/472). D.A. Chart, *The Register of John Swayne* (Belfast 1935), p. 115.
42. R.I.A. MSS nos. 1269/III A (B/iv/1b); 743 (A/iv/3), p. 691; McKenna, *Aithdioghluim Dána*, no. 18; T. Ó Donnchadha (ed.), *Leabhar Cloinne Aodha Buidhe* (Dublin 1931), pp 59-86.
43. 'Muir*cert*ach ruagh rogha an i*ar*sma . Aedh buide le mbreathnaigh siad cosmail mei*ne* an mogal c*ur*adh . tob*ur* feili ul*adh* iad
    Ag Aed buidhe as f*err* a n-onoir . ord fil*edh* na feadhna tall . . .'
    (R.I.A. MS no. 1269/III A).
44. Ó Donnchadha, *Leabhar Cloinne Aodha Buidhe*, pp 59-64; D.A. Binchy (ed.), *Corpus Iuris Hibernici*, p. 1289; T. Ó Raithbheartaigh, *Genealogical tracts* i (Dublin 1932), p. 30.
45. 'Cia tharla mar thu dod shliocht?' R.I.A. MS no. 743, p. 693.
46. McKenna, *Aithdioghluim Dána* no. 18, verse 21.
47. *Ibid.*, verse 36.
48. Ó Donnchadha, *Leabhar Cloinne Aodha Buidhe*, p. 73 line 67.

49. *Ibid.,* p. 76 line 14.
50. *Ibid.,* p. 82 line 21.
51. *A.F.M.*; J. O'Donovan, 'The annals of Ireland . . . by . . . Duald MacFirbis' in *Miscellany of the Irish Archaeological Society* i (Dublin 1846), p. 201.
52. *A.U., A.F.M., Ann. Conn., A.L.C.*; S. Ó hInnse (ed.), *Miscellaneous Irish Annals* (Dublin 1947), p. 114; O'Donovan, 'Annals . . . by . . . MacFirbis', pp 203, 208.
53. Ó Donnchadha, *Leabhar Cloinne Aodha Buidhe,* pp 76-86.
54. *Ibid.,* p. 85; K. Simms, 'Guesting and Feasting in Gaelic Ireland' in *R.S.A.I. Jn.* cviii (1978), p. 92.
55. 'Ná deunadh rí do fhréimh Chuinn . eineach is é ar a ghualainn láimh re hAodh ó fhior eile . mion gach taom dá thaidhbhsighe. (Ó Donnchadha, *Leabhar Cloinne Aodha Buidhe,* p. 64) (My translation.)
56. 'Déis a ttiobhra ar ttoc*ht* na ndá*mh* . ní bú hiomdha ga fholt cláon ní gnáth ion*n*mhas ag an fhial . cách dá ríar as ion*n*las d'Aodh' (R.I.A. MS no. 743, p. 692) (My translation.)
57. Good examples of the use of this device in the absence of real kingship come in McKenna, *Aithdioghluim Dána* no. 4 and J. Carney (ed.), *Poems on the O'Reillys* (Dublin 1950), no. xxxiv.
58. See F.J. Byrne, *Irish Kings and High-Kings* (London 1973), p. 15.
59. K. Simms, ' "Gabh umad a Fheidhlimidh" — a fifteenth-century inauguration ode?' in *Ériu* xxxi (1980), p. 136.
60. K. Simms, 'Propaganda use of the *Táin* in the later middle ages' in *Celtica* xv (1983), pp 142-9.
61. L. McKenna, 'To Art MacMurchadha Caomhánach' in the *Irish Monthly* lvi (1928), p. 99; MacCionaith, *Dioghluim Dána* no. 100.
62. M. Dillon (ed.), *Lebor na Cert* (Dublin 1962), p. 123.
63. L. McKenna (ed.), *The Book of Magauran* (Dublin 1947), pp 379, 387.
64. *Ibid.* no. xi, verse 26.
65. Bergin, *Irish Bardic Poetry,* no. 45; McKenna, *Aithdioghluim Dána,* no. 29.
66. MacAirt, *Leabhar Branach,* pp 108-115.
67. Ó Donnchadha, *Leabhar Cloinne Aodha Buidhe,* pp 65-9; *Ann. Conn.,* 1415 A.D.
68. McKenna, *Book of Magauran,* pp 379-80.
69. T. Ó Máille, 'A poem to Tuathal Ó Máille' in *Revue Celtique* xlix (1932), pp 175-6.
70. See B. Ó Cuív, *The Irish Bardic Duanaire or 'Poem-Book'* (Dublin 1973).
71. Williams, *Poems of Giolla Brighde,* p. 121; K. Simms, 'The O'Hanlons, the O'Neills and the Anglo-Normans in Thirteenth-Century Armagh' in *Seanchas Ardmhacha* ix (1978), pp 79-80.
72. P. Breatnach, 'The Chief's Poet' in *R.I.A. Proc.* lxxxiii (1983), pp 60-66.
73. *A.L.C., A.F.M.* 1185 A.D.
74. *Ann. Conn., A.U.,* 1350 A.D.
75. L. McKenna, 'Some Irish Bardic Poems' in *Studies* xxxvii (1948), p. 323.
76. *Ann. Conn.,* 1415:2.
77. Williams, *Poems of Giolla Brighde,* p. 2.
78. *Ann. Conn., A.L.C.,* 1435 A.D.; *Misc. Ir. Ann.,* p. 112; 'Ionmhuin taisi ata a nDoire', Book of O'Conor Don, fo. 138b; R.I.A. MS 2 (23/F/16), p. 140; 'Ciondas do roighfinn rí Oiligh?' Franciscan Library, Killiney, MS A/25, p. 149.
79. J. O'Donovan (ed.), *The Tribes of Ireland: a satire by Aenghus O'Daly* (reprint Cork 1976), p. 55.

80. D. Greene, 'The Professional Poets' in *Seven Centuries of Irish Learning* ed. B. Ó Cuív (Dublin 1961), p. 47; McKenna, *Dioghluim Dána*, no. 67 verse 46.

81. B. Ó Cuív, 'A sixteenth-century political poem' in *Éigse* xv (1973-4), pp 267-71, 273.

82. J. Carney, 'Society and the bardic poet' in *Studies* lxii (1973), pp 246-7.

83. Above, pp 60-63.

84. Carney, *The Irish Bardic Poet,* p. 15.

85. Williams, *Poems of Giolla brighde,* no. x.

86. *Ibid.*; McKenna, as above, note (75); *Aithdioghluim Dána,* nos. 34, 40; Knott, *Poems of Tadhg Dall,* no. 15.

87. McKenna, *Book of Magauran,* nos. ii, iv, x, xvii (*A.L.C.*, 1315, 1349 A.D.); MacAirt, *Leabhar Branach,* nos. 16, 47, 53, 59, 60, 61.

88. Evidence for the political influence of the Méig Shamhradháin lies chiefly in their marriage alliances — see McKenna, *Book of Magauran,* p. ix. On Uí Bhroin see B. Bradshaw, 'Native reaction to the Westward Enterprise' in *The Westward Enterprise* ed. K.R. Andrews, N.P. Canny and P.E.H. Hair (Liverpool 1979), pp 65-80.

89. e.g. MacAirt, *Leabhar Branach* no. 18; McKenna, *Aithdioghluim Dána,* nos. 21, 37-40.

90. E.C. Quiggin, 'O'Conor's House at Cloonfree' in *Essays and Studies presented to William Ridgeway* ed. E.C. Quiggin (Cambridge 1913), pp 333-52; McKenna, *Dioghluim Dána,* no. 119; Knott, *Poems of Tadhg Dall,* nos. 5, 6, 11; Simms, 'Medieval kingdom of Lough Erne', p. 135.

91. e.g. McKenna, *Aithdioghluim Dána,* no. 3; 'Beg nár bháith Aodh oighidh Coinn' R.I.A. MS 743 (A/iv/3), p. 792.

92. B. Bradshaw, note (88) above; B. Cunningham and R. Gillespie, 'The East Ulster Bardic Family of Ó Gnímh' in *Éigse* xx (1984), pp 106-114; while N. Canny has, of course, broached the study of post-bardic literature in *Past and Present* xcv (1982), pp 91-116. Professor Ó Concheanainn has lately emphasized the valuable research already done by literary editors (*Celtica* xvi, pp 15-25), but this cannot excuse the long negligence of the historians themselves.

ADDENDUM

In listing the seven bardic poems and a fragment on Aodh Buidhe II Ó Néill in footnote (42), I omitted by some oversight an eighth, attributed to Maoilsheachlainn na nUirsgéal Ó hUiginn, in R.I.A. MS 743, p. 688. This celebrated author is careful to point out that his patron has not been inaugurated as Ó Néill, though King of Ireland were a fitting title for him.

Edmund Spenser on Justice
and Mercy

BRENDAN BRADSHAW

What follows is ultimately intended to support a suggestion I made some years ago that the drastic scheme for the reformation of Ireland outlined in Edmund Spenser's *A View of the Present State of Ireland* finds its intellectual source in his protestant world-view.[1] The suggestion was subsequently dismissed as airily as it was, no doubt, originally proposed. On the contrary, it has been claimed that protestantism is largely irrelevant to Spenser's reform programme, that the suggestion of a simple major determining influence is methodologically unsound,[2] and that, in any case, examination reveals that Spenser's practical proposals were inconsistent with his (conventional) reform theory.[3] This riposte will take the form of an attempt to provide chapter and verse for the original suggestion. It seeks to demonstrate that Book V of the *Faerie Queene* elaborates a theory of justice which is directly related to protestant doctrine and which provides a rationale for the practical scheme of reform outlined in the *View*, the two works having been written contemporaneously. The study has also, however, a more immediate purpose. It is intended to demonstrate a method of analysing Spenser's poem which to my knowledge has not been attempted before, and in the process to draw attention to a *genre* of Renaissance discourse that receives all too little attention from historians interested in the use of literature as a historical source.

Every undergraduate who has faced the daunting task of understanding Spenser's massive and intricate poem knows that it operates at three levels of meaning all at once. At one level it is a chivalric tale in six books, each narrating the quest of a doughty knight for a fair lady who is held captive by a wicked giant. At another level it presents an allegory on the virtues, each of the six chivalric quests providing a figurative account of the way to perfection in a particular virtue. At a third level it elaborates a historical epic, in the tradition of Virgil's *Aeneid*, which celebrates the reign of Elizabeth I as the fulfilment of England's imperial destiny, foreshadowed in the nation's origin legends.[4] Probably what the undergraduate will not know, because its significance seems to have been lost on the commentators as well, is that the *Faerie Queene* belongs to a *genre* of discourse now no longer cultivated, described by its practitioners in classical antiquity and in the Renaissance as Eloquence.[5] This entailed the attempt to realise the Ciceronian ideal of reconciling wisdom and rhetoric by conveying philosophical knowledge through the techniques of art. In making sense of the *Faerie Queene,* therefore, the crucial task is to decode the rhetoric of literature in terms of wisdom or philosophy. The poem must be read in the same way as Professor Patrick Boyde has taught us to read the *Divine Comedy,* as an intellectual discourse.[6]

Read in this way, the notorious bleakness of Book V reveals its precise implications. Here in the quest of Sir Artegall for the Lady Irena, Spenser presents his discourse on Justice. The introduction immediately indicates the philosophical tradition within which his reflections are developed. It provides Artegall with a formation under the tutelage of the goddess Astraea — the goddess of Justice — which cultivates in him the attributes of power, awesomeness and strictness so that

> Even wildebeasts did fear his awful sight
> And men admyr'd his overruling might.[7]

and he gives his protagonist a sword taken from the armoury of Jupiter himself, the Chrysaon symbol of sovereignty and the capacity to enforce it. In similar vein he depicts Talus, the groom bequeathed to Artegall by Astraea when she fled the earth, as an *Iron Man,* i.e. strong and unrelenting, carrying an iron flail, the symbol of retribution. In this way Spenser associates himself with a voluntarist tradition of thought relating to justice which in the treatises of the time was characterised by the epithet severe, a tradition which pivoted on the notions of sovereignty, power and order, and which envisaged the exercise of justice in terms of coercion, punishment and retribution.[8]

As the narrative of the quest proceeds and the characterisation of Artegall and his groom is developed Spenser's conception is filled out and its extremity becomes increasingly apparent. Thus Talus acts out his role of groom in such a way as to give three characteristics special prominence. One is a disposition towards violence; he invariably fulfils his master's behests by bringing irresistible force to bear and without any indication of rational reflection. The second is ruthlessness: Spenser is even willing to describe him as cruel — as cruel as the other monsters in the narrative but distinguished from them by the exercise of cruelty in the service of justice. Thirdly, and most ominously, Talus is endowed with a capacity for arbitrary conduct: in face of the forces of anarchy Artegall withdraws and allows his groom to exercise unrestrained violence. Here, then, in Talus, is portrayed Spenser's view of the function of power as an instrument of justice. How radical it is may be observed in one well-known episode which brings Talus into special prominence and which, in virtue of its theme, holds special significance. This is the account in the second canto of the confrontation between Artegall and a popular demagogue which took the form of a debate over the criterion or measure of justice. Artegall and the demagogue each rehearse a side of the conventional argument as between a criterion of equality, which the demagogue defends by appeal to the inequity of social privilege, and a criterion of due proportions which Artegall advances by appeal to the cosmic order:

> Thou that presumist to weigh the world anew,
> And all things to an equall to restore,
> In stead of right we seemes great wrong dost shew,
> And far above thy forces pitch to sore.
> For ere thou limit what is lesse or more
> In every thing, thou oughtest first to know,
> What was the poyse of every part of yore:
> And looke then how much it doth overflow,
> Or faile thereof, so much is more than inst to trow.[10]

The episode is revealing partly for Artegall's elaboration of the conventional Christian classical notion of justice as consisting in due proportion and the middle way between extremes. However, its deepest significance is revealed in the apparent incongruity of such a conception with the manner chosen by Spenser to resolve the confrontation. This is achieved not by rational argument but by the violent intervention of Talus who throws the demagogue to his death over a cliff and proceeds to suppress the ensuing 'tumultous rout' by laying about him with his flail. Emphasising the point, Spenser has Artegall eschew any function in these proceedings apart from authorising Talus's intervention:

> For loth he was his noble hands t'embrew
> In the base blood of such a rascall crew.[11]

The message is that justice based on reason is insufficient of itself to sustain that rational order to which it is directed as to its end. Paradoxically, it must allow arbitrary violence to intervene on its behalf when confronted with the forces of anarchy.

Before proceeding, attention should be drawn to the significant difference in Spenser's attitude which the foregoing episode serves to highlight as between justice considered as a means and as an end. In regard to the end of justice the episode shows him espousing the conventional ideal, the Christian-classical conception of a duly proportioned harmonious order. However, in relation to means, in relation to the question of how justice is to act to attain its end, the episode points up the radical implications of Spenser's commitment to the conception of 'severe justice', the conception, it is relevant to note, which the narrative structure of Book V is designed to elaborate. The characterisation of Talus, the groom, in effect, provides Spenser's radical answer to a question that is central to the consideration of justice as a means, its relationship to power, specifically, in the domain of public justice, its relationship to the coercive instruments of the state. The corollary to Spenser's radically voluntarist conception of that relationship is provided in the characterisation of Artegall which Spenser develops into a disquisition on the relationship between justice and mercy.

Here clearly we come to the central issue of the philosophical discourse because we also come to the crisis of the chivalric narrative. That narrative is structured around the testing of Artegall through a series of trials in which the knight is required to prove himself a 'true champion of Justice' by overcoming in turn the virtue's enemies. In accordance with the conventions of chivalric narrative the crisis is provided by Artegall's failure in one of the tests. The episode is recounted in canto five where Artegall, having shown himself proof against partiality and corruption is now tested for constancy of purpose. The terms in which the crisis is presented and the manner of its resolution require careful elucidation since, as always, the interpretation of the philosophical discourse must proceed by decoding the rhetoric. In this connection attention must first of all be drawn to the two basic features of Spenser's brilliant rhetorical strategy. The first in his allegorization of the crisis in terms of a conflict between justice and mercy. The second is his manipulation of the allegorical categories in a way that enables him to construct the narrative as a polemic against pity and clemency, the two attributes which served in the classical, rationalist tradition, to mitigate the rigours of justice by appeal to the claims of mercy. The procedure here involves three conventional tropes: the allegorization of justice and mercy in sexual categories, identifying justice as a male attribute and mercy as a female one; the allegorization of the sexual categories in turn in terms of physical and moral attributes, associating man with strength and discipline and woman with weakness and licentiousness; finally the device of role-reversal which allows the allegorical categories to be inverted as a way of heightening the perception of abnormality. From these elements Spenser constructs a moral tale that revolves upon the consequences of Artegall's choice of mercy before justice. The moral is what holds the key to the philosophical interpretation of the episode but that can only be grasped by following the story as Spenser unfolds it in three sequences: the defeat of Artegall, his deliverance, and his confirmation in knightly virtue.

The first sequence, canto five, tells of Artegall's encounter with Radigund, 'Queene of the Amazons', whom he seeks to overcome in order to free the knights held captive by her in revenge for unrequited love. Victory turns to defeat for Artegall, when, having knocked Radigund to the ground, he is overcome by pity at sight of her face and throws down his sword. Radigund promptly recovers and Artegall, now defenceless and in fear for his life, submits and pleads for mercy. The mercy he receives is to be dressed in women's weeds and set to spinning.[13] Artegall's act of mercy, therefore, is disastrous both in its personal and in its public consequences. It enables injustice to prevail and causes him to forfeit his manhood. In canto seven the story of Artegall's deliverance is recounted in such a way that the allegorical categories are inverted while the moral remains the same.

Artegall's deliverer is a woman who, however, acts like a man. She is Britomart, Artegall's faithful lover but also a valorous warrior. She now does battle with Radigund and shows no compunction in dealing the fatal blow which 'with one stroke both head and helmet cleft'.[14] The redoubtable Talus completes the task by settling upon Radigund's terrified followers with his flail. In the sequel Britomart not only sets Artegall at liberty and restores him to his knightly estate, she also accomplishes his task: firstly, the liberation of the captive knights; secondly the restoration of Radigund's misruled commonwealth to a just order by the repeal of the liberty of women and their restoration to the subjection of men.[15] Thus what Artegall lost by displaying the womanly attribute of mercy Britomart restores by displaying the manly attribute of justice.

In the final sequence, narrated in canto nine, King Arthur brings Artegall to the court of Mercilla, the goddess of Mercy, where they witness the trial of the 'false Duessa' on a charge of conspiring to usurp the office of Mercilla herself.[16] Thus Spenser brings the allegory full circle: the allegorical characters now conform to type and Mercy confronts Licence. In accordance with literary convention the final resolution is required to show firstly that Artegall has overcome the fault that produced his fall and is, therefore, ready to complete his quest; secondly that the apparent conflict of virtues involves a misconception, mercy must be reconciled with justice. Additionally, however, the resolution must serve the needs of the intellectual discourse: the moral tale must produce a denouement that will clinch Spenser's polemic against pity and clemency. Spenser manages to encompass all of these designs within the final sequence by resolving the issue in Duessa's case into the moral dilemma on which the earlier sequences had pivoted, the choice between cruel justice and merciful injustice. The issue emerges from the way the case is argued. Zele of justice, for the prosecution, demands death as the due penalty in respect of Duessa's manifold treasons — which include, as well as the conspiracy to usurp Mercilla's place, conniving at the subversion of the political and social order.[17] The defence implicitly admits the charge but pleads for clemency on grounds that do not extenuate Duessa's guilt but elicit an emotional response to her predicament: *Pittie, Regard* of womanhood, *Dannger* threatening hidden dread, *Nobilitie* of birth, 'And lastly, Griefe did plead many teares forth powre'.[18] Once more Spenser has engineered a situation in which the trial of vice becomes reflexively the trial of virtue. On this occasion Argegall comes through with flying colours; his constancy is highlighted by the perplexed response of Arthur who waxes 'sore empassionate' at Duessa's 'dreadful fate'.[19] Artegall, however,

> with constante firme intent
> For zeale of Justice was against her bent.[20]

Artegall has now learned to discern the false claims of mercy and to reject them. To complete his instruction he must learn to discern mercy's true claims and how to reconcile them with justice.

The instruction is provided by the judgment of Mercilla which, at the same time, points up the moral of the tale and clinches the polemic. Lying behind that judgment is the Aristotelian principle that virtue lies in the middle between extremes. However, what is instructive — for the reader, as well as for Artegall — is Mercilla's application of the principle. This has two dimensions. One concerns subjective dispositions — the relationship between will and passion in the exercise of virtue. Here Spenser reminds us of Mercilla's susceptibility to an emotional resolution of the case, by succumbing either to manly anger, as the injured party, or to womanly pity in virtue of her sex and Duessa's peculiarly pathetic circumstances.[21] However, Mercilla yields to neither passion but rather exercises moderation in handing down her judgment 'without grief or gall':[22] mercy as a disposition does not consist in the passion of pity but in a virtuous moderation that ensures the dispassionate exercise of justice. The other

dimension of Mercilla's use of the golden mean in dispensing mercy relates
to the objective criterion as end of the virtue — specifically to the relationship between due punishment and mercy. Here, once more, Mercilla is confronted with the problem in extreme form in the arguments presented by
the opposing advocates. *Zele* bases the case for the prosecution on the
claims of retributive justice and demands the imposition of the strict penalty as the exaction of 'just vengeance'.[23] The case of the defence, in contrast, is based on the principle of *epikeia* which holds that it is better to save
than to destroy and which requires, therefore, that the strict requirements
of justice be tempered by reason and moderation in their application in individual cases. Paradoxically, Mercilla displays mercy by exacting the due
penalty and handing Duessa over to execution. In fact, as Spenser's commentary explains, Mercilla here treads a middle way between the rigorist
and the laxist extremes. She does so, in effect, by inverting their arguments.
She seeks to save rather than to destroy with the laxists and, therefore, rejects the rigorist conception of justice as directed to retribution. However,
in order to save it is necessary to reform injustice not to tolerate it and,
therefore, she adheres to the strict application of due punishment against
transgressors.

> For if that Virtue be of so great might,
> Which from just verdict will for nothing start,
> But to preserue inviolated right,
> Oft spilles the principall, to save the part;
> So much more then is that of powre and art,
> That seekes to save the subject of her skill,
> Yet never doth from doome of right depart:
> As it is greater prayse to save, than spill,
> And better to reforme, than to cut off the ill.[24]

Spenser's platitudinous verse hides a paradox which contains his solution
to the dilemma posed by the claims of justice and mercy: the necessity to be
cruel in order to be kind.

In sum, Spenser's treatment of the relationship between justice and mercy in the episode of Artegall's testing, neatly complements his earlier treatment of the relationship between justice and power in his depiction of
Talus's function. In both cases he adheres to a conventional conception of
justice in terms of its *finis*, its end or object, i.e. right order (distributive
justice) and reformation (commutative justice). The severity of his conception relates to justice as an *esse,* as a means or process, directed to right
order and reformation. In this respect his earlier emphasis on the coercive
function of justice is here complemented by a radical reformulation of its

relationship with mercy. The significant feature of this is the way in which the function of mercy in mitigating the severity of justice is neutralised. Through the tale of Artegall's testing a conjuring trick of drastic implications is effected. One part of the trick is to dissociate mercy from two of its traditional attributes, pity and clemency: in Spenser's presentation these are consistently denigrated by association with the womanish vices of weakness and licentiousness. The other part of the trick is to reconcile the virtue with punitive justice: thus the superb denouement in which Mercy is made to consign licentiousness to execution. By means of these rhetorical ploys and a capacity for fine distinctions that a scholastic might envy Spenser conjures into existence a mercy merciless.

A major anomaly in Spenser's moral tale remains to be considered. It is constituted by the deliverance of Artegall. Had Artegall received his deserts in accordance with the norm of severe justice the moral tale must have concluded with the account of his unmanning and captivity by Radigund. This irony was not lost upon the author. Indeed it is central to his message. The explanation offered within the text itself lies in an aspect of the episode that has not been discussed so far, its place in the historical epic of imperial Britain. Critical is the account with which the sequence of Artegall's deliverance is introduced in canto seven, Britomart's mystical experience at the Church of Isis.[25] The effect of that experience is to transform her natural desire to rescue her lover into a divinely ordained mission, imposed by the exigencies of her special destiny, now for the first time revealed, to become, as Artegall's spouse, the eponymous founder of the imperial British kingdom.[26] Artegall is exempted, therefore, from the decrees of justice by a special dispensation of divine providence in view of his role in the fulfilment of England's imperial destiny. The implications of this explanation need to be explored. They direct attention to a dimension of Spenser's thought on the theme of justice and mercy that provides a necessary corollary to the one already elaborated.

Here the task of decoding the rhetoric must be embarked upon once more for it is clear that the episode of Artegall's deliverance is freighted with allegorical significance crucial to the meaning of the intellectual discourse. The first significant feature concerns the implications of removing the episode to the sphere of historical epic. The effect is to set it apart from the chivalric narrative as a whole. A new moral order is found to prevail. The narrative is now propelled by a decree of destiny not by a free agent in pursuit of virtue. Most anomalously, the overriding claims of justice which the chivalric tale is designed to affirm, are here transcended by a special dispensation of mercy: the deliverance of Artegall is initiated by the summons of Britomart to the sanctuary of Mercy, personified by Isis, and it concludes with the summons of Artegall himself to the throne of Mercy, personified by Mercilla.[37] Spenser manipulates the epic theme, therefore, to raise in that context the central problem of the discourse, the relationship between justice and mercy. However, precisely by raising it in that context he is enabled to address a dimension of the question excluded from the discussion conducted through the medium of the chivalric tale, the relationship between human justice and divine mercy.

The second philosophically significant feature of the episode, and the key to Spenser's thought on the subject of human justice and divine mercy is the characterisation of Artegall. He now manifests a totally different aspect to the protagonist of the chivalric narrative. The difference may be reduced to three elements. Firstly, the external persona is transformed from a figure of strength to one of weakness: the knight in armour becomes a captive in women's weeds.[28] Secondly, the moral persona is correspondingly transformed from one of external to internal virtue: the exponent of public justice becomes in captivity an exponent of humility and fidelity, exhibited through acceptance of his fate and continuing love for Britomart.[29] Finally, Artegall's role is transformed from active dispenser of human justice to passive recipient of supernatural mercy: his deliverance is effected wholly by Britomart without any contribution on his own part;[30] Talus, symbol of human power, is replaced as Artegall's helpmate throughout the sequence of his deliverance by the supernatural figure of Britomart.[31]

Having established the characteristics of Artegall as presented in the episode of his deliverance the next step is to ask who he is intended to represent. The answer lies in the commonplace observation that the *Faerie Queene* is to be interpreted not simply as a humanist but as a Christian text, and not simply as a Christian text but as a Protestant one as well. Viewed from this perspective the features of Artegall became immediately recognizable. They assume the precise contours of the three states involved in Christian conversion according to the classic Protestant description: bondage of the will; conviction of sin and trust in divine mercy; justification by supernatural grace alone. Furthermore, the contours of the entire episode conform to the account of the three stages of justification discerned in the Protestant doctrine of salvation: predestination-election at the Church of Isis; conversion — at Radigund's castle; sanctification — at the court of Mercilla.[32] By manipulating the narrative of the historical epic, therefore, Spenser succeeds in providing not only an allegory of human justice but an allegory of supernatural justification as well.

It remains to draw the moral of the allegory. It is contained in the opening verse of canto ten where Spenser explicitly ponders the question of the relationship between justice and mercy. His response is to accord mercy a status equal to justice. Howver, in five pregnant lines he indicates that mercy is a divine not a human virtue and that it is mediated to humankind by divine means.

> This well I wrote, that sure she [Mercie] is as great,
> And meriteth to have as high a place,
> Sith in th' Almighties eurlasting seat
> She first was bred, and borne of heavenly race;
> From thence pour'd down on men, by influence of
> grace,[33]

The practical implications of that conception are expressed in the protestant doctrine of the two kingdoms which provides the key to Spenser's treatment of the episode of Artegall's deliverance, and to his view of how human justice and divine mercy are reconciled. According to that doctrine a sharp distinction must be made between the spiritual and the temporal domains, God's will being effected in the former through grace and the mediation of the Word, and in the latter through power, and the mediation of the Sword. Accordingly, it is held, Mercy belongs to the domain of grace: it is a divine prerogative which human government must not usurp. In the latter sphere justice must prevail: the magistrate is to regard himself as the left hand of God.[34] Thus, by endowing Artegall with a dual persona and a dual role Spenser carefully distinguished between the dispenser of human justice and the recipient of divine mercy. In doing so his point is not to indicate that Artegall represents two different people. In fact the message hinges on the fact that the two personas coexist in the same individual. He wants to demonstrate the paradox that the necessary condition for becoming a 'true champion of Justice' is to experience in one's life the grace of divine mercy.

It has been argued here that Book V of the *Faerie Queene* is to be read as an attempt to elaborate, according to the mode of Renaissance Eloquence, a philosophical vindication of 'severe justice'. In particular it has been argued that the centre-piece of the Book, the account of Artegall's crisis (cantos five to nine) is to be read as a polemic against the traditional, classical-Christian appeal to mercy, whether human or divine, as a virtue that mitigates the rigours of strict justice. The final section of the Book (cantos nine to twelve) provides an opportunity to locate Spenser's rationale in its polemical setting. Here Artegall, now proven in virtue, at last completes his quest by slaying the giant Grantarto and liberating the Lady Irena. The details of the exposition need not concern us since they merely add Spenser's q.e.d. to all that has gone before: the combination of unflinching violence (Talus) and unflinching justice (Artegall) proves irresistible against injustice. The interest lies, rather, in the identification of the Lady Irena, since in her Spenser locates the ultimate object of the entire enterprise. In this regard the commentaries assign two identities. One is philosophical, i.e. peace, the ultimate object of justice. The other is historical, i.e. Ireland, the immediate object of Spenser's concern with pacification.[35] It will suffice by way of conclusion to draw out the implications of the approach provided here for this double identity.

First of all, it may be noted, that, Irena, as peace, brings the philosophical discourse to its logical conclusion by moving the discussion from a consideration of the *esse* (means) and *finis operis* (the immediate end) of justice to its final end (*finis operantis*). Secondly, however, it does not seem that Spenser's polemical purposes in offering such a discourse can be confined to his concern with the pacification of Ireland. The important consideration here is the function of the *Faerie Queene* as a historical epic celebrating the imperial destiny of England, and identifying that destiny with the success of the protestant Reformation in England. In that light it would be reasonable to assume that Book V, like the rest of the poem, is intended, in the first instance, to advance the cause of reformation in England. In fact, reference to the concerns of reformers in England readily offers a polemical context for Spenser's discourse. That is the debate that originated during the regime of Protector Somerset (1547-9) precisely on the issue of coercion as an instrument of social reform, in which English protestantism — supported by Calvin himself — aligned itself on the side of severe justice.[36] In the mid-1580s, under the stress of a mounting socio-economic and political crisis, the debate was re-opened with new vigour by the Puritan vanguard, with treatises by leading spokemen such as Thomas Lupton and John Stubbles.[37] This was the intellectual environment in which Spenser first conceived the idea of the *Faerie Queene* and in which he began to write it, proposing Artegall as an example of 'a good gouernour and a vertuous man'. It cannot reasonably be doubted that Book V was written with the issue of social order and social reform in England at the centre of Spenser's pre-occupations.

Against that background we may turn thirdly and finally to consider Book V in the context of Elizabethan Ireland. It will now be clear that the relationship of the Irish crisis to Spenser's 'bleak view' requires more subtle formulation than has recently been offered.[38] No doubt it is reasonable to postulate a causal connection between the extremity of socio-political crisis that Spenser encountered in Ireland and the extremity of his proposal for resolving it, expressed in his *View of the Present State of Ireland.* In the light of the study presented here, however, two further observations suggest themselves. Firstly, it is clear that Spenser's perception of the Irish crisis and his response to it was conditioned by the intellectual framework — the world-view — that he brought with him. That 'world-view' was the result of Spenser's English protestant formation. Secondly, Book V of the *Faerie Queene,* may now be seen to provide the moral and philosophical vindications of Spenser's radical programme. In fact the programme conforms to the formula for social control patterned in the activities of Talus and Artegall: relentless, arbitrary violence as the antidote to anarchy, and severe justice as the ordinary means of achieving and maintaining social harmony — the Word, meanwhile, being proclaimed as the means of inner, spiritual renewal. In the light of Spenser's refined philosophising in Book V of the *Faerie Queene* the charge of intellectual incoherence recently made against the *View* will hardly stand. That the exoneration of Spenser from such a charge serves to enhance the reputation of the 'gentle humanist' may be doubted.

NOTES AND REFERENCES

1. B. Bradshaw, 'Sword, Word and Strategy in the Reformation in Ireland' in *Historical Journal,* xxi (1978), pp 475-502, especially pp 482-3, 490-1, 498-9.

2. Nicholas Canny, 'Edmund Spenser and the Development of an Anglo-Irish Identity', in *The Yearbook of English Studies,* xiii (1983), pp 1-19, especially p. 1.

3. Ciaran Brady, 'Spenser's Irish Crisis: Humanism and Experience in the 1590s', in *Past and Present,* forthcoming. I am grateful to Ciaran for supplying me with a typescript of his forthcoming article and for vigorous criticism of the present piece. I am also grateful to Geoffrey Elton's Tudor Seminar for allowing me to address them on the subject and for criticisms made at the time.

4. A rather dated but reliable introductory study is Graham Hough, *A Preface to the Faerie Queene* (London, 1962). See also M. Pauline Parker, *The Allegory of the Faerie Queene* (Oxford, 1960). For a learned explication of the allegorical motifs of Book V see T.K. Dunseath, *Spenser's Allegory of Justice in Book Five of The Faerie Queene* (Princeton, New Jersey, 1968).

5. Gerrold E. Seigel, *Rhetoric and Philosophy in Renaissance Humanism* (Princeton, New Jersey, 1968). W.K.C. Guthrie, *A History of Greek Philosophy,* iii (Cambridge, 1969), pp 176-225. I have earlier used the method of analysis applied here to a quite different Renaissance humanist text, Erasmus's *Antibarbari.* See my 'The Christian Humanism of Erasmus', in *The Journal of Theological Studies,* new series, xxxiii (1982), pp 411-47.

6. Patrick Boyde, *Dante Philomythes and Philosopher* (Cambridge, 1981). Nearer home, it might be said, the idea is reflected in Sir Philip Sidney's *Apologie for Poetrie* in which he advances the argument that poetry excels moral philosophy in that it not only sets forth what is good but does so in such a way that men are allured to follow.

7. *Faerie Queene,* V.i, 8.

8. *Faerie Queene,* V.i, 12. The epithet derived from a mistaken view of the judicial reforms of the emperor Alexander Severus, Madeleine Doran, *Endeavors of Art* (New York, 1954), p. xlv.

9. For a particularly gruesome example of Talus's 'pitylessness' see the account of his dismemberment of Pollente's daughter, *Faerie Queene,* V.ii, 25-7.

10. Ibid., ii, 34.

11. Ibid., ii, 52.

12. On Artegall's incorruptibility see the episode of the brigand Pollente, ibid., ii, 4-28. On his impartiality see the account of his arbitration between the two sons of Milesio, ibid., iv, 4-20.

13. Artegall's defeat by Radigund is recounted in ibid., v, 4-21.

14. *Faerie Queene,* vii, 34. The account of the confrontation is at vv, 25-43.

15. Ibid., vii, 37-43.

16. Ibid., ix, 34-50.

17. Ibid., ix, 39-44, 47-8.

18. Ibid., ix, 45.

19. Ibid., ix, 46.

20. Ibid., ix, 49.

21. Ibid., ix, 50.

22. Ibid., x, 4.

23. Ibid., ix, 50.

24. Ibid., x, 2.

25. Ibid., vii, 1-24.

26. Ibid., vii, 22-4.

27. See *Faerie Queene,* vii. 6-8, 12 and ix, 27, 34-5. The point is underscored in the Church of Isis episode where a priest explains to Britomart that the significance of the crocodile at the feet of Isis is to show her capacity to restrain Osyris i.e. justice.

    Clement oft in things amis,
    Restraines those sterne behests, and cruell doomes of his.

28. Ibid., v, 20-4.

29. Ibid., v, 26-57.

30. The sequence of Artegall's release is at *Faerie Queene,* vii, 37-41.

31. For the severance of Artegall and Talus, see ibid., v, 19. They rejoin when Artegall departs from Britomart, ibid., viii, 3.

32. On Luther's theology of justification by faith alone see Bernard M.G. Reardon, *Religious Thought in the Reformation* (London, 1981), pp 55-85, especially pp 80-5.

33. *Faerie Queene,* V.x, 1.

34. On this aspect of protestant political thought see W.D.J. Cargill Thompson, 'The "Two Kingdoms" and the "Two Regiments": Some Problems of Luther's *Zwei Reiche Lebhre',* in idem., *Studies in the Reformation* (London, 1980), pp 42-59. Also, Reardon, *Religious Thought in the Reformation,* pp 85-7.

35. For this identification see Parker, *Allegory of the Faerie Queene,* p. 224.

36. See M.L. Bush, *The Government Policy of Protector Somerset* (London, 1975), pp 61-73, 110-11, 127-61. C.S.L. Davies, *Peace, Print and Protestantism* (St Albans, Herts, 1976), pp 265-8. A.B. Ferguson, *The Articulate Citizen*, pp 263 ff., especially p. 269.

37. See Doran, *Endeavors of Art*, p. xlv. Donald McGinn, 'The Precise Angelo' in *J.Q. Adams Memorial Studies* (New York, 1948), pp 129-39.

38. See above, p. 76 and references 2, 3, p. 87.

Irish National Character
1790-1900

SEAMUS DEANE

The aim of this essay is to trace the history of an idea through a series of mutations over a span of about one hundred years. Much of the material is taken from literary sources because it is in these that the sometimes elusive but always potent force of the idea of a national character is most frequently and most memorably articulated. In the nineteenth century the stereotyping of this idea is particularly noticeable. The caricaturing of national types was an important instrument of propaganda warfare during and after the French Revolution; the brilliant and savage tradition of Rowlandson and Gillray was carried on through the century, becoming more and more closely bound up with the development of the popular (finally the Yellow) press.[1] Although this form of ideographic representation is pertinent to my theme, I do not intend to pursue its development here. L.P. Curtis and R.N. Lebow have already analysed its nature and function in relation to English and Irish affairs.[2] My interest is to observe some of the ways in which it registered itself in the literature of the time and to trace therein the contribution made by the idea of an Irish national character to political attitudes and ideologies.

Although there had been, since medieval times, contrasting versions of British and of Irish national character, they did not achieve their ultimate definition until the eighteenth century. As part of the British response to the Glorious Revolution of 1688, a number of writers — Dryden, Sir William Temple, Defoe, Addison, Steele, Pope and Horace Walpole most prominent among them — constructed a version of the English literary tradition and of the English national character which had, as one of its primary purposes, the attribution to the island kingdom of a unique historical destiny which distinguished it from its continental contemporaries.[3] As England distinguished itself from the continent (particularly France) in the early decades of the century, so Ireland learned to distinguish itself from England in the later decades. Although this summarises the process in a crude shorthand, it does call attention to the swiftness of the interchange and to the fact that the idea of an Irish national character took shape in response to the earlier and aggressive English (or British) definition.

English historical writing in the eighteenth century was remarkably free of the preoccupation with national character which is so pervasive in the country's literature. The idea of a philosophic history, the chief use of which was 'to discover the constant and universal principles of human nature'[4] survived at least into the French Revolutionary decade. This characteristically enlightened vision was, nevertheless, closely allied with the current of anglomania in France, impelled by Voltaire and Montesquieu and by the view that the dramatic events of seventeenth-century England provided the historian with an incomparable opportunity for narrative reflection.[5] The writing of history and the writing of literature were not then so widely separated as they were later to become. But literature, burdened by the need to formulate a specifically English aesthetic to counteract the cultural hegemony of France, sought for and found a symbol in which the English genius for the conciliation of liberty with order could be represented. That symbol was the English garden, the predominant literary trope of the age. From Sir William Temple's essay 'Upon the Gardens of Epicurus; or, Of Gardening, in the Year 1685' to Addison's long allegorical discourse in *The Tatler* of 20 April 1710 and *The Spectator* papers of 21 and 25 June 1712, the features of the ideal English landscape garden are established, both as a political and aesthetic ideal. Temple described what he called the 'Chinese' garden, although he unwittingly used the Japanese word 'sharawadgi' to identify its chief characteristic — 'studied disorder'. He thereby inaugurated that vogue for the new landscape garden which was to oust the fashion for the symmetrical gardens of Italy and France (particularly those of Versailles).

The English garden is a protest against despotic order, geometrical regularity and uniformity. Along with the later and associated development of the 'Gothic' taste in architecture, it is seen to be, like the British constitution itself, a 'natural' institution in which the general principle of order is combined with the most eccentric individualism. This was a new and influential gloss on the theme of 'ars celare artem'. With its open vistas, its picturesqueness and its asymmetry, it rebuked the artificial restrictions of Versailles and its imitations at Schonbrunn, Peterhof, Herrenhausen and elsewhere. Pope's garden at Twickenham and William Kent's Rousham and Stowe and, finally, the great achievements of Capability Brown and Humphry Repton led to the adaptation throughout the continent of the *jardin anglais* and the accompanying philosophy of the picturesque. Of immediate interest here is the notion that the studied disorder of the so-called Chinese garden was repeatedly associated with the English character as a typical emanation of its peculiar genius.[6] The publication in 1757 of Edmund Burke's second book, *A Philosophical Inquiry into the Origin of our Ideas of the Sublime and Beautiful*, transformed several decades of aesthetic speculation by asserting a dualism between its two key terms and by ceding to the Beautiful all that was ordered and symmetrical and to the Sublime all that was wild, grand or magnificent. Shadowing his discussion, especially in relation to landscape, is the distinction between the formal garden, the *jardin anglais* and the wild nature of 'mountain gloom and mountain glory'. The link between national character and the English garden became extended to the open (and preferably 'wild') landscape. Insofar as this is an aesthetic issue, it has clear and well-known reverberations.[7] But the aesthetic aspect is never entirely detached from the political in the treatises and discussions of the period. The central term, politically speaking, is freedom; but Burke's success in giving the whole question of aesthetics a psychological emphasis enforced the relationship between feelings of awe, terror and reverence and the idea of freedom. Burke's 1790 version of the British national character existed as an aesthetic formulation over forty years earlier.

However, between 1760 and 1765, Burke wrote his unfinished *Tracts on the Popery Laws* in which he repudiated the slanders on the Irish national character perpetrated by English historians like Clarendon and Temple (the father of Sir William Temple). The Irish were not by nature a 'turbulent people'; they had been made so by 'the most unparalleled oppression'.[8] Yet Burke was not thereby rejecting the idea of a national character as such. It would have been difficult for a Whig and a disciple of Montesquieu to do so. Burke's knowledge of and admiration for Montesquieu is well-known.[9] *L'Esprit des Lois* (1748) had attempted to clarify the influence of physical and political conditions on the development of national character and had also, of course, given a famous, laudatory and inaccurate description of the British Constitution as a model of liberty. But its technical inaccuracy in this respect was much less important than the emphasis upon *les moeurs,* upon custom, habit and precedent, on the character of a people and the link between these and their chosen form of government. Montesquieu was laying the basis for a political sociology and his dependence on the idea of national character was later to be enhanced by Burke and by Mme de Staël, two of his greatest disciples. Thus, the French Enlightenment and the English Whig tradition, the new aesthetics and the new political science, all contributed to Burke's growing apprehension of the particular and traditional characteristics of any given nation's character. In his writings some of the long-term implications of this belief are expounded with consequences for both Britain and Ireland.

In his various crusades and causes — of the integrity of parliament against the influence of the King's Friends, of India against the rapacity of Hastings and the East India Company, of America against the policy of George III, of Ireland against the bigotry of the Ascendancy and of the France of the ancien régime against the Jacobins — one consistent theme may be discerned. Put simply, it is that the integrity of an established culture should not be violated by the intrusion of an external force hostile to or contradictory of its habits and customs. All factions within a state threatened to disturb traditional modes of behaviour and with that, traditional modes of feeling; these, because they were traditional, represented some of the deepest and most natural aspirations of mankind. His theme achieves its highest definition after 1790, with the publication of the *Reflections on the Revolution in France,* in which he makes his most memorable and polemical contrast between the national character of the British and that of the French. In doing so, he asserts, more openly than anyone before him, that the connection between British national character and the British constitution is a normative one and that deviations from it, like the French, are radically unnatural and dangerous. The British differ from the French in that

(1)   they cherish and nurture their 'natural affections'.

(2)   they preserve these out of a sense of natural awe and reverence for constituted authority which ultimately derives from God.

(3)   they have little time for speculators, theorists and intellectuals and certainly never allow such men — especially as they are deists or infidels — into power.

(4)   they are bonded together by habit, custom and precedent and therefore suspect simplicity of organisation and uniformity of practice. They are exponents, in short, of studied irregularity — sharawadgi — and in being so reveal the conformity of the 'Gothic' British constitution to national character.

(5)   they are morally and sexually conservative and stable. In favouring the family as a natural unit, they distinguish themselves from the French who have recently sponsored groups like the philosophic cabal and the Parisian mob against the French Royal Family.

This is a brilliant redaction of Temple, Addison, Montesquieu and a whole host of minor writers who had been helping to formulate for the idea of national character a specific national destiny. Burke transforms the idea into a counter-revolutionary notion, even exploiting the fact that it had its origins in the revolution of 1688. But he goes further by making a respect for antiquity, complexity and asymmetry an essential feature of the traditional nation, while the countering features of the revolutionary culture were seen to be novelty, simplicity and an overweening respect for mechanical regularity. The standard attacks of the early century upon despotism were now transferred to radicalism. The intimate alliance between this new ideology and the aesthetics of the landscape garden, the sublime and the numinous presence in wild nature, the sentimental appeal of the ancient edifice and of the ruin, is perfectly visible in the rich texture of Burke's rhetoric.[10]

This highly politicised version of the British national character was achieved at a time of heightened national consciousness in Ireland. The first Celtic revival, effectively launched by the Ossian forgeries in 1758 and more respectably if less popularly supported by the work of Evan Evans (*Specimens of the Poetry of the Antient Welsh Bards* (1764)), Thomas Percy (*Reliques of Ancient English Poetry* (1765)), Sylvester O'Halloran, Charles Vallancey, Charles O'Conor, Sir Laurence Parsons and many other Irish scholars, had benefited from the new appreciation of the Sublime and its projected landscape of lonely and mountainous places, and from the perceptible shift — which they helped to accelerate — from the pejorative associations of the idea of the primitive and barbaric to the benign connotations of the spontaneous and original. Vigour and freshness of feeling, a rural traditionalism, a rediscovered antiquity, a religious feeling which was doctrinally vague but emotionally powerful, an almost complete freedom from either intellectual theory or sexual promiscuity — these were not only traditional or 'Celtic' virtues, they were also indisputably non-revolutionay characteristics. The new primitivism was not French, nor was it radical. It was British, but not wholly so. In Ireland, the emergence of the differentiation between British and Irish national character, although begun in the last decades of the eighteenth century, did not fully emerge until after the Union. But the hostility of both conceptions of national character to doctrinaire revolution is at first more important than any subsequent differences between them. Irish national character was at first an idea without a sufficient history, most especially without an origin. The various attempts by people like Vallancey and, in the next century, Sir William Betham, to provide one are absurd historical fictions with a serious purpose — the ratification of a specific Irish character and destiny, a Carthaginian rather than a Roman or British nation.[11] The origin tended to be exotic because, for purposes of reconciliation, it had to be distant. Nothing specifically Gaelic or British, Catholic or Protestant, would do. Antiquarianism was consistently a more political avocation for countries with an unsettled history than for those who had already achieved an enduring political system.

The amateurishness of the scholarship of the early revival should not disguise the reality of its achievement. The new alliance between Irish poetry and Irish music, anticipated in works like Joseph Cooper Walker's *Historical Memoirs of the Irish bards* (1786), Charlotte Brooke's *Reliques of Irish Poetry* (1789) and, in 1796, Bunting's first series of the *General Collection of Ancient Irish Music* (1796), found its fullest expression in Moore's *Irish Melodies,* published in ten numbers between 1807 and 1834. Moore made the connection with national character explicit in a well-known letter to Sir John Stephenson, his collaborator

But we are come, I hope, to a better period of both politics and music; and how much they are connected, in Ireland at least, appears too plainly in the tone of sorrow and depression which characterises most of our early songs . . . The poet who would follow the various sentiments which they express, must feel and understand that rapid fluctuation of spirits, the unaccountable mixture of gloom and levity, which composes the character of my countrymen, and has deeply tinged their music.[12]

It may be that, as Hazlitt said, 'Mr Moore converts the wild harp of Erin into a musical snuffbox'.[13] But it is the very synthetic and artificial element in his work, the determined emasculation of the Gaelic originals, which enabled him to mobilise the political power of their appeal. By 'refining' Gaelic music, he made it fashionable and made the idea of a Celtic cultural difference an acceptable literary and eventually an acceptable political idea to both Irish and English. Moore's songs, like the 'vulgar ballads' which James Hardiman complained at for having 'displaced the native lyrics so effectually'[14] were crucial in the awakening of the notion that Ireland had a unique character, a unique destiny and a glorious past, all of which differentiated it from Britain. He was as amateurish in scholarship as his eighteenth-century predecessors but in an age which was more affected by James MacPherson's Ossian than by Evan Evans' scholarship, amateurishness was no bar to success. It was, in fact, a prerequisite. All those rediscovered countries of the eighteenth century — the Gothic, the medieval and the classical as well as the Celtic — were the product of a new aesthetic and political dispensation in Europe.

The local Irish background to the writings of Burke's last seven years is, therefore, important in helping us to see how influential his version of a traditionalist British national character could become in this context. However, it is incomplete unless we also take into account two other issues. The first of these is Burke's view of the role played in the Irish situation by the Protestant Ascendancy and its response to the increasing demands of the Irish Catholics for admission to political life, demands increasingly favoured by an English government anxious to placate them in the dangerous revolutionary decade. Burke's attack on the Ascendancy becomes increasingly violent as a comparison between his letters to Sir Hercules Langrishe of 1792 and 1795 shows. In that of 1792, two points are central to our consideration here. The first is that the Ascendancy is not an aristocracy in the accepted sense of the word — or at least, not in the sense which Burke assigned to it.

We know that the government of Ireland (the same as the British) is not in its constitution *wholly* aristocratical . . . If it had been inveterately aristocratical, exclusions might be more patiently submitted to. The lot of one plebeian would be the lot of all . . . But our constitution has a *plebeian member,* which forms an essential integrant part of it. A plebeian oligarchy is a monster: and no people, not absolutely domestic or predial slaves, will long endure it. The Protestants of Ireland are not *alone* sufficiently the people to form a democracy; and they are *too numerous* to answer the ends and purposes of *an aristocracy*. Admiration, that first source of obedience, can be only the claim or the imposture of the few. I hold it to be absolutely impossible for two millions of plebeians . . . to become so far in love with six or seven hundred thousand of their fellow-citizens . . . as to see with satisfaction, or even with patience, an exclusive power vested in them, by which *constitutionally* they become the absolute masters; and by the *manners* derived from their circumstances, must be capable of exercising upon them, daily and hourly, an insulting and vexatious superiority.

The second point is that, in this state of exclusion, the Catholics are not even virtually represented.

Virtual representation is that in which there is a communion of interests, and a sympathy in feelings and desires, between those who act in the name of any description of people, and the people in whose name they act, though the trustees are not actually chosen by them.

Without that, the existing state of affairs, claims Burke, cannot but

produce alienation on the one side, and pride and insolence on the other.[15]

Ireland, therefore, has no homogeneity of interest between the governed and the governors; the governors are not a true aristocracy; the mass of the people are excluded from the benefits of the Constitution. The system is formally British, but in spirit not so. The reason for this violation of the spirit or, as Montesquieu would have said, the *principe* of the British system is that the Irish Protestants constitute a faction within the state. By 1795, he can declare to Langrishe, in a famous condemnation which embraces all that he fought against throughout his career:

I think I can hardly overrate the malignancy of the principles of Protestant Ascendancy, as they affect Ireland; or of Indianism as they affect these countries, and as they affect Asia; or of Jacobinism, as they affect all Europe and the state of human society itself . . . Whatever tends to persuade the people, that the *few* . . . are of opinion that their interest is not compatible with that of the *many*, is a great point gained to Jacobinism.[16]

The lack of connection between the ascendancy and the people, the failure to adapt the British system of government to the character of the Irish, and the very dubious status of the ascendancy itself were to remain a matter of concern in Anglo-Irish writing from Burke to Yeats.[17]

It is in the early nineteenth century that the idea of national character becomes a crucial cultural category and the subject of intense dispute in Europe at large as well as in Ireland. Part of the reason for this is the reaction to and the attempted analyses of the Franch Revolution and the Napoleonic regime which succeeded it. In Ireland, there was, in addition, the changed circumstances which obtained after 1798 and the union. Having lost her briefly-won political identity, Ireland produced writers who were correspondingly more anxious to assert the existence of a cultural coherence which would provide an alternative to or compensation for that loss. In England, writers as opposed as Coleridge and Hazlitt were inclined to assign the failure of the Revolution or, in Hazlitt's case, the defeat of Napoleon, to the fatal weakness of the French national character which they thought to be at root attracted to despotism and authoritarianism. In this respect, it was, of course, the antithesis of the English national charcter with its ineluctable bias towards liberty and a mixed constitution.[18] A more interesting analysis and proposed remedy was provided by Mme de Staël whose novels and critical writings are largely preoccupied with the search for a reconciliation between the forces of contemporary nationalism and of the older eighteenth-century and Enlightenment ideal of cosmopolitanism. The oppositions in terms of which she pursues this reconciliation are in part derived from Montesquieu, but they have also the unmistakable flavour of the age of nationalism. German profundity and solemnity is seen as the counterbalance to French gaiety and elegance; the Protestant North of Europe is recruited to harmonise its virtues with those of the Catholic South; prudence seeks its reciprocal virtue in spontaneity and enthusiasm. Mme de Staël is indeed the earliest exponent of the theme of reconciliation between the Enlightenment and the Revolution. Nationalism and cosmopolitanism are interpreted by her as the motive principles of the age and their mutual interdependence is her favourite theme.[19] In Ireland, the same preoccupation is evinced in the novels of Maria Edgeworth and, in muted form, in later novelists, although in them the terms of the debate are more localised and tend to dwell on the desired merging of factions — Ascendancy and peasantry, Protestant and Catholic — and, equally, tend also to a final disillusion with the possibility of their final compatability. But Edgeworth in particular is, like de Staël, confident that the starting point of her great project should be the idea of a national charcter, something which she regards as an indisputable sociological fact. This conviction is by no means unique to her, although she is probably the most optimistic of all those who commented upon the national characer, being convinced, at least for a time, that it was capable of improvement. The belief that the Irish national character was degraded beyond the point of recovery was more likely to be found in the writings of English literary men, although the fear that this was the case is a pronounced feature of much Irish writing too, especially among those who regarded Daniel O'Connell with disfavour and who felt that his demagogic crusades had had a deleterious effect on the character of the peasantry. First, though, it will help to set much of this Irish writing in perspective if we look at some of the evidence adduced by English writers on the Irish national character. The perspective is not false since so much Irish writing — especially Irish fiction — of the early nineteenth century was written with an eye to the English audience and took many of its assumptions from that audience's beliefs about the Irish character.

In *The Morning Post* of January 1800 — the same month that *Castle Rackrent* appeared — Coleridge followed up on Burke's 1795 attack on the Protestant Ascendancy:

The Irish national character we have ever contemplated with a melancholy pleasure, as a compound of strength and vivacity: an amalgam of the qualities of the two rival nations, England and France. Ireland itself is placed in the most enlightened part of the world, the sister of, perhaps, the most enlightened kingdom in it . . . What indignation, then, must not every good mind feel against that parricidal faction, which has contrived, as it were, to mock a miracle of God, and make a *Goshen* of darkness in a land surrounded by dawning or noon-day light![20]

Fourteen years later, Coleridge had changed his mind about the Ascendancy. By then it had become for him a necessary bastion of British rule in an Ireland which could not conceivably be separated from Britain, largely because it was in Britain's interest that the Union should be maintained. Interestingly, he miscalls the Ascendancy the 'Orange Confederacy' and on another occasion describes the Orangemen as having begun as Defenders. Essentially, Coleridge sees the Irish situation through the eyes of one whose mind was dominated by the fear of Jacobinism and he was ready to attack any group which seemed to be in any way sympathetic to or supportive of that cause. Therefore the United Irishmen become the focus of the attack he launched on Mr Justice Fletcher's 'Charge' to the Grand Jury of Wexford at the Summer Assizes in 1814. In six newspaper articles (or 'Letters'), signed by 'An Irish Protestant', Coleridge gives an exaggerated account of the advance of Jacobinism among a people of Ireland, 'at once the most numerous, and with few exceptions . . . the least civilised of Christian Europe'.[21] Coleridge's importance here has little to do with his versions of Irish history, but with his recurrent emphases on the conditions and circumstances which had led to the degradation of the Irish character and the near-impossibility of rescuing it by any programme of legislative or social reform.

In a similar vein, Carlyle wrote of the Irish national character in his essay 'Chartism' (1839):

The Irish national character is degraded, disordered; till this recover itself, nothing is yet recovered. Immethodic, headlong, violent, mendacious: what can you make of the wretched Irishman? Such a people works no longer on Nature and reality; works now on Phantasm, Simulation, Nonentity; the result it arrives at is naturally not a thing but no-thing, — defect even of potatoes. Scarcity, futility, confusion, distraction must be perennial there. Such a people circulates not order but disorder through every vein of it; — and the cure, if it is to be a cure, must begin at the heart: not in his condition only but in himself must the Patient be all changed. Poor Ireland![22]

The last sentence here seems to indicate that Carlyle believed that character was independent of conditions and that both must be changed. However, it is difficult to elicit from his writings any determinate views on this issue. By 1850, in 'Downing Street', one of his *Latter-Day Pamphlets*, the Irish question has become part of the English question as the famine hordes descend upon England — 'The Irish Giant, named of Despair, . . . advancing upon London itself, laying waste all English cities, towns and villages.'[23] What troubles Carlyle most is that this apocalypse, visited upon England because of its misrule in Ireland, will lead to a social upheaval in England if the Irish take work at substandard wages and thus increase English unemployment and unrest.

It is possible to find among English writers some who would not only chastise this view of the Irish national character's wildness and turbulence, but who would throw doubt on the validity of the idea of a national character as such. John Stuart Mill had done this in relation to the English view of the French national character in the first number of *The Westminster Review* in 1824 and his comments on Ireland tended in the same direction thereafter. Most outspoken of all was the famous wit and reviewer for the *Edinburgh Review*, Sydney Smith, whose *Peter Plymley's Letters* (1807-8) supplied a tonic alternative to the current hysteria and propaganda on both France and Ireland. On the latter he wrote:

Before you refer the turbulence of the Irish to incurable defects in their character, tell me if you have treated them as friends and equals? . . . Nothing of all this. What then? Why, you have confiscated the territorial surface of the country twice over; you have massacred and exported her inhabitants: you have deprived four-fifths of them of every civil privilege; you have at every period made her commerce and her manufactures slavishly subordinate to your own: and yet, the hatred which the Irish bear to you is the result of an original turbulence of character, and of a primitive, obdurate wildness, utterly incapable of civilization.[24]

Like Burke, forty years earlier, and Coleridge in 1800, Smith recommended the conciliation of the Irish Catholics by admitting them to full rights under the British Constitution, even if this had to be done at the expense of and in face of what he called the 'Orange tyranny'. But Smith was writing against the tide. National character, either of itself or as the product of oppressive conditions, was increasingly identified as the unchanging and unchangeable element in the Irish problem. Although Matthew Arnold was later — especially in the years 1878-1882 — to remodel the Irish character as Celtic temperament and to explain the failure of English rule in Ireland as the result of an incompatability between it and the Murdstonian British middle classes — the nature of the diagnosis was unchanged.[25] Nor was it an English diagnosis only. No group believed it more readily than the Irish writers and no body of literature is more preoccupied with national character than that produced in Ireland in the first half of the nineteenth century.

But they softened the vision of national character by attaching it to the first Celtic revival's romantic note. The word 'romantic' has had some strange effects when it is brought into contact with the notion of representation, especially in fiction. Generally, to cast a romantic hue upon the matter represented is, in effect, to misrepresent it by lending it an aura or attraction not essentially its own. The Irish novelists of the early nineteenth

century recognised and exploited the fact that they were writing for an audience which would regard the ordinary circumstances of Irish life with incredulity. But this also imposed a heavy burden. The actuality of Irish life
was regularly viewed as a romantic representation. In such circumstances,
it was difficult to write realistic fiction. In the Preface to *Castle Rackrent,*
Maria Edgeworth addresses herself, apologetically, 'to those who are
totally unacquainted with Ireland' and admits that for them, 'the following Memoirs will perhaps be scarcely intelligible, or, probably they may appear perfectly incredible'.[26]

William Carleton says of his account of the Famine in *The Black Prophet* (1847) that he has understated rather than overstated the case. Again
he looks to his foreign audience:

. . . the reader — especially if he be English or Scotch — may rest assured that the
author has not at all coloured beyond the truth. The pictures and scenes represented
here . . . not only have escaped contradiction, they defy it.[27]

Even in works which are not (consciously) fictional, the same theme recurs.
W. Stuart Trench prefaced his well-known sketches in *Realities of Irish
Life* (1868) — written by this industrious land agent to give the English
public an idea of some of the problems faced by an improving landlord in
Ireland and to persuade it that 'Ireland is not altogether unmanageable' —
with the avowal that

. . . it has been my lot to live surrounded by a kind of poetic turbulence and almost
romantic violence which I believe could scarcely belong to real life in any other
country in the world.[28]

The incredulity of the audience for Irish fiction and memoirs, insofar as
they are distinguishable — the life presented by Jonah Barrington is
perhaps even more remarkable than that presented by Edgeworth in *Castle
Rackrent* — is one of the standard features in the literature of Irish romanticism. The English audience lives in the everyday world; the Irish writer
and the Irish culture belong to a surreal world. The artist, as mediator between these two, even as apologist for one to the other, is beset by a plight
which is a political as well as an imaginative one. A favoured explanation
for the difference between the two worlds is the national character of each.
Although this by no means excludes consideration of other factors —
political, social, economic — it does always manage to provide that surplus
labour which more pragmatic analyses cannot generate. Interestingly,
though, the hostile use of the unfavourable view of the Irish national
character gives emphasis to the untrustworthiness of Irish witness to

historical fact, especially when the evidence is unfavourable to the British. This is the other side of the 'romantic' coin. Romantic misrepresentation may be passed off as something which can be expected of a poet or novelist, but it is a more serious matter when historical evidence is at issue. Thomas de Quincey provides a startling example of the political implications of misrepresentation and its putative roots in the national character in his *Autobiographic Sketches*. Three chapters of this work were devoted to de Quincey's visit to Ireland at the time of the Union. He wrote down his memories of this and of the stories he heard then about the rebellion of 1798 somewhere between 1832-33. In 1853 he added a long footnote to the earlier published account he had given twenty years before of the character and behaviour of Castlereagh and of the brutal behaviour of British troops in Mayo in 1798. That account had been given him by the then Protestant Bishop, Dr Stock. In the demurring footnote of 1853, de Quincey declares:

I myself had seen reason to believe, indeed sometimes I knew for certain, that, in the *personalities* of Irish politics, from Grattan downwards, a spirit of fiery misrepresentation prevailed, which made it hopeless to seek for anything resembling truth.

Dr Stock was, it appears, a liar. De Quincey goes on:

I shrink from the bishop's malicious portraiture of our soldiers, sometimes of their officers, as composing a licentious army, without discipline, without humanity, without even steady courage. Has any man a right to ask our toleration for pictures so romantic as these? [29]

Thus, by the de Quincey law of re-, not to say detraction, the Irish were by nature subject to 'fiery misrepresentation' which led to the production of 'romantic' pictures. There was, therefore, a perfect safety device for the English audience. Ireland could be as romantic as it pleased in fiction or in fact; that was acceptable. But when the extremity of Irish conditions was attributed to English misrule, that was 'misrepresentation' and was not acceptable, although it was very much to be expected from so unreliably romantic a race. This placed the Irish writer in an impossible position in relation to his audience. He could — like Maginn, Sylvester O'Mahony, Lover, Lever and many others — portray Ireland as 'a humorist's arcadia'; [30] or he could — like the Banims, Griffin, Carleton and Maria Edgeworth — portray conditions which were in dire need of improvement for a race that would, as a result, be perfectly normal. But he could not safely attribute the evils of his country to English misrule. That would be 'misrepresentation' of the de Quincey species.

Any survey of the fiction of the period from 1800 to 1850 shows how difficult it is clearly to separate it from the sub-genres of travel literature, written by foreigners, and of folk or folksy reminiscences and reports, written by natives. From Arthur Young's early *A Tour in Ireland* (1780), through Eyre Evans Crowe's *Today in Ireland* (1825), Cesar Otway's *Sketches in Ireland* (1827), the Banims' *Tales of the O'Hara Family* (1825-6) and of course Crofton Croker's *Fairy Legends and Traditions of the South of Ireland* (1825), we discover a strange admixture of antiquarianism, sociology and fiction, most of it concerned to cast some light on the linkages between Irish national character and Irish conditions. History, geography, climate are frequently brought into consideration but the senior category in all these accounts and appraisals is the national character. It is both cause of and caused by the other factors. It is both a product of history and an abiding metaphysical essence. Most important of all, perhaps, is the often tendered opinion that the uniqueness of Irish conditions is finally attributable to the uniqueness of the national character. This can be meant either as compliment or insult; its most enduring assumption, that of uniqueness, is perhaps more important than the particular uses to which any individual writer subjected it.

Moreover, just as the English literary commentators on the Irish national character were preoccupied with its degradation, so the Irish writers were preoccupied with its redemption. The novelists were pre-eminent in this respect and received most of the praise, in the latter part of the century, for having achieved it. National character, it was believed, exhibited itself most strongly and visibly in the Irish peasantry. To rescue them from the degradation they had suffered at the hands of English misrepresentation was, in retrospect, one of the most memorable achievements of the Irish novelists. In 1882, Alexander M. Sullivan, one of the notorious 'Bantry Gang', looked back on the changes which had taken place in the representation of Irish peasant life since the days of the Famine:

The Irish peasant of forty years ago — his home, his habits, manner, dress; his wit and humour, his tender feeling, his angry passions, his inveterate prejudices — all these have been portrayed with more or less of exaggeration a hundred times. Caricature has done its worst with the subject; but justice has sometimes touched the theme. One of the changes most pleasing in our time is the fact that in England the clumsy "stage Irishman" of former days is no longer rapturously declared to be the very acme of truthful delineation. The Irish are keenly sensitive to ridicule or derision; and to see the national character travestied in miserable novel or brutal farce — the Irish peasant as a compound of idiot and buffoon — for the merriment of the master race, was an exasperation more fruitful of hatred between the peoples than the fiercest invective of those 'agitators' whom it has been the fashion to credit with the exclusive manufacture of Irish sedition.

Banim and Griffin, Mrs. Hall and Carleton, have left pictures of Irish life and character which on the whole cannot be surpassed for fidelity and effectiveness.[31]

Yet when we look at the manner in which the Irish peasant or, indeed, the national character in general was redeemed by the novelists we find that the prescription is very similar to that recommended by Mme de Staël and by all those who wished to discover some means of reconciling European romantic nationalism with the European Enlightenment. In effect, this meant that two stereotypes would recur; one would be the standard version of an old, relatively untutored 'wildness'; the other an equally standard representation of civility brought to the point of anaemia or dullness. The old, disreputable wildness belonged to the past. To take three representative samples, in *Castle Rackrent, The Collegians* and *Traits and Stories of the Irish Peasantry,* the wildness is associated with a group which is part of a dying culture. In Edgeworth's novel it is the Ascendancy class of the Rackrents; in Griffin's it is the class of the 'half-sirs', the Cregans; in Carleton's stories, it is the peasantry of his native Tyrone. Retrospect is important in these works. It allows us to witness the disappearance of a class while retaining our affection for it. The historical features which lend disenchantment to the nostalgic view are, respectively, the Union, Catholic Emancipation and the degradation of the peasantry which Carleton believed O'Connell had brought about by turning a truthful race into a conniving, dishonest band. In each case an alternative to this wildness is proposed. Instead of the Rackrents, 'The best that can happen will be the introduction of British manufacturers in their places.'[32] So too, in *Ennui* (1809) and *The Absentee* (1812), Edgeworth recommends Irish landlords to forego their second-rate life of absenteeism in England and to return to their estates in Ireland, bringing utilitarian common sense to their dilapidated and romantic homes. Even more clearly, in *Ormond* (1817), the eponymous hero is faced with a choice between three modes of life — that of his Rackrentish uncle Ulick O'Shane, a corrupt politician; that of Ulick's brother, Corny O'Shane, king of the Black islands, trapped in his Jacobite-Gaelic time-lock; and that of the Annaly family, representing all that is steady, thrifty and respectable in English civilisation. Her dream of order relied for its foundation upon an alliance of the wild Irish aristocratic type (Catholic or Protestant) with the pragmatic English spirit. The consequence of its realisation would be, in her view, the improvement of the condition of the people and the winning of their devotion. But Edgeworth's dream soon faded in the face of actual circumstance. She wrote nothing of consequence after 1817 and, in 1834, in answer to her brother's query on her long silence answered:

It is impossible to draw Ireland as she now is in the book of fiction — realities are too strong, party passions too violent, to bear to see, or care to look at their faces in a looking glass. The people would only break the glass, and curse the fool who held the mirror up to nature — distorted nature in a fever.[33]

Ireland marked out the limits of her idea of mimesis. History had passed beyond the range of representation in fiction. It is a telling moment.

Part of what it tells is embodied in Griffin's famous novel. *The Collegians* promotes the replacement of the reckless and violent world of the Squireen Cregans, epitomised in Hardress, with the sober respectabilities of the Catholic middle-class, epitomised in Kyrle Daly. That replacement can only be achieved, in the terms of this novel, by marriage between the noble inheritor of the Ascendancy tradition, Ann Chute, and young Kyrle. It is the first of many Irish dreams of the noble and the bourgeois man in alliance against disreputable, violent, hard-drinking rapscallion life. Like Edgeworth, Griffin too is conscious of the English reader, for he has his eye on the respectability Emancipation will confer on the Catholic bourgeois and wishes to present them in as winsome a light as possible. Even more than she, he is entirely given to the idea of national characteristics. 'National' is, in fact, one of his stock epithets. Mr Daly 'had a national predilection for Irish history'; Lowry Looby had 'the national talent for adroit flattery'; Dr Leake has 'a national turn of character' and Mr Cregan 'possessed all the national warmth of temperament and liveliness of feeling'.[34] Like most of the 'romantic' Irish novels of this period, Griffin's is as anxious to offer a political solution to the 'wildness' of the national character by tempering it with the sobriety of the new Catholic middle-class dispensation as it is ready to exploit those wild elements in catering to the taste of the incredulous English reader. His attempted balance between these elements is entirely lost in the Boucicault stage adaptation *The Colleen Bawn* (1860) and in Benedict's operetta, *The Lily of Killarney* (1862).

It is hardly necessary to say that William Carleton was, more than any other writer, the beneficiary and the victim of the age's obsession with the Irish national character. Not only did the Irish peasantry achieve an undisputed prominence in literature with his *Traits and Stories* but they also gained it in the eyes of an Irish as well as an English audience. The new energy in the Irish publishing trade helped him to survive as a writer for his own people as well as for the English audience which received him as warmly as he could have wished. Dr Barbara Hayley has analysed in detail all of the issues which Carleton touches upon in his famous 'general introduction' to the 1842 edition of the *Traits and Stories* — national character, language, the treatment of the Irish personality in literature and especially in literature written by Irishmen, the importance of a 'national literature' and the impulse given to it both by himself and magazines like the *Dublin University Magazine*.[36] But Carleton was also the victim of the circumstances he describes. For all its virtues, his writing was marred by a series of stylistic ruptures which repeated revisions could not heal. Most of these were caused by his uncertainty about how best to represent on the page the varieties and vagaries of Irish peasant speech; how to present himself as narrator; how to pass from dialect to standard speech in a smooth transition. As with so many Irish writers, the problem of representation was almost insuperable. A direct representation (if such a thing exists) of what he knew was constantly parried by a consciousness of what he ought to present to his audience. Moreover, he had the alertness to recognise that he, like the recorders of folk tales, customs and habits, was actually altering, even destroying the very thing he recorded by the very act of writing it down. Therefore, in him the perils of nostalgia are particularly acute. The Tyrone of his childhood is a much more threatened culture than that of Edgeworth's Rackrents or the prosperous decade of Griffin's eighteenth-century background in *The Collegians,* for it has no alternative political programme of redemption comparable to theirs. The best Carleton can offer, in the 1830 Preface to the First Series of his stories, is the hope,

. . . — his heart's desire and anxious wish — that his own dear, native mountain people may, through the influence of education, by the leadings of purer knowledge, and by the fosterings of a paternal government, become the pride, the strength, and support of the British empire, instead of, as now, forming its weakness and reproach.[36]

Yet Carleton's one theme — Irish national character, as evinced in the Irish peasantry — finds its only appropriate form in the tale and, in the larger frame of the novel, tends towards those melodramatic exploitations which he, among others, had been so eager to replace. He, like his portrait of the Irish national character, degenerated into caricature and a considerable degree of incoherence after mid-century. *The Squanders of Castle Squander* (1852) and the fatally popular *Willy Reilly and his Dear Colleen Bawn* (an early version in 1850-51, a later one in 1855) are sufficient indications of his decline.

Yet it may be argued that Carleton's touching trust in the power of education was not entirely misplaced in an era which had seen the setting up of the National Schools and the first attempt to provide a university education for Catholics. The necessity of education was a constant theme in the writings of Thomas Davis, even though he wished to direct the Irish people away from Westminster and the Empire towards a new conception of themselves and their nationality. 'The Library of Ireland', one of his best-known articles for *The Nation,* is a typical example of his variation upon the already worn opposition between utilitarian England and romantic Ireland. Even in its threadbare state in the 1840s, this opposition was used over and over again to dress up the national character in its implacable appearances upon every literary occasion.

Westminster ceased to be the city towards which the Irish bowed and made pilgrimage. An organisation, centring in Dublin, connected the People; and oratory full of Gaelic passion and popular idiom galvanised them. Thus there has been, from 1842 — when Repeal agitation became serious — an incessant progress in Literature and Nationality. A Press, Irish in subjects, style and purpose, has been formed — a National Poetry has grown up — the National Schools have prepared their students for the more earnest study of National politics and history . . .

Yet the power of British utilitarian literature continues. The wealthy classes are slowly getting an admirable and costly National Literature from Petrie, and O'Donovan, and Ferguson, and Lefanu, and the *University Magazine.* The poorer are left to the newspaper, and the meeting, and an occasional serial of very moderate merits. That class, now becoming the rulers of Ireland, who have taste for the higher studies, but whose means are small, have only a few scattered works within their reach, and some of them, not content to use these exclusively, are driven to foreign studies and exposed to alien influence . . .

To give to the country a National Library, exact enough for the wisest, high enough for the purest, and cheap enough for all readers, appears the object of "The Library of Ireland".[37]

Although this may be regarded as a characteristic specimen of what Yeats was later to call 'the school-boy thought' of Young Ireland, it is a useful reminder of the centrality given by two intellectual movements — that of Young Ireland in the forties and that associated with *The Dublin University Magazine* in the thirties — to the idea of national character and the need to provide it with a wider and deeper cultural base. In this context, Carleton's work can be more clearly seen, for the two movements, which appeared to have a single cultural aim, were seriously divided in politics — one nationalist, the other unionist — and catered, as Davis mentions, to different classes. If national character were to be educated, if the romantic wildness could be subdued into enlightened rationality, to what end would it be directed? All seemed to agree that the end would not be utilitarian, but that did not necessarily mean that it would be Irish in the political sense the nationalists gave the term. The great exponent of the marriage between cultural nationalism and unionism was Sir Samuel Ferguson. We may see Carleton more clearly if we regard him as a figure caught between the revivalist politics of Ferguson and Davis, each equipped with a theory of education and each confident of the transformation it could have in practice upon the national character.

Ferguson's importance is acknowledged but it has never been estimated with sufficient care. He extends the eighteenth-century antiquarian revival, not merely by the production of his influential translations from the Gaelic, but by the provision of a new context for their reception. The famous credo of 1840, published in the *Dublin University Magazine,* is his version of Davis's 'Library of Ireland', founded on the claim that Ireland can be taught to recover a lost cultural unity through

. . .the disinterring and bringing back to light of intellectual day, the already recorded *facts*, by which the people of Ireland will be able to *live back*, in the land they live *in,* with as ample and as interesting a field of retrospective enjoyment as any of the nations around us.[38]

But this new programme envisions a very specific form of reconciliation. Ferguson, horrified by the demagoguery of O'Connell and hostile to the spectacle of the populist and emergent Catholic nation, sought a relationship between Catholic and Protestant which would reveal to the former their true identity and to the latter their true role. The fire and passion of the Celtic and Catholic heritage could be absorbed into the modern, civil and civic forms of the Protestant tradition, once the Catholic had been freed from the 'spiritual thraldom' of his religion and the Protestant from the 'civil degradation' he had undergone at the hands of the British government. In other words, Ferguson wants to provide a Protestant intellectual and political leadership to a Catholic and Gaelic people before that people is transmogrified into a mob (by O'Connell and the priests) and before the Protestant Ascendancy is reduced to a dying caste, a foreign garrison in its own country. In his remarkable essay of 1833, also in the *Dublin University Magazine,* entitled 'A Dialogue Between the Head and Heart of an Irish Protestant' he acknowledges the Protestant rationale for refusing sympathy to the Catholic claims. But there is also the heart's claim:

I love this land better than any other. I cannot believe it a hostile country. I love the people of it, in spite of themselves, and cannot feel towards them as enemies.[39]

Ferguson, therefore, sees the alliance between Romantic Ireland and Enlightenment Ireland in Catholic and Protestant terms. Further, he sees it as the only alliance which can effectively put a halt to the degradation of the national character by a populist nationalism which would sharpen sectarian strife and a provincial, philistine culture. This attitude is of a piece with the counter-revolutionary movements in Europe, all of which were, in their neo-Burkean fashion, attempting to recreate the notion that there was a natural and traditional fellowship between the old aristocratic leadership and the people. Feguson is also influenced by Mme de Staël's crusade for a merger between the Nordic Protestant spirit and the Southern Catholic one. Most of all, Ferguson is important for the manner in which he anticipates the form which this debate is to take in Irish writing thereafter. He successfully separates the Protestant ideal from the utilitarian ethos with which it was to be so often identified later (e.g. by Matthew Arnold) and he distinguishes between Gaelic civilisation and Catholic nationalism with a decisiveness that neither Standish O'Grady nor Yeats was to equal. In brief, he begins the rewriting of the idea of Irish national character. Rather than belonging exclusively or pre-eminently to the peasantry, it now becomes the future product of a new mutuality between Catholic and Protestant, peasantry and ascendancy. Ferguson counters Burke's attack on the Ascendancy by restoring it to the centre of traditional Irish culture and refuses entirely any imputation of a similarity between it and Jacobinism or any such foreign body in the ancestral system.

It is in the light of Ferguson's ideal that we can observe more sympathetically the dark passages in the writings of Standish O'Grady. O'Grady's long and furious lament for the failure of the Irish landlord class to assume the political and intellectual leadership of the Irish people is not simply a characteristic specimen of late nineteenth-century neo-feudalism. It is a lament for the lost opportunity in Ireland of creating a new and heroic dispensation which would not be marred by the vulgarities of the commercial, industrial and liberal-democratic world of nineteenth-century Britain.[40] But O'Grady's historical writings and pamphlets, like Yeats's essays and poems, carried on the debate about national character and about the alliance between the ascendancy and the people in an intellectual climate profoundly different from that of the thirties and forties. Since Renan and Arnold, Irish national character had begun to define its Celtic difference more and more at the expense of the British national character. British national character was now identified with the British middle classes and their philistine, utilitarian, and allegedly shallow liberalism or cosmopolitanism was now coming under attack from all quarters. The Irish, now the Celtic, character was the beneficiary of most of these attacks. For, by the eighties of the last century, it was customary to find that egalitarian societies, based on the principles of liberal democracy, were criticised as manifesting, in mass form, all the symptoms of decadence. The adversarial position, increasingly adopted in literary and scientific circles, promoted the idea that spiritual health could be restored to British, indeed Western, culture by the emergence of a new aristocracy operating within an hierarchical social structure. The history of this complicated repudiation of mass democratic society is far beyond the scope of this paper, but its bearing upon the transformation of the idea of national character and of the uses to which this idea was put is immediately obvious in the writings of men as diverse as Shaw, Yeats, Pearse and Synge. It is in fact an integral part of the story of Irish nationalism's resurgence at the turn of the century.

One way of approaching the issue is to look at the treatment of the theme of national degeneration, as observed above in Coleridge, Carlyle and others when writing on the Irish problem, when its range if widened to include the degeneration of the species as a whole or, with faint modesty, the degeneration of the white races. The traditionalist Romantic advocacy of the need for a spiritual leadership or intellectual 'clerisy' (to use Coleridge's term) was drastically altered by the impact of Darwinism. The theory of Evolution, treated by many as a doctrine, added a new dimension to the conception of the clerisy or, as it came to be called, of the elite. The most influential formulations of this new development were achieved in the writings of Darwin's cousin, Francis (later Sir Francis) Galton, whose book *Hereditary Genius* (1869) proclaimed the need to produce a 'highly gifted race of men'. Although it was 1883 before Galton coined the word 'eugenics' for 'the breeding of human beings who were hereditarily endowed with noble qualities', the notion of selective breeding was already widely canvassed by then. With that came the intensification of the attacks on modern degeneration and the necessity to recover from it. E. Ray Lankester's *Degeneration* (1880), Lombroso's *Man of Genius* (translated 1888) and Max Nordau's *Entartung* (1892-3), translated as *Degeneration* in February 1895, with its publication timed to coincide with the trial of Oscar Wilde for 'degenerate' offences, had profound consequences in literature, especially at first on the literary criticism of men like Alfred Orage and Havelock Ellis.[41] Ellis in particular refashioned the old oppositions found in Mme de Staël, between the Nordic and the Celtic spirit. His essay of 1906, 'The Celtic Spirit in Literature' should be read in sequence with Arnold's 1867 lecture, 'The Study of Celtic Literature', the 1893 translation of Renan's book *The Poetry of the Celtic Races* and Yeats's 1897 essay 'The Celtic Element in Literature' to reveal the increasingly racial and pseudo-scientific basis upon which the idea of Irish national character rested by the turn of the century. But it is of course in Shaw that Irish literature registers the impact of evolutionary theory on the notion of national character, British and Irish, and provides us with the definitive left-wing theory of the authoritarian elite formed by a process of natural selection by the Life Force.

The apparently scientific approach of the evolutionist school of writers would seem to make any rapprochement between it and the fashionable new pseudo-science of the eighties unlikely. But Evolutionism found an ally, however uncomfortable, in Occultism. That word too was coined in the eighties, 1881 to be exact, by A.P. Sinnett, author of *Esoteric Bhuddism*, but less well remembered than Madame Blavatsky, whose disordered tomes *Isis Unveiled* (1877), *The Secret Doctrine* (1887) as well as the more lucid *Outline of Theosophy* (1891) became magic books for Yeats and the various occult circles in which he moved. Occultism announced the existence of a world totally opposed to all that egalitarian mass democracies represented. It dismissed utilitarian rationality, secularism, commercialism and liberalism with contempt. On joining the Order of the Golden Dawn in 1890, Yeats became a member of a secret society which believed in a secret doctrine, orally transmitted through the ages in cryptic and symbolic forms. Through magic, he became a believer in the essential link between the wisdom of the people and the inner cadre of the spiritual aristocrats. This was Ferguson and O'Grady in form but with the substance of their thought radically transformed. Yeats kept it within the limits of recognisability by making Ireland and the national character of the Irish people, the peasantry, as well as that of the Ascendancy, the essential Celtic preserve for this ancient, non-utilitarian and non-British wisdom. As he set out on his astonishing intellectual journey through nineteenth-century literature, he recognised the need to counter the old opposition between parochial and cosmopolitan by invoking the new esoteric version of Irish national character. In doing so, he brings a strange history to an unexpected conclusion:

I would have Ireland recreate the ancient arts . . . arts like these. I think indeed I first learned to hope for them myself in Young Ireland Societies, or in reading the essays of Davis. An Englishman, with his belief in Progress, with his instinctive preference for the cosmopolitan literature of the last century, may think arts like these parochial, but they are the arts we have begun the making of.[42]

Ancient Ireland had finally arrived in Irish literature as the ultimate rediscovery of modern Ireland. The people and the ascendancy were now, as possessors of the national character, in a new alliance to rescue the degenerate modern world from the secular-commercial triumphs of the British national character against which they had both struggled to define and distinguish themselves since the eighteenth century.

NOTES AND REFERENCES

1. See D. George, *English Political Caricature 1793-1832: A Study of Opinion and Propaganda* (Oxford, 1959); D. Hill (ed.), *Fashionable Contrasts: Caricatures by James Gillray* (London, 1966); R. Paulson, *Rowlandson: A New Interpretation* (London, 1972); E. Rickwood (ed.), *Radical Squibs and Loyal Ripostes: Satirical Pamphlets of the Regency Period, 1819-1821, Illustrated by George Cruikshank and Others* (Bath, 1971).

2. R.N. Lebow, *White Britain and Black Ireland: The Influence of Stereotypes on Colonial Policy* (Philadelphia, 1976); L.P. Curtis, *Apes and Angels: the Irishman in Victorian Caricature* (Washington and London, 1972).

3. See Rene Wellek, *The Rise of English Literary History* (New York, 1966), pp 24-35.

4. David Hume, *Essays Moral, Political and Literary* ed. T.H. Green and T.H. Grose, 2 vols (London, 1875), II, p. 68.

5. See L.L. Bongie, *David Hume: Prophet of the Counter-Revolution* (Oxford, 1965), pp 5-8.

6. For a fuller account, see Ciaran Murray, 'Intellectual Origins of the English Landscape Garden' (unpublished Ph.D. thesis, University College, Dublin, 1985); B. Sprague Allen, *Tides in English Taste, 1619-1800*, 2 vols (London, 1937); D. Clifford, *A History of Garden Design* (London, 1962); C. Hussey, *English Gardens and Landscapes 1700-1750* (London, 1967); E. Hyams, *The English Garden* (London, 1966); O. Siren, *China and the Gardens of Europe of the Eighteenth Century* (New York, 1950).

7. The standard work is still S.H. Monk, *The Sublime* (New York, 1935).

8. *The Works of The Right Honourable Edmund Burke*, 8 vols (London, 1877-78), VI, p. 45.

9. See especially C.P. Courtney, *Montesquieu and Burke* (Oxford, 1963).

10. See J.T. Boulton, *The Language of Politics in the Age of Wilkes and Burke* (London and Toronto, 1963).

11. See N. Vance, 'Celts, Carthaginians and Constitutions: Anglo-Irish Literary Relations, 1780-1820', *Irish Historical Studies*, XXII (1980), pp 216-230. Betham's best-known works are *The Gael and the Cymbri* (1834) and *Etruria-Celtica* (1842); see also J. Sheehy, *The Rediscovery of Ireland's Past: the Celtic Revival, 1830-1930* (London, 1980).

12. W.S. Dowden (ed.), *The Letters of Thomas Moore*, 2 vols (Oxford, 1964), I, p. 116.

13. P.P. Howe (ed.), *The Complete Works of William Hazlitt*, 21 vols (London, 1910-34), VII, p. 154.

14. J. Hardiman, *Irish minstrelsy: or, Bardic Remains of Ireland with English Poetical Translations*, 2 vols (London, 1831), I, p. v.

15. *Works*, III, pp 304-5. See also, S. Deane, 'Edmund Burke and the Ideology of Irish Liberalism' in *The Irish Mind* ed. R. Kearney (Dublin, 1985), pp 141-56.
16. *Works*, XI, p. 58.
17. See W.J. McCormack, *Ascendancy and Tradition in Anglo-Irish Literary History from 1789 to 1939* (Oxford, 1985).
18. See Hazlitt, *Works*, X, pp 99, 166, XIII, p. 56.
19. See especially *De La Littérature considerée dans ses rapports avec les institutions sociales* ed. P. Van Tieghem, 2 vols (Geneva and Paris, 1959).
20. D.V. Erdman (ed.), *The Collected Works of Samuel Taylor Coleridge: Essay on His Times*, 3 vols (London, 1978), I, p. 120.
21. Ibid., II, p. 413.
22. *The Works of Thomas Carlyle*, 30 vols (London, 1898-99), XXIX, p. 137.
23. Ibid., XX, p. 194.
24. See G. Bullett, *Sydney Smith: A Biography and a Selection* (London, 1951), p. 224.
25. See S. Deane, *Celtic Revivals: Essays in Modern Irish Literature, 1880-1980* (London, 1985), pp 17-28.
26. *Castle Rackrent* (ed. G. Watson, London, 1964), p. 4.
27. *The Black Prophet*, introduction by Timothy Webb (Shannon, 1972), pp vii-viii.
28. *Realities of Irish Life* (2nd ed., London, 1869), p. vii.
29. *De Quincy's Works*, 15 vols (Edinburgh, 1863), vol. 14, p. 285 n.
30. The phrase is Yeats's, quoted in Thomas Flanagan, *The Irish Novelists, 1800-1850* (New York, 1959), p. 174.
31. *New Ireland: Political Sketches and Personal Reminiscences of Thirty Years of Irish Public Life* (Glasgow, 1884), p. 3.
32. *Castle Rackrent* (ed. G. Watson), p. 97.
33. A.J.C. Hare, *The Life and Letters of Maria Edgeworth*, 2 vols (London, 1894), II, p. 550.
34. *The Collegians* (London and Dublin, 1942), pp 20, 31, 81, 173.
35. *Carleton's Traits and Stories and the 19th Century Anglo-Irish Tradition* (Gerrard's Cross, 1983), pp 357-363.
36. Ibid., p. 24.
37. Thomas Davis, *Prose Writings; Essays on Ireland* (Dublin, n.d.), p. xiii.
38. M.C. Ferguson, *Sir Samuel Ferguson in the Ireland of his Day*, 2 vols (Edinburgh and London, 1896), I, p. 47.
39. *Dublin University Magazine*, 2 (1833), p. 588.
40. See especially *Toryism and Tory Democracy* (London, 1886) and *Selected Essays and Passages* (Dublin, 1918).
41. For an interesting sketch of this literature, see T. Gibbons, *Rooms in the Darwin Hotel* (London, 1978).
42. W.B. Yeats, 'Ireland and the Arts' (1901) in *Essays and Introductions* (London, 1961), p. 206.

Sanditon:
A Regency Novel

OLIVER MacDONAGH

I

Whether we define the Regency period strictly, as 1811-20, or, more loosely, as the first quarter of the nineteenth century, *Sanditon* belongs to it, unquestionably, in date. In fact, it is close to the meridian. The entire fragment of the projected novel, a mere 22,000 words, was written — by a dying woman — between 17 January and 18 March 1817. These two months have as high a claim as any to represent the climax of the post-war freneticism which the term, Regency, generally connotes; and indeed it is the scramble for innovation, riches and self-realization, at the expense of duty, integrity and social peace, which engrosses *Sanditon* and constitutes the target in Jane Austen's sights. But is the exactitude of the chronological attribution more than an antiquarian's curiosity? Does *Sanditon* illuminate or improve our image of the Regency? Does the very concept of a 'Regency period' add to our understanding or evaluation of *Sanditon*? Do either or both help us with the most fundamental historiographical issue opened up by such thoughts, the legitimacy and the fruits of historical phasing?

One can, I think, say boldly and simply that the historian must periodize or perish. He can only avoid the labelling of groups of years or lengths of time by falling to the depths of sightless positivism or the undifferentiated chronicle. Of course, having made his choice, he must next undertake a critique of the particular periodization which he is making. He has to consider its deficiency as an entity; the reproduction, before or after its temporal limits, of some of its supposed ideosyncrasies; and its spatial, even districtal, limitations. But in the end he will either surrender his category as hopelessly riddled by exceptions or continue to employ it, however qualified. What *is* ruled out is the abandonment of the use of labels. 'The Age of Reason', 'the French Revolutionary period', 'the mid-nineteenth century', 'La belle époque', are indispensable frames of references — or, if not these, whatever better general titles can be found to serve as an historical shorthand. The tag says *ars longa*, not *ars sine termino*.

'The Regency' is far from secure as a periodization. Strictly, it describes the mere nine years, 1811-20; and these were years, moreover, of extraordinary variations in Britain's international power, levels of employment and state expenditure. The Regent himself was to reign, in his own right, for another decade. The dominant prime minister of his regency, Liverpool, was to govern for almost as long after 1820 as he had before it. Furthermore, the word 'Regency' is debauched, from the historian's standpoint, by its appropriation by the connoisseurs of furniture and arefacts. They use the word with great chronological licence, moving freely over half-a-century at least, between 1790 and 1840, concerned with common forms rather than contemporaneity. None the less, the term has certain important unities and certain special characteristics for historians. Among the more obvious are these: a phase of inflation, extravagance, conspicuous consumption, debt, speculation, joblessness, rising class consciousness, rising class conflict, speed and speed of change, and a phase in which Coleridge, Wordsworth, Shelley, Byron, Keats, Scott, Cruickshank, Repton, Nash, Constable and Turner were all producing work of high significance.

Byron — and who had a better claim to do so? — sang the requiem in 1822. In Canto XI of *Don Juan*, composed in the autumn of that year, he wrote:

> Talk not of seventy years as age; in seven
>   I have seen more changes, down from monarchs to
> The humblest individual under heaven,
>   Than might suffice a moderate century through.
> I knew that nought was lasting, but now even
>   Change grows too changeable, without being new:[1]

This points to two definers of the 'Regency'. First, it bore the marks of a post-war burst of relaxation, indulgence and liberation. Literally, such a delimitation would tie it to the years 1814-20 — I say 1814 because the Hundred Days of 1815 were an unforeseeable as well as a very brief reversal. But the break following the Peace of Amiens in 1802 had already shown several of these characteristics in the higher ranges of society; and still more important, from about 1808 onwards a generation, which had grown up perpetually embattled in (so far as Continental Europe was concerned) an island fortress, was coming to maturity. They were eager to make good their life-long deprivations. Secondly, Byron's stress upon the rapidity and totality of change points to the feverish, reckless, jazz-like strain in the concept 'Regency'. No one captured, and posthumously preserved, this quality as well as he.

Then dress, then dinner, then awakes the world!
Then glare the lamps, then whirl the wheels, then roar
Through street and square fast flashing chariots, hurl'd
Like harness'd meteors . . .[2]

'Meteor' is of course the master image. The 'Regency', for the upper ten thousand at least, burned brightly but briefly in its swift, hectic passage.

The archetypal standard work covering these years is, I suppose, Steven Watson's volume of the Oxford History of England, *The Reign of George III;* the relevant section of Watson's work is headed, 'The restlessness of the Regency' and nothing could be more apropos *Sanditon:* restlessness is at once its leit motif and its key stylistic note. The twelve short chapters of the fragment are tense with movement — in the utmost contrast to, say, the pace and circumscription of *Emma*'s Highbury — and in a sort of mimicry the writing of *Sanditon* is — quite uncharacteristically — staccato, rushing, impressionistic and elliptical. Watson goes on to select as the three exemplars of the Regency spirit, building, fashion and what he calls 'the new fad' of the seaside holiday. Regency building, he writes, was distinguishable by its gaiety, lightness and (often) superficial shoddiness. 'The balance of taste was precarious. The success of the regency period was a prelude to a disastrous decline in architecture as novelty and pastiche swamped the sense of form . . .'[3] He might almost be describing Sanditon New Town.

Trafalgar House [begins a memorable passage of the fragment] . . . was a light elegant building, standing in a small lawn with a very young plantation round it, about an hundred yards from the brow of a steep, but not very lofty cliff — and the nearest to it, of every building, excepting one short row of smart-looking houses, called the Terrace, with a broad walk in front, aspiring to be the Mall of the place . . .

Charlotte having received possession of her apartment, found amusement enough in standing at her ample Venetian window, and looking over the miscellaneous foreground of unfinished buildings, waving linen, and tops of houses . . .[4]

Mr Parker — the prime mover in *Sanditon*, in every sense — has let his solid, comfortable family home, 'well fenced and planted', as Jane Austen says, 'and rich in the garden, orchard and meadows which are the best embellishments of such a dwelling';[5] and is now the proud owner of Trafalgar House. He has but one regret, however — his precipitate choice of name; for as he himself observes, 'Waterloo is more the thing now'.[6] At any rate, when he is chided by his wife upon the loss of the woods and shade which had surrounded their old country place, he jauntily responds, 'but we have the canvas awning, which gives us the most complete comfort within doors — and you can get a parasol at Whitby's for little Mary at any time, or a large bonnet at Jebb's'.[7] Long-grown grace we are being told, was not so much lost as thrown away for flimsy novelty.

Raiment followed the same course. Almost to the year, the regency inaugurated a new epoch. It was about 1810 that female fashion turned towards gauzification and scattered bedeckment, and that the customary layers of petticoats and the high necklines vanished. Even so undemanding a censor as Byron was disturbed:

> Like Mother Eve our maids may stray unblam'd
> For they are naked — and are not ashamed.

Jane Austen in her annual descriptions of the London modes for the benefit of her sister, Cassandra, also marked the reign of frivolity and licence from 1812 on; and in turn, though more obliquely, *Sanditon* made substantially the same comment on the age. 'Look at William Heeley's windows', exclaimed the delighted Mr Parker, 'Blue shoes and nankin boots! — Who would have expected such a sight at a shoemaker's in old Sanditon!' In the new town, of course, things were still more advanced, with bright displays of 'straw hats and pendant lace', 'smart trinkets', and 'drawers of rings and brooches'.[8] As for Steven Watson's third piece of litmus, the rise of the seaside holiday resort, this was the very vehicle chosen by Jane Austen for her satire. Watson's master categorization, restlessness, is echoed by the heroine, Charlotte Heywood, when she describes one of her encounters at Sanditon as 'Activity run mad!'.[9] Indeed, the stage is set in the opening pages by Mr Parker's,

All done in a moment; the advertisements did not catch my eye till the last half hour of our being in town; when everything was in the hurry and confusion which always attend a short stay there. One is never able to complete anything in the way of business, you know, till the carriage is at the door.[10]

It is certainly striking that a middle-aged spinster in a Hampshire village should, half-way through a little epoch, discover and deploy the same distinguishing marks for it as the Oxford History of England was to do more than a century and a half later. *Sanditon* was clearly meant as a satirical study of modernization; and to select and connect such still-developing features of contemporary life as its exemplars manifests extraordinary acuteness of observation — the writer as witness in a high degree. But Jane Austen could — and did — cut much more deeply than this. If I might parody Paine — a thing I have long wished to do! — she not only mocks the plumage, she also anatomizes the living bird. Buildings, clothes, pleasure places and motion are all externalities, comparatively easy to track in their new courses, and then to classify. Ideology, temper and frames of mind are much more difficult affairs; but these subtleties are equally hunted down, bound, and pilloried in *Sanditon*. Here Jane Austen is not so much anticipating the verdict of posterity upon her final years as furnishing us with new and far more fundamental definers of the Regency as a separate age. I would select three in particular in the novel — Political Economy, the Romantic Mode and the pursuit of the body's health, for special notice; and I shall try to deal with each of these three in turn.

II

We are scarcely launched into the opening chapter of *Sanditon* before the political-economical debate begins. The first protagonist, the squire Mr Heywood, stands as a type of the old values, and as such deplores the mushrooming of watering-places on his native Sussex coast. Their 'growing the fashion', and his 'wonder' '*Where* people can be found with money or time to go to them!', are clearly pejorative comments, implying idleness and waste. The gravamen of Heywood's charge however is that the new resorts are inflationary and socially subversive. They were 'Bad things for a country; — sure to raise the price of provisions and [to] make the poor good for nothing'. The argument between Heywood and the speculating promotor of Sanditon, Mr Parker, is thereafter complicated by the mutual courtesy of two gentlemen-strangers. Heywood politely allows that Sanditon (of which he knows nothing) may be exceptional — or at least that it may be no worse than any other seaside venture. With similar good manners, Parker grants that Heywood's strictures may be justified in the case of the 'large, overgrown' established places, the Brightons and the Eastbournes. It is true that in his eagerness as drummer, Parker contradicts himself absurdly. In the same sentence that he speaks of Sanditon's security in being small, he looks forward confidently to 'the growth of the place, the buildings, the nursery grounds, the demand for everything'; and he immediately goes on to describe those who are trying to add to the number of Sussex seaside resorts — a group in which he is patently a leading member — as persons 'excessively absurd, . . . [who] must soon find themselves the dupes of their own fallacious calculations'. None the less, he does present Political Economy's counter to the traditionalists like Heywood: the new Sanditons, he contends, would excite 'the industry of the poor and diffuse comfort and improvement among them of every sort'[11] — or, in our jargon, they would increase employment and raise the basic standard of living and levels of consumption.

Later, substantially the same debate takes place but now with Parker's confederate in speculation, Lady Denham, arguing the conservative case. Avarice rather than fanaticism has driven Lady Denham to join Parker in promoting Sanditon, and she greets the news that a Creole family will holiday there with some satisfaction initially.

'That sounds well. That will bring money'.

'No people spend more freely, I believe, than West Indians.' observed Mr Parker.

'Aye — so I have heard — and because they have full purses, fancy themselves equal, may be, to your old country families. But then, they who scatter their money so freely, never think of whether they may not be doing mischief by raising the price of things . . . and if they come among us to raise the price of our necessaries of life, we shall not much thank them, Mr Parker.'

'My dear madam, they can only raise the price of consumable articles, by such an extraordinary demand for them and such a diffusion of money among us, as must do us more good than harm. — Our butchers and bakers and traders in general cannot get rich without bringing prosperity to *us*. — If *they* do not gain, our rents must be insecure — and in proportion to their profit must be ours eventually in the increased value of our houses.'

'Oh! — well. — But I should not like to have butcher's meat raised, though — and I shall keep it down as long as I can.'[12]

Lady Denham is no economist. She understands so little of her own enterprise, or even of her own greed, as later to complain that since Sanditon had become 'a public place',

'Families come after families, but as far as I can learn, it is not one in an hundred of them that have any real property, landed or funded. — An income perhaps, but no property. Clergymen may be, or lawyers from town, of half pay officers, or widows with only a jointure. And what good can such people do anybody? — except just as they take our empty houses — and (between ourselves) I think they are great fools for not staying at home.'[13]

But Parker is a primitive Keynesian, a Keynesian, so to say, before the modern state. For all his folly, he argues consistently for investment, for expenditure, for inflation, for consumerism, and for economic growth as the basis of general prosperity; he even foreshadows, in rudimentary form, Kahn's multiplier! The naivety of the economic language, and the lilliputian scale and farcical nature of the speculative activity, should not deceive us. By 1817 the great depression of the nineteenth century, so far as

Britain was concerned, was well on its way, with mass demobilization, a drastic reduction in public expenditure and the money supply, catastrophic falls in demand, and galloping unemployment. There were few Mr Parkers and many Mr Heywoods in the consequent economic controversy; but Jane Austen could find at least one reflationist and give him a fair run for his — to say nothing of other people's — money.

We might note in passing the Malthus's *Enquiry into the nature and progress of rent,* which underpinned theoretically his famous *Essay,* was published less than two years before *Sanditon* was composed, while Ricardo's *Principles of political economy* first appeared in 1817 itself.

III

It is notorious that Jane Austen ridiculed the Romantic mode. Every schoolboy, or at any rate every schoolgirl knows that *Northanger Abbey* was a sustained satire upon Gothicism. Most would also have been told that *Sense and Sensibility* was an elaborate indictment of the second quality in the title. With neither view can anybody quarrel; and indeed *Sanditon,* so far as it goes, continues in both these strains. The note of mockery of the pseudo-picturesque is struck immediately. In the opening scene Parker sprains his ankle but, discerning a delightful little house at a distance, is convinced that it is the dwelling of the surgeon whom he is seeking. '*There,* I fancy lies my cure', he exclaimed, 'pointing to the neat-looking end of a cottage, which was seen romantically situated among wood on a high eminence . . .' [14] Heywood soon sets him right: 'as to that cottage, I can assure you sir that it is in fact — (in spite of its spruce air at this distance) — as indifferent a double tenement as any in the parish, and that my shepherd lives at one end, and three old women at the other'. [15] This is plainly *Northanger Abbey* in parvo, romantic illusion punctured by the hard-following reality.

As to the *Sense and Sensibility* strain, the mock-hero of *Sanditon,* the handsome young baronet, Sir Edward Denham, bids fair to turning out a foolish and even comic version of the villain Willoughby. Sir Edward had been nurtured on Richardson and his successors as sentimental novelists, especially those specializing in the conscienceless pursuit and ruin of young women. Denham's great object in life, Jane Austen writes,

was to be seductive. With such personal advantages as he knew himself to possess, and such talents as he did also give himself credit for, he regarded it as his duty. He felt that he was formed to be a dangerous man — quite in the line of the Lovelaces. [16]

Sir Edward's selected victim, Clara Brereton, a poor relation of his aunt-in-law, Lady Denham, fitted the classic pattern. She was 'young, lovely and dependent', an orphan and practically defenceless, for Lady Denham's patronage was capricious and would certainly not extend to inconveniencing herself. Clara's seduction, the fragment continues,

was quite determined on. Her situation in every way called for it . . . He [Sir Edward] had very early seen the necessity of the case, and had now been long trying with cautious assiduity to make an impression on her heart, and to undermine her principles . . . If she could not be won by affection, he must carry her off. He knew his business . . . If he *were* constrained so to act, he must naturally wish to strike out something new, to exceed those who had gone before him — and he felt a strong curiosity to ascertain whether the neighbourhood of Timbuctoo might not afford some solitary house adapted for Clara's reception; — but the expense alas! of measures in that masterly style was ill-suited to his purse, and prudence obliged him to prefer the quietest sort of ruin and disgrace for the object of his affections, to the more renowned.[17]

Thus, Jane Austen's customary mockery of contemporary Romanticism was thoroughly sustained in *Sanditon*. In fact it was carried forward into virtually a new genre, what we might even term the Fiction of the Absurd. The dignified parody of place to be found in *Northanger Abbey* — after all, the Abbey itself could not be faulted either as pile or as gentlemen's estate — is practically parodied in itself, as the cottage *ornée* stands revealed as a rural slum dwelling, or when Mr Parker argues the superiority of the gimcrack New Town to the solidity and settled comfort of his hereditary home. In fact the point is silently emphasized in the last paragraph which Jane Austen ever wrote. Sanditon House, Lady Denham's manor, approached through grounds of 'beauty and respectability',

was large and handsome . . . everything had a suitable air of property and order . . . They were shown into the usual sitting room, well-proportioned and well-furnished — though it was furniture rather originally good and extremely well kept, than new or showy . . .[18]

How very fitting somehow that Jane Austen's penultimate sentence should be partly spent on putting down the 'new or showy'. Similarly, *Sense and Sensibility* presents seduction, actual and potential, in half-tragic terms; *Sanditon*'s would-be seducer is merely silly, a futile figure of fun. Jane Austen's final assault upon Romanticism turns its grotesque side upwards.

But again by now, by 1817, she could work also at a deeper level. Her most penetrating reworking of the Romantic theme is probably her treatment of the poetry of passion. In the Austen canon proper, she had dealt with this most fully in the writing of *Persuasion* two years before. Captain Benwick is a highly respectable devotee of the verse of feeling. Anne Elliot tries gently to persuade him of the moral danger of excessive indulgence in literature of this form and tone; and she later smiles privately at the prospect of the hearty Louisa Musgrove being metamorphisized into a young lady of sensibility and sentiment under the influence of love and Captain Benwick's reading list. But it is only the extravagance of its followers, and not the substance, of the new poetry which *Persuasion* satirizes — and even that most mildly.

In *Sanditon*, however, the egregious Sir Edward is cast as the expounder and justifier of Romantic verse. 'Do you remember', he begins,

'Scott's beautiful lines on the sea' Oh! what a description they convey! . . . That man who can read them unmoved must have the nerves of an assassin! Heaven defend me from meeting such a man un-armed.'

'What description do you mean' said Charlotte. 'I remember none at this moment, of the sea, in either of Scott's poems.'

'Do not you indeed? Nor can I exactly recall the beginning at this moment'.

Burns, the erotic Burns, was Sir Edward's hero.

'If ever there was a man who *felt*, it was Burns Montgomery has all the fire of poetry, Wordsworth has the true soul of it. Campbell in his pleasures of hope has touched the extreme of our sensations — "Like angel's visits, few and far between". Can you conceive anything more subduing, more melting, more fraught with the deep sublime that that line? But Burns — I confess my sense of his pre-eminence Miss Heywood. If Scott *has* a fault, it is the want of passion, Tender, elegant, descriptive — but *tame*. . But Burns is always on fire. His soul was the altar in which lovely woman sat enshrined, his spirit truly breathed the immortal incense which is her due.'

'I have read several of Burns' poems with great delight,' said Charlotte as soon as she had time to speak, 'but I am not poetic enough to separate a man's poetry entirely from his character; and poor Burns' known irregularities, greatly interrupt my enjoyment of his lines. I have difficulty in depending on the *truth* of his feelings as a lover. I have not faith in the *sincerity* of the affections of a man of his description. He felt and he wrote and he forgot.' [19]

It is noteworthy that Sir Edward fails to mention Byron. Yet he is meant to be an up-to-the-moment young man of fashion. Certainly, his conversation is replete with the latest literary jargon and affectations. Prefixes such

as 'hyper' or 'pseudo' or 'anti' were then the vogue — they were to leave a
lasting legacy, alas — and Sir Edward speaks dutifully in the current cant.
'It were hyper-criticism, it were pseudo-philosophy to expect from the soul
of high-toned genius, the grovellings of a common mind',[20] is a prime example. Elsewhere, he extols 'the anti-puerile' man, the compound being
Jane Austen's final substitution for what she originally wrote 'sagacious'.
Yet he has apparently read no Byron. The explanation may very well have
been that Jane Austen herself had read no Byron: he had after all only just
burst upon the firmament. The latest-written poetry quoted in Sanditon
(or indeed, I think, in any of her novels) comes from *The Lady of the Lake*,
which was published in 1810.[21]

None the less Jane Austen was well aware that early Byronic man
(whether or not she thought of him in some such terms) had recently turned
up upon the literary scene. He is quite evident in *Sanditon*. Sir Edward has
marked, if ludicrous, aspirations in this direction. Not for nothing does he
juxtapose 'the soul of high-toned genius' and the grovellings of the common mind. The Corsair, as the glorious embodiment of male power, and
capability to force the world into the shape he wills, would fill every corner
of Sir Edward's fantasies. It is the *Übermensch* mentality, that of the
piratical hero standing above and outside all morality, which is the target
for (in my view) *Sanditon*'s most deadly shafts. I think that we can safely
speak of Corsairism as the most abhorrent expression of the Romantic
mode, in Jane Austen's judgment.

IV

War is the promoter of health, and of talk and thought about health. At
least, one could reasonably invite an undergraduate to discuss such a proposition with relation to (as the examination papers say) the conflicts of
1793-1815. In these years the struggle between France and Britain was in no
small degree a trial by medicine. In certain theatres, the Low Countries in
1794-5 or the West Indies at all stages, to take but two examples, the losses
in combat were negligible compared to the death-roll from disease.
Perhaps the crucial reason for Britain's ultimate success was her master-
ing, between 1796 and 1802, the problem of keeping tens of thousands of
sailors, cooped up for months on end in men-of-war, alive and even fit. Effective sea-power, and in particular the critical blockades, rested upon
preventive medicine. The long Peninsular campaign was a forcing ground
for other medical advances, chiefly in surgery perhaps, but also in dietary,
sanitary and hospital organization. From the beginning, the Revolutionary

Wars had vastly increased the demand for medical practitioners: even in 1793 the Army was forced to recognize Scottish and Irish qualifications in order to make up the necessary numbers in their medical corps. Various scandals, and their successor inquiries in 1805-10,[22] changed profoundly the basis of medical training and professional behaviour.

The upsurge in serious medicine was of course accompanied by an upsurge in quackery, as the subject attracted ever more general attention. During these years, the sales of the notorious Dr Solomon's *Guide to Health* (a popular sexual textbook) were reputed to be running second only to Paine's *Rights of Man*,[23] so much so that by 1817 Solomon could construct his massive Palace of Health in London. Meanwhile the wartime tax on patent medicines had proved unexpectedly remunerative, producing several millions for the exchequer by the time of which I speak.

Certain of the effects of these advances — good and bad — are taken up for sceptical scrutiny in *Sanditon*. Possibly Jane Austen's own disease directed her attention thither. 'What we have here . . .', it has been urged recently, 'is a dying woman treating the subject of illness with amusement and raillery . . . Was she trying to cheer herself up by making fun of her condition? Or was she . . . so absorbed in the subject of ill health, that the subject presented itself irresistibly?'[24] Her letters of 1817 — not to add, her habitual disposition — suggest nothing of the kind. She wrote calmly, hopefully yet — if need be — resignedly to her family and friends up to a few weeks before she died. But who can speak with certainty on such a point? What cannot be questioned is that, having selected the new watering place as her vehicle for lampooning modernization, Jane Austen was committed also to lampooning one aspect of the medical revolution, the cult of physical well-being, self-doctoring and hypochondria. Orthodox medicine was spared; neither physicians nor criticism of physicians appear in *Sanditon*; it is only imaginary health and illness which is sent up.

Salubrity was the seaside resort's chief selling point in the first instance. Very early in the fragment, Parker gives it the full salesman's pitch.

He held it indeed as certain, that no person could be really well, . . . could be really in a state of secure and permanent health without spending at least six weeks by the sea every year. The sea air and sea bathing together were nearly infallible, one or the other of them being a match for every disorder, of the stomach, the lungs or the blood; they were anti-spasmodic, anti-pulmonary, anti-septic, anti-bilious and anti-rheumatic. Nobody could catch cold by the sea, nobody wanted appetite by the sea, nobody wanted spirits, nobody wanted strength. They were healing, softening, relaxing — fortifying and bracing — seemingly just as was wanted — sometimes one, sometimes the other. If the sea breeze failed, the sea-bath was the certain corrective; and where bathing disagreed the sea breeze alone was evidently designed by nature for the cure.[25]

Conversely, to denigrate a rival resort to Sanditon, Parker points to its 'ridge of putrifying sea weed . . . most insalubrious air . . . [and] water brackish beyond example, impossible to get a good dish of tea within three miles of the place'.[26] Thus, Jane Austen deals very simply with the claims that the seaside raises the body to its highest pitch, while acting also as a prophylaxis, by allowing Mr Parker's faith in his sovereign slogan — 'saline air and immersion'[27] — to topple over by the weight of its own absurdity.

But the seaside as speculation depended on more than the craze for fitness and the preventive measure. The invalid was its second clientele. Here again Parker demonstrated the superiority of his economic sense to that of his co-entrepreneur, Lady Denham. He saw the absence of any resident physician as a brake upon Sanditon's development; the ill, the feeble and the convalescent would fight shy of a place unable to provide them with their customary medical attendance. His search for a surgeon was in fact the initial motivator of his adventures. But Lady Denham, still smarting under the memory of ten fees charged by the practitioner who (as she put it) 'sent *him* [her husband] out of the world',[28] reasoned otherwise.

It would be only encouraging our servants and the poor to fancy themselves ill, if there was a doctor at hand. Oh! pray, let us have none of the tribe at Sanditon.[29]

Besides, she herself had two milch asses, whose produce she wished to palm off privately on some consumptives, and a chamber-horse (evidently the Regency equivalent of the exercise bicycle) for hire. But Mr Parker was justified in the event. When at last a West Indian heiress was inveigled to Sanditon, her chaperon, Mrs Griffiths, would have nothing to do with asses' milk or chamber-horses.

'Miss Lambe [she said] was under the constant care of an experienced physician; and his prescriptions must be their rule' — and except in favour of some tonic pills, which a cousin of her own had a property in, Mrs Griffiths did never deviate from the strict medicinal page.[30]

Until Miss Lambe's arrival, Sanditon appears to have had no success in tapping the invalid market — that is to say, the regular invalid market, for Mr Parker's two sisters and his youngest brother, Arthur, who arrived together, were so to say, independent operators. 'Invalids indeed', exclaimed the dominant sister, Diana, 'I trust there are not three people in

England who have so sad a right to that appellation'.[31] But she had worked her way through doctors and was now effectively in practice on her own account.

We have entirely done with the whole medical tribe. We have consulted physician after physician in vain, till we are quite convinced that they can do nothing for us and that we must trust to our own knowledge of our own wretched constitutions for any relief.' [32]

Diagnosis was Diana's forte. When her sister Susan had been suffering from headache and six leeches a day for ten days on end, Diana, on 'being convinced on examination that much of the evil lay in her gum, . . . persuaded her to attack the disorder there' and to have three teeth extracted. Meanwhile, 'Arthur, [is] more languid than I like, . . . I fear for his liver.' [33] When she turned up at Trafalgar House it was without Susan and Arthur. She had persuaded them to remain in their hotel for, as she said, Susan had suffered hysterics when she came in sight of 'poor old Sanditon', while Arthur was assured that it would be imprudent for him to expose himself to the elements: 'there is so much wind that I did not think he could safely venture, for I am *sure* there is lumbago hanging about him'.[34] Immediately she turned her hand, literally, to Mr Parker's ankle — with rather more cheering results on this occasion: 'that's right; all right and clean. The play of your sinews a *very* little affected', though 'I see by the position of your foot, that you have used it too much already'.[35]

When Mr Parker and Charlotte paid their return visit to the other Parkers, there were, Jane Austen writes, 'almost as many teapots etc as there were persons in company' on the supper tray. For, while the visitors were treated to ordinary fare, 'Miss Parker [drank] one sort of herb-tea and Miss Diana another', and Arthur what was meant to be a 'large dish of rather weak cocoa'. Susan Parker, more worn down (we are told) by medicine, was in every sense a pale version of Diana, but Arthur struggled hard for a more comfortable form of valetudinarianism. He fought, for example, to be allowed to butter his own toast, with

his sisters . . . declaring he was not to be trusted, and he maintaining that he only eat enough to secure the coats of his stomach . . . Charlotte could hardly contain herself as she saw him watching his sisters, while he scrupulously scraped off almost as much butter as he put on, and then seized an odd moment for adding a great dab just before it went into his mouth.

As Jane Austen drily notes his invalidism was 'by no means so spiritualized' as his sisters', and Charlotte was surely right in her conclusion that he had adopted it in order to indulge 'an indolent temper . . . determined on having no disorders but such as called for warm rooms and good nourishment'.[36]

It is all summed up in a passage of what Graham Hough has called her 'coloured narrative', the peculiarly Austenesque form in which the thoughts of character and author blend gradually and inextricably.

It was impossible for Charlotte not to suspect a good deal of fancy in such an extraordinary state of health . . . The Parkers were no doubt a family of imagination and quick feelings — and while the eldest brother found vent for his superfluity of sensation as a projector, the sisters were perhaps driven to dissipate theirs in the invention of odd complaints . . . Some natural delicacy of constitution in fact, with an unfortunate turn for medicine, especially quack medicine, had given them an early tendency at various times, to various disorders; the rest of their sufferings was from fancy, the love of distinction and the love of the wonderful. They had charitable hearts and many amiable feelings — but a spirit of restless activity, and the glory of doing more than anybody else, had their share in every exertion of benevolence — and there was vanity in all they did, as well as in all they endured.[37]

Thus the wheel of *Sanditon* comes full circle. Imaginary roads to health and imaginary disease are satirized to the edge of farce. But in the end they are caught up and interwoven with the general biting analysis of restless activity, love of distinction and above all vanity — with the larger indictment of the England of 1817.

V

In many ways, *Sanditon* differs startlingly from Jane Austen's earlier work. No one can say how it would ultimately have developed, although the outcome of her other fragment, *The Watsons,* written probably in 1804, is quite predictable, and its relationship to various stretches of *Mansfield Park, Emma* and *Persuasion* unmistakeable. It is true of course that the manuscript of *Sanditon* was uncorrected, apart from the overwriting of alternative words and phrases. Yet the pitch and tone of the twelve draft chapters are absolutely consistent, *and* consistently extraordinary in the corpus of Jane Austen's work.

The most striking difference between *Sanditon* and the rest is — ironically enough perhaps — its modernity. As Margaret Drabble observes,

There are plenty of melodramatic trappings — with the beautiful heroine in distress, Clara, and the half mulatto heiress Miss Lambe, we are almost in the romantic atmosphere of Charlotte Bronte, and would be well into it were it not for the irony with which Jane Austen handles her material. But the material attracts her, nevertheless. The future beckons.[38]

In the final chapter, the best (if not the only) known image in *Sanditon,* Charlotte's glimpse over the palings through the mist of 'something white and womanish in the field on the other side',[39] gives off decidedly Bronteish emanations. Stranger still, I think, is the faint foreshadowing of Dickens. At times, Sir Edward's speech seems almost a pre-echo of Micawber's, and Mr Parker's that of Mr Jingle. What of these jerking sentences of Parker's, for example, 'the dissolution of a partnership in the medical line — in your own parish — extensive business — undeniable character — respectable references — wishing to form a separate establishment — you will find it at full length, sir';[40] or, 'The finest, purest sea breeze on the coast — acknowledged to be so — excellent bathing — fine hard sand — deep water ten yards from the shore — no mud — no weeds . . .'[41] One can, I suppose, easily make too much of this verbal form of resemblance; but two others seem really significant and substantial. One is the unwonted savagery and even coarseness of the irony in *Sanditon,* the other, its systematic use of comic exaggeration. While there is no question of replication, there are undoubted family resemblances between Lady Denham and Lady Catherine de Bourgh, Sir Edward and Willoughby, Mr Parker and Mr Weston; and the younger Parker sister and Emma's father. But how much harder and harsher, how much crueller and less delicate, is the mockery of folly and vice in the case of the first character of each coupling? Again, how magnified, how melodramatic, even how grotesque, are not the embodiments of the qualities in *Sanditon* — even to the extent, in the case of Willoughby and Sir Edward, of the novelist repeating herself first as near-tragedy and then as farce? If not in exuberance or plotting, at least in certain strategies of attack, is there not some sort of cousinhood between the Austen of 1817 and the young Dickens of two decades later?

Nonetheless, there are crucial differences. The economy of style and composition, the ease of the penetration, and the freedom from sentimentality, all distance *Sanditon* from Dickens, Charlotte Bronte and their entire generation. Combined with the other qualities of the fragment, these render it, I believe, an exactly contemporary work in a sense beyond that of any of the completed Austen novels. The resultant tone or temper of *Sanditon* seems — to me at least — much more akin to some of the greatest literature of the immediate post-war years than to any Early Victorian writing. In reading *Sanditon* I am reminded most of Peacock's *Nightmare Abbey* and Byron's *Don Juan*, both of which were completed within four years of Jane Austen's fragment. The material reasons for the association are different in either case. *Nightmare Abbey* — and let me add *Crochet Castle*, for despite its later date, it is identical in technique — are akin to *Sanditon* upon the intellectual plane. It is Romantic posturing and the ideological fads, trends and claptrap of the day, the March of Mind and its accompanying *argot* and camp followers, which Peacock excoriates. Conversely, the Byron of *Don Juan* is a moralist, discerning unerringly and pitilessly contemporary vanity and deceit. These two signals of the *fin-de*-Regency, so to say, seem to converge and intersect in *Sanditon*. But all three works meet completely in a special sort of amalgam of wit, economy, exactitude and ruthlessness. Perhaps we can best 'place' this peculiar genre by describing it — more properly this time! — as later Regency in form and temper.

VI

What finally of the writer as witness and — perhaps we might add — the historian as presiding magistrate? First, let us for the moment invert the relationship and consider how the historian may help in understanding what the writer says. In the case of *Sanditon,* he can proffer a moderately well-established category, bearing the label of convenience, 'Regency'. Like all other periodizations, this concept has been forged as a historian's working tool. That is to say, he has bound together a cluster of characteristics and associated them with a particular stretch of time, in order to describe, analyze and argue more economically and efficiently. In the special instance of 'Regency' the general connotations are hecticness, levity, restlessness, speculation, conspicuous waste and consumption, and the like. All this is also both symbolized and actualized in the historian's imagination, by specific phenomena such as those selected by Steven Watson, buildings, dress and manners and the seaside holiday. With these models, readymade, before us, we see *Sanditon* in a new light. The hectic, the restless, the speculative, the shallow and the vain are epitomized by and concentrated in the chosen centrepiece, the new watering place. How clever is the choice of the device! It opens the way to satirizing shady speculation, doubtful building ventures, the mushroom leisure industry and more generally all the Brave New World of facades, insatiation and display.

In short, the historian's working device, the template which he has selected to clarify and speed up his work, gives us immediate access to a deeper level of interpretation and a more complex, and interlocked, reading of Jane Austen's fragment. On the one hand, our abstraction,

Regency, serves as a burning glass, concentrating the scattered rays into a new intensity of insight. On the other — if I may adhere to the metaphor of optics — it acts also as a prism, lighting up fresh facets of implication as we twist *Sanditon* this way and that under the exterior illumination.

But our primary concern, as laid down by this Conference's theme, is what *Sanditon* has to offer the historian. Again, I select three elements for your consideration. First, it vivifies, personalizes and renders concrete what the historian already holds. It is something to know numerical utilitarianism, but more to know Gradgrind too; it is something to know the 1861 Decree, but more to know *The Cherry Orchard* also. *Pari passu*, certain of the conventional characteristics of our image of post-Napoleonic War Britain gain in solidity, and begin to take on — so to say — a third dimension in our minds, from the happy chance that they have been particularized by such an artist as Jane Austen. Next, by a sort of nuclear breeding, this very particularization suggests fresh ranges of historical investigation, *precisely* because it is so firmly located in the very day of its composition. Striking the imagination with a force, colour and *haeccietas* far beyond what the prescribed historical sources can provide, particularities such as *Sanditon*'s start up chains of useful questions. Who were the speculators who laid out and — in all senses including the perjorative — developed the new resorts? Should we not merely laugh at Mr Parker's puffing of Sanditon's comparative proximity to London and his ill-fated quest for a seaside doctor but also see in these the germs of hypotheses to explain the boom? Who has investigated the rise of proprietary pharmaceuticals? Who has investigated the origins of the cult of fitness? Who has considered the seven-eights of the late Romantic movement which lay beneath the surface but supported its great, exposed expressers? Who has considered the laity to whom the high priests of political economy preached, who — on the evidence of *Sanditon* at least — were by no means mere passive or supine auditors? In short, the seeds of many doctoral dissertations and fresh or revisionary books may be scattered through the pages of the fragment, awaiting — as is I suppose the case with all great fiction — the right reader to set them in generation, even if it be centuries hence.

Finally, *Sanditon* refines the periodization with which this paper opened. I do not for a moment claim that the *Zeitgeist*-manifestations which I have discerned in the fragment, early economic, literary and salubrietary forms of modernization, are the only ones to be discovered, or perhaps even the most important. But they are certainly there: and once we distinguish and define them, correspondences with actualities in the second half of the second decade of the nineteenth century begin to crowd in upon us. In other words, our piece of historical shorthand, the phrase, Regency period, is enriched and sensibly enlarged. It can now operate at a much deeper level. The calibration of the historian's new reference-frame is finer, the range of his preliminary calculator multiplied.

By an unlucky accident perhaps, the actual term 'Regency novel' has been — for half a century or more — attached to the romances of Georgette Heyer and her various inferior imitators. But even if the tag itself is soiled through years of misappropriation, *Sanditon* has earned it truly in its proper, chronological sense. For it is an epitome of its little age. To say that *Sanditon* is the fragment of a Regency novel is, I believe, to illuminate both what was written and the exact time of writing. Of course, Jane Austen left no more than the opening of an uncorrected draft, only one-fifth or one-sixth perhaps of the projected whole. But it was *she* who wrote it. To use the language of the stage — sometimes abhorrent though this was to her — there are only small actors, there are no small parts.

NOTES AND REFERENCES

1. V. de Sola Pinto (ed.), *Byron's Poems,* 3 vols (London, 1963), iii, p. 344.
2. Ibid., iii, p. 340.
3. J. Steven Watson, *The Reign of George III, 1760-1815* (Oxford, 1960).
4. *Sanditon*, in R.W. Chapman (ed.), *The Works of Jane Austen,* 6 vols (London, 1954), vi, p. 384.
5. Ibid., p. 379.
6. Ibid., p. 380.
7. Ibid., p. 381.
8. Ibid., pp 389-90.
9. Ibid., p. 410.
10. Ibid., p. 367.
11. Ibid., pp 368-9.
12. Ibid., pp 392-3.
13. Ibid., p. 401.
14. Ibid., p. 364.
15. Ibid., p. 366.
16. Ibid., p. 405.
17. Ibid., pp 405-6.
18. ibid., pp 426-7.
19. Ibid., pp 396-8.
20. Ibid., p. 398.
21. When Charlotte Heywood spoke of 'either of Scott's poems', the reference was probably meant to be to *Marmion* (1808) and *The Lady of the Lake.*
22. The first relevant inquiry was set afoot under 45 Geo. III c. 47 on 5 June 1805 and the last, into the Scheldt expedition, in 1810. The reformed Army Medical Board was appointed during 1810.

23. F. Barry Smith, 'Sexuality in Britain 1800-1900: Some Suggested Revisions' in Martha Vicinus (ed.), *A Widening Sphere: Changing Roles of Victorian Women* (London, 1977), p. 194.
24. Margaret Drabble in her Introduction to Jane Austen, *Lady Susan; The Watsons; Sanditon* (Harmondsworth, Middlesex, 1974), p. 24.
25. *Sanditon*, p. 373.
26. Ibid., p. 369.
27. Ibid., p. 367.
28. Ibid., p. 394.
29. Ibid., p. 393.
30. Ibid., p. 422.
31. Ibid., p. 410.
32. Ibid., pp 386-7.
33. Ibid., p. 387.
34. Ibid., p. 407.
35. Ibid., p. 411.
36. Ibid., pp 416-18.
37. Ibid., pp 412-13.
38. Drabble, *Lady Susan; The Watsons; Sanditon*, p. 30.
39. *Sanditon,* p. 426.
40. Ibid., p. 366.
41. Ibid., p. 369.

Fiction as 'the best history of nations': Lady Morgan's Irish novels*

TOM DUNNE

In so far as there is a modern image of Lady Morgan, it tends to reflect that common among her contemporaries, of a rather bizarre society hostess, who wrote romantic and eccentric historical novels, all of whose heroines resembled herself, while she in turn imitated the best known of them, Glorvina of *The Wild Irish Girl* (1806), in terms of dress and ornamentation, and a proclivity for bringing her harp to parties. Her Irish novels, four in all, published between 1806 and 1827,[1] are precisely the kind of literature from which most historians tend to recoil, as wildly imaginative and essentially frivolous, while literary critics have ignored them as badly written popular romances. This paper hopes to show that Morgan was less a romantic than a realist writer, one whose flamboyance masked a serious intent, and whose novels should be seen by historians as valuable documents for understanding important elements of Irish political culture and intellectual life between the Union and the Famine. It may also be of interest to those who work in the highly specialised and exciting area of historical inquiry, which literary criticism is, at least in part, because these novels offer a particularly interesting case study of a novelist who employed historical perspectives to explain, and even to influence, contemporary reality. Her argument that fiction constituted 'the best history of nations', made in the preface to her second Irish novel, *O'Donnel* (1814), referred less to its ability to recreate the past, than to the fact that it 'exhibited a mirror of the times in which it is composed: reflecting morals, customs, manners, peculiarities of character and prevalence of opinion'.[2] This view that the imaginative writer is, of necessity, a historian of his or her own time, however much this may be disguised by the nature of the literary genre involved, must form the basis of any belief in the value of literature as historical evidence. It is also basic to some modern hermeneutic approaches to literary theory and criticism. Paul Ricoeur has

*I am grateful to the students who took my pre-famine novels course during the past two years for many new insights, and to Clare O'Halloran, Pat Coughlan, Roy Foster, Kevin Barry and Charlotte Wiseman for their help and encouragement.

tried to provide a common theoretical framework for both disciplines, arguing that history writing and fiction are related and comparable forms of discourse, in terms of narrative structure, as well as the location of each in historical time.[3] Marxist literary critics, like Frederic Jameson, make the connection in a different way, in arguing for a historically informed criticism, and especially for 'the priority of the political interpretation of literary texts'.[4]

Concern about the relationship between writings which were subjectively imaginative and those which claimed to be objectively historical, had a particular importance in the evolution of the novel in the eighteenth century. Awareness of a resistance on the part of readers to the very idea of invented or imagined worlds led novelists like Defoe, Richardson and Fielding to disguise their works as autobiographies, memoirs, real-life adventures or eyewitness accounts. The new popular historical works they counterfeited, on the other hand, were regarded as a branch of literature and only slowly developed critical approaches to evidence and documentation.[5] While very influenced by the eighteenth-century tradition, Morgan did not go so far as to claim that her novels were 'true' histories, but she constantly interwove her fiction with historical 'facts', and appealed to the authority of historians and historical documents. She described her novels as 'my Irish histories', and herself as a 'collator of Irish chronicles', an 'Irish antiquarian', and was mocked by Hazlitt for 'strutting the little Gibbon of her age'.[6] Her failure to make any absolute distinctions between fiction and history can also be seen in the ease and pragmatism with which she moved from one genre to the other. She began what became her biography of the Italian painter-patriot Salvator Rosa as a novel, while what was begun as a history of the Belgian revolution was turned instead into a novel, called *The Princess*.[7] Her Irish novels, in particular, combine three distinct but interdependent texts. As well as the fictional text, and the inevitable authoritative authorial voice commenting on it, there is a large and often obtrusive historical subtext, made up of references to and quotations from both historians and historical sources, and in the form of footnotes or end of volume notes. This subtext, acting in support of the authorial commentary, directs the reading of the fictional text, and has a wide and interesting range of reference, reflecting the intense and, as Donal McCartney has shown, increasingly partisan contemporary debate among historians.[8] This paper is concerned mainly with the nature of Morgan's historical understanding, and its relationship to her political attitudes and intent, but it will also discuss an important shift in her later novels, from an appeal to the eighteenth-century Catholic antiquarians, the so-called 'native historians' like O'Halloran and O'Connor, to an ever-greater reliance on the work of more modern historians, mainly Irish Protestant and English. This was, doubtless, influenced by the new critical approach to sources begun by Ledwich, though Morgan's liberal Protestantism disdained the sectarian obsession with the 1641 rising, to which this was mainly applied. Nevertheless, her novels, like the histories to which they appealed, can properly be regarded, in Oliver MacDonagh's phrase, as 'politics by other means'.[9]

While she wrote only one Irish historical novel, in the conventional sense — *The O'Briens and the O'Flahertys* (1827), set in the 1770s and 1790s — the rest, although they had contemporary settings, were dominated by historical perspectives and obsessed with historical explanations. The first of them, *The Wild Irish Girl*, while romantic in tone, was heavily didactic in intent, and this tendency was intensified when in the next Irish novel, *O'Donnel: a national tale,* she moved away, as the preface put it, from 'pure abstraction', to concentrate on 'the flat realities of life'.[10] In fact, all her novels, including the first, belong properly to the realist tradition and their concern with history owed less to romanticism than to a recognition that clashing perceptions of Irish history formed a central element of the reality she wished to confront and to influence. In this, as in other respects, her fiction reflected the profoundly colonial nature of Irish society, and her primary concern was to encourage a reappraisal of the colonial past, as an essential means of dealing with its contemporary legacy of conflict and division. Her perspective was a liberal colonist or ascendancy one, akin to Maria Edgeworth's in important respects, but in a distinctively different tradition,[11] closer to Thomas Davis whose proposal of a dialogue between past and present as the key to reconciliation, she anticipated. Terry Eagleton has argued recently, that modern hermeneutic theory, which proposes a similar type of dialogue, has the problem that it cannot 'tolerate the idea of a failure of communications . . . It cannot, in other words, come to terms with the problem of ideology'.[12] Such a failure, charged with ideological difference, led, as we will see, to Lady Morgan's ultimate disillusionment with the healing potential of history within Ireland. At the same time, the achievement of Catholic Emancipation robbed her of the cause that she had long urged on English liberal opinion. This English audience was, for her, the primary one, and thus the one which most shaped her fiction. Following in the long tradition of Irish colonial writing, her main concern was to explain the Irish historical experience, and through it, contemporary violence and poverty, to English readers, who would thus be persuaded to support the demand for Irish reforms, particularly Catholic Emancipation. This tradition was reinforced by the Act of Union which made Irish affairs the direct responsibility of the Westminster Parliament.

It involved, among other things, a sensitivity to English historical perspectives, in this case the English Whig tradition, with which Morgan, in any case, identified and appealed to as an Irish Whig. The nature and purpose of her appeal to this English opinion changed from a favourable presentation of the Gaelic past to combat traditional anti-Irish prejudice, in her first novel, to a harsh but limited indictment of 'six centuries of oppression' in the remaining three, 'a series of national tales', as she described them, 'undertaken with a humble but zealous view to the promotion of a great national cause, the emancipation of the Catholics of Ireland'. She defended this overt political ambition for fiction, on the basis that, 'Novels, like more solid compositions are not exempted from the obligation to inculcate truth. They are expected, in their idlest trifling to possess a moral scope, and politics is but morals on a grander scale'.[13]

Morgan used history in three principal ways. Most simply, and often most memorably, it provided colour or atmosphere — history as entertainment. In all of her novels this was associated particularly with her passion for ruined castles, abbeys and churches, 'at once so melancholy and so interesting'.[14] While *The Wild Irish Girl* was the most colourful of her novels in this respect, even here, history had a second and more serious purpose, that of explanation and authority; the key to understanding the present. 'The causes of Ireland's misfortunes are so deep-rooted', declared her hero in *Florence Macarthy* (1818) 'that every page in her history is a palliation of her faults'.[15] Morgan's marshalling of evidence and authority for her historical account recognised the persistence of the tendency in the reading public to distrust fiction on important matters, while deferring to historians — a tendency long since reversed! It also underlined the political as well as the literary purpose of her novels. The third, and perhaps most interesting use of history by Lady Morgan was as a dynamic element in the story — historical understanding forwarded the action, and transformed situations and lives. When the Anglo-Irish hero, Mortimer, in *The Wild Irish Girl* arrived on the estate of his absentee father in the west of Ireland, he discovered a locked study, full of books on Irish history, and in liberating them, so to speak, he began the process of freeing himself from his prejudiced views of Gaelic Ireland. He was soon 'deep in the study of the language, history and antiquities of this ancient nation', helped by a series of lectures from the Prince of Inismore, the descendant of the 'Milesian' lord, dispossessed and indeed killed by Mortimer's ancestor. This novel largely comprises a series of such lectures, and whatever their effect on the modern reader might be, they galvanised the hero into a determination to reconcile his father and the Prince.[16] In a key scene of her second

Irish novel, *O'Donnel,* the hero of that name used the 'few shrivelled parchments and mouldering papers' that remained from his ancestors, the Gaelic lords of Tír Conaill, to prove the legal rights of an English heiress to lands alienated from his father by the penal code.[17] In *Florence Macarthy,* ancient documents are also important in a court case, when an attempt to frame the local Whiteboy leader for an entirely fictitious 'rebellion', was foiled by one of the judges demonstrating that the key prosecution document was from the sixteenth century.[18] Finally, in *The O'Briens and the O'Flahertys,* the hero's father, Terence O'Brien became a wealthy lawyer due mainly to his antiquarian lore, and resurrected his family title 'on the evidence of an old tombstone'.[19] In his case, the fruits of historical research were to be megolomania and ruin, though even in this last and most pessimistic of her Irish novels Morgan preserved the primary dynamic function of her characters' confrontations with the past and its legacy — that it should be a healing process, and lead to reconciliation. This found its ultimate symbol in all the novels in the marriages of hereditary enemies — that of the Gaelic Glorvina and 'Cromwellian' Mortimer in *The Wild Irish Girl,* of the Gaelic heroine, Florence Macarthy, to the Norman Fitzadelm, of O'Donnel and his English Duchess, and of Murrough O'Brien to Beavoin O'Flaherty. In her account of why she had abandoned her original project of a historical novel based on the life of Red Hugh O'Donnel, she explained that history *had* to have a healing effect, or it had no place in her fiction. Once convinced that the story of Red Hugh instead of promoting 'conciliation' would let loose 'discord', she abandoned it in favour of a story of 'more modern and more liberal times'.[20]

This emphasis on Morgan's *uses* of history helps to point up the contrast between her fiction and that of her great contemporary, Sir Walter Scott. Both were preoccupied with historical explanation, and Scott too provided an authoritative, if less pedantic, subtext of historical references and footnotes. The central historical event for both was the destruction of traditional Gaelic societies over the previous three centuries, and the complex social and political revolution which accomplished and accompanied this. The explanation provided by both aimed at a reconciliation of past and present, in part to aid a national consensus, in part to explain the author's country to an English audience. Both were essentially conservative and supporters of the status quo. The differences between them, however, are more revealing, and go much further than Victor Hugo's acid judgment that Morgan had 'much more love of celebrity than love of her country', and that, 'beside Scott's pictures, full of life and warmth, Lady Morgan's studies were only pale and chilly sketches'.[21] They had fundamentally different approaches to, and understandings of, historical process, reflecting in part, perhaps, their different political allegiances. While Scott's Toryism encouraged an emphasis on organic growth and continuity, Morgan's Whiggism saw history more as a series of revolutions leading to the achievement of 'liberty'. Scott's theme was no less than the nature of historical change itself, as Lukacs has argued so brilliantly.[22] His characters represented major historical forces and social trends, and his emphasis was on the transformation of social life at all levels, and the interaction of class interests with political events. Morgan lacked Scott's depth of historical understanding, as well as his sophistication in handling historical themes. Scott, as recent research has emphasised, was aided by a remarkable school of eighteenth-century Scottish 'philosophical' historians, like Stewart, Hume, Fergusson and Smith.[23] The contrast with the traditionalism and limited concerns of the historians on which Morgan had to rely can be seen at a glance in that between titles, such as Adam Ferguson's *An essay on the history of civil society* (1767) or John Miller's *Origins of ranks* (1771) compared with John Curry's *A historical and critical review of the civil wars in Ireland* (1775) or *Ierne defended* (1774) by Sylvester O'Halloran. The revolution in Irish historiography from the 1790s, despite its more critical approach to sources, continued with the narrowly political and partisan concerns of the antiquarians. For Morgan, as for most Irish historians, history was a storehouse of argument to be used, rather than a process to be understood. Her main concern, as she put it, was to explain 'national grievances' as 'borne out by historic fact'. Thus, even though she also tried to portray characters, 'such as identify a class or represent a genus',[24] she could not, as Scott did, root her characters in a sustained way, in the historical process. This failure, common to most contemporary Irish novelists, to transcend the particularism of the Irish experience and produce fiction of universal appeal, can also be explained in tems of the nature of Irish society. While Scott was the product of a society which was relatively prosperous, self-confident and socially cohesive. Morgan's more fractured historical sense reflected a divided and impoverished country, traumatised as well as mesmerised, by a revolution few felt to be complete or secure. The Irish Whig interpretation of history could not have the self-confidence long developed by the English. Ireland's abrasive and continuing colonial experience, in marked contrast to the experience of Scotland, ensured that historical conflicts persisted into current politics. Thus, Morgan could accept the historical necessity and ultimate benefit of the Irish 'revolution', but could not shut it up in a 'completed' past, as Scott did that of Scotland. This may be why Scott could write historical novels, while Morgan, for the most part, could only write contemporary novels suffused with history — though she could write historical novels on non-Irish themes.[25] The Irish experience, and the Irish Whig tradition also meant that Morgan's heroes, rather than coming from the common people, as so many of Scott's do, were all aristocratic, and indeed she saw historical change largely in terms of a conflict between aristocracies, and its ultimate resolution in the substitution of an enlightened for a corrupt ruling class.

There were other and perhaps more prosaic influences, which helped to shape Lady Morgan's historical perspectives; notably her family background, her Whig politics, her adoption by Dublin's Viceregal society, and her involvement with the Catholic emancipation campaign. Daiches has explained Scott's psychology and outlook in terms of the tensions between his mixed aristocratic and bourgeois ancestry.[26] Those inherent in Morgan's origins were far more complex, and extreme, and yet, as we will see, there is little enough evidence for tensions flowing from her mixed Gaelic, Anglo-Irish and English background, in her novels. The tradition that she was born on the Irish Sea, as her bourgeois English methodist mother travelled to Dublin to join her flamboyant Connaught father, an actor-singer who specialised in stage-Irish parts, has at least a symbolic validity. In her *Memoirs*, she gave this mixed parentage a characteristically romantic gloss, 'My father was a Celtic Irishman, my mother was a Saxon',[27] but the reality was more confused. She obviously disliked her mother, though she was glad ultimately to have inherited her practical common sense. Her mother's early death was a decisive event, bringing her even more strongly under her father's influence, and accelerating the collapse of the family's fortune, which in the end drove the young Sydney Owenson to become a writer. Her engaging, impractical and ultimately pathetic father was the centre of her life, 'my child as well as my father, the object for which I laboured and wrote and lived', as she wrote after his death.[28] The comparison in this, as in so many other respects, with Maria Edgeworth, is interesting, and in her strong distaste at being mentioned in the same breath as Lady Morgan, Edgeworth pitied her for having a father so different from her own and saw this influence as the basis of the contrast in their literary styles.[29] Morgan, however, seemed proud of him and was certainly protective. Her account of his history seems a romanticised version of his own and centred on the transformation of Robert MacOwen, Irish-speaking son of a Catholic tenant farmer and a harp playing mother from the Protestant gentry family, the Croftons, into Robert Owenson, a moderately successful actor on the English stage, with the help of his distant cousin, Oliver Goldsmith. Her pride in her ancestry came to be focused almost entirely on her paternal grandmothers' Protestant connections, and the influence on her of the Anglicised Gaelic background of her father, while clearly great, was also complex.[30] He had a fund of folklore and legend, as well as a notable repertoire of Gaelic songs, which formed the basis of his daughter's important collection of Irish airs, with English words, published the year before *The Wild Irish Girl*, and an influence on Moore. It was clear, however, from her introduction, and other comments,[31] that despite being so close to this authentic Gaelic source, her attitude was that of the sympathetic outsider, as distanced in its own way as that of Charlotte Brooke from the Bardic poetry she published. Even though she mimicked her father's Irish in her singing, she clearly had no understanding of the Irish language, beyond a few phrases used to charm servants.[32] Similarly, while her father's background gave her a romantic interest in the west of Ireland, her perspective on it was more that of Longford House, the residence of her Crofton relations, where she stayed while gathering materials for *The Wild Irish Girl*.[33] This ambivalent attitude to her Gaelic background only reflected that of her father, who was a fascinating combination of the authentic and theatrical — even to the extent of singing traditional songs in Irish while playing stage-Irish parts.[34] His major dramatic roles, like Sir Lucius O'Trigger or Major O'Flaherty, clearly influenced his daughter's writing and characterisation, and in a more general sense, both her fiction and her view of history retained a theatrical quality. Her father also introduced her to Whig politics. His reconstruction of the Fishamble Street theatre, renamed The National Theatre Music Hall, was inspired, his daughter believed, by the 'Irish nationality' of the Volunteers and the corps to which he belonged filled the pit in full uniform on the opening night in 1784. Later that year, a benefit performance, organised by Napper Tandy for an imprisoned patriotic printer led to the theatre losing its licence.[35]

This political connection was strengthened by the support given to her by the Irish Whig establishment after *The Wild Irish Girl* became the object of Tory attacks. Looking back to that time in 1846, in the preface to the new popular edition of the novel, she proudly listed those of 'her gallant and liberal countrymen' together with 'the English members of the Irish government', who had come to her aid, and in a remarkable footnote, she added,

Last and least of the "mere Irishry" drawn within the English pale of this truly delightful society, was an obscure girl, whose sole passport into circles so brilliant was that she had written an Irish tale, in the Irish interest, sung Irish songs, translated by herself from Irish poems and played the Irish harp.[36]

Her adaptation of her father's 'Irish' performances, both genuine and theatrical, from the stage to the pages of the novel, and to Dublin drawing-rooms, was certainly a major factor in her social success in Whig and Viceregal circles. However, though she may have been at first simply another focus for the current aristocratic fashion for the Gaelic past, she eventually became an insider and a major political hostess. Her description of herself as one of the 'mere Irishry' was more colourful than accurate, and the rapidity of her absorption into Dublin society can be seen in another opening night audience, this time for her 'impromptu little play', written as a vehicle for her father, and produced three years later, in 1809. Her description of that scene can be read as a paradigm of her vision of Irish society as a whole.

The Viceregal box and dress circle were exclusively occupied by the court and officers of the garrison, who were headed by the commander-in-chief. The whole of the liberal part of the Irish bar, and their friends, filled the upper circle, and the pit and galleries were filled by a popular Catholic Irish audience, whose fun and humorous sallies filled up the intervals of the acts, while their frequent cheers for the Lord Lieutenant, and frequent calls for "Patrick's Day" and "Kate Kearney" . . . produced a sort of national drama.[37]

At the end of the same year, her social metamorphosis was completed when she accepted the invitation to live in the household of the great Tory magnate, Lord Abercorn, putting up with the irritations of being patronised as an exotic family retainer for the entrée it gave her into the highest social circles in England, and which she later extended to those of the Continent. The Abercorns also rather bullied her into marriage with their family doctor, Charles Morgan, and by procuring him a knighthood gave her the necessary independent social standing of a title. However, even before Sydney Owenson became Lady Morgan, her politics, like her views of history were markedly aristocratic.

   The extension of her promotion of Catholic emancipation from writing novels to some involvement with O'Connell's campaign underlined her Whiggism. In 1826, together with her English and 'ultra liberal husband', she became part of the liberal Protestant support group, 'the friends of civil and religious liberty', as she described them. Deeply distrustful of O'Connell, and 'that nest of hornets', the Catholic Association', her role, even by her own exaggerated account[38] was confined mainly to providing part of the social milieu in which some of the Catholic leadership met their

Protestant supporters, and sympathetic members of the Irish government. Her only attendance at a Catholic Association meeting was at the final one which, to her relief, decided on 'the prompt extinction of this great engine of popular opinion'. She hoped that the granting of emancipation would end popular agitation and her chagrin when this proved not to be the case, and her alarmism during the years following about 'revolution . . . from below', showed the extent to which she regarded emancipation as a boon to be conferred by the English government, at the instigation of liberal Protestant opinion in both countries.[39] This was not only in the Irish Whig tradition of her beloved Grattan, but also in a particular colonial tradition going back to the early sixteenth century and beyond. If, as I have argued elsewhere, Maria Edgeworth belonged to the Spencer tradition of colonial writing about Ireland, Morgan belonged to that of Anglo-Irish reformers and historians of the Pale.[40] Thus, her portrayal of Irish history featured the Anglo-Irish of Norman origin as both heroes and victims, a corrupt and essentially 'New English' aristocratic clique as villains, while the passive Gaelic Irish were patronised as well as sympathised with, and the English both castigated and appealed to. Lady Morgan may have belonged to this Anglo-Irish tradition less simply than Edgeworth belonged to hers, but it nonetheless offers an indispensable key to her writings.

The influence of Morgan's aristocratic and Whig ambiance on her fiction and politics was evident in her second Irish novel, *O'Donnel*, dedicated to the Duke of Devonshire who was described as the foremost among Ireland's

great English landholders . . . whose conduct towards a grateful and prosperous tenantry best evinces in its effects how much the happiness and improvement of the lower classes of the nation depend upon the enlightened liberality and benevolent attentions of the highest.[41]

The preface revealed her decision to change to a more overtly political and realist ficiton, and explained why she had abandoned her initial plan to base the novel on 'the romantic adventures and unsubdued valour of O'Donnel the Red, Chief of Tir Conaill in the reign of Elizabeth', in favour of one which featured his latterday descendant.[42] She had, in fact, done a lot of research on Red Hugh, and had written one volume of the projected historical novel, before she abandoned it, partly under the influence of her newly acquired and fastidiously rationalist husband. 'As for me, I am every inch a wife', she wrote to a friend, 'and so ends the brilliant thing that was Glorvina'.[43] The death of her father, the original of 'the Prince of Innismore', in the same few months, may also have been a factor. Most important, however, was her changing historical perspective, which reflected the Anglo-Irish tradition of deep hostility to as well as fascination with the Gaelic world. In her own explanation, as well as the fear of encouraging 'discord' rather than 'conciliation', she instanced the disappointment of her hope 'to extenuate the errors attributed to Ireland, by an exposition of their causes, drawn from historic facts'. Instead, she found that she would be holding up 'a glass to my countrymen, reflecting but too many fearful images . . . for I discovered, far beyond my expectations, that I had fallen upon "evil men and evil days" '.[44] It is clear from the synopsis of her original plot, which she preserved in the text of the rewritten novel as the O'Donnel family history, that she had recoiled from the ultimate response of Red Hugh to the appalling injustices he had suffered, his joining with O'Neill in a major rebellion against the Crown, a response that 'the interests of humanity require to be buried in oblivion'.[45] O'Flanagan has argued that *O'Donnel* broke new ground in having a Gaelic Catholic aristocrat as hero,[46] but it is even more significant that, unlike his famous ancestor, the modern O'Donnel not only accepted the colonial settlement, but also helped to preserve it.

Morgan's retreat from the largely favourable view of the Gaelic world and the Gaelic past in *The Wild Irish Girl* was also influenced by the new critical approach to the Gaelic sources, evident in contemporary historians, and which was reflected in the increasingly hostile portrayal of antiquarians in her novels. Even in *The Wild Irish Girl*, the Prince's romantic antiquarianism, with its constant references to Keating and O'Halloran, is balanced somewhat by his daughter Glorvina's defence of McPherson's translations of Ossian. While her 'fancy is sometimes dazzled' by reading them in the original, she also thinks them spoiled by 'wildly improbable' and 'ridiculously grotesque details' and often prefers 'the refined medium of McPherson's genius.[47] The heroine of *Florence Macarthy*, a writer of Irish novels like her creator, has an antiquarian library and lives in the half-ruined castle of her MacCarthy More ancestors. Yet she declares that, 'the present state of this poor country interests me more than its ancient, real or fabled, greatness'. In this novel Morgan's attack on Irish antiquarians commenced in earnest in her portrayal of Terence Oge O'Leary, pedantic schoolmaster and author of the 'Genealogical history of MacCarthy More, written in the Phoenician tongue, vulgo-vocato Irish, it being more precise and copious than the English and other barbarous dialects', as he described it. He is an archaic figure, though having some influence on the peasant mind, and is portrayed as in turn ludicrous, fanatical, pathetic, and sinister. Lest the reader miss the point, the author explains that O'Leary is 'an ancient Seanachy' of Ireland, 'credulous of her fables and jealous of her ancient glory; ardent in his feelings and fixed in his prejudices . . . living only in the past, contemptuous of the present and hopeless of the future'.[48] The father of Murrough O'Brien, the hero of *The O'Briens and the O'Flahertys* is 'a profound Seanachy, antiquarian and an Irish Philologist'. Despite his learned contribution to the recently established Royal Irish Academy, he too lived in the past, 'knowing nothing of modern Ireland but her sufferings and her wrongs', knowing little of ancient Ireland but her fables and her dreams'.[49] The reader is hardly too surprised to learn that he was also a secret Jesuit, dedicated to restoring the ancient high-kingship in the Catholic cause! Even after Lady Morgan, like Maria Edgeworth ten years earlier, had found both the Irish present and the Irish past too disturbing as subjects for fiction, she continued her attack on Ireland's 'learned and patriotic antiquarians', most notably in an interesting essay on 'Irish historians' published in 1841. This made the perceptive point that 'the native antiquarians stop short where fable ends and history begins, at the English invasion', and that most of the history of the later period and up to the present was written by Englishmen whose work gave them access to official records. She was also at pains to defend her own use of 'such images from the vasty deep of doubtful story' as she described material taken from Keating, O'Halloran and others, arguing that it was 'not only patriotism but sound policy' to use 'rhyme and reason, fact and fable, poetry and prose alike', to achieve the indispensable reform, Catholic Emancipation. This done, however, Ireland should look to the future, and not to the past,[50] — a naive if understandable hope, and a nice example of the fallacy that there can be a clear dividing line between 'history' and 'the present'.

Having, thus far, looked at the relationship of history to fiction in Lady Morgan's writings, and having discussed the main factors which influenced her historical understanding, it remains to examine her version of the Irish past, and the consequences for her of the ultimate failure of Catholic Ireland to share it. Her novels have contemporary settings, except for *The O'Briens and the O'Flahertys,* and even that is set within the timespan of her own lifetime. Instead, each reflects on the Irish historical experience over centuries, as a commentary on contemporary problems. Nonetheless, it is possible to construct from them her cumulative portrayal of that experience, which for the purposes of this paper, can be divided into three distinct phases:

(a) Her account of the conquest from the twelfth century to the seventeenth, and in particular, its impact on the old Gaelic elite.

(b) Her depiction of the more recent past, especially of 1782-1800, as the golden age of Irish Whiggism, its frustration and betrayal.

(c) The history of the Catholic cause and its championship by Irish Whigs, the final phase, as she believed, or rather hoped, of Ireland's revolution.

The regret of the hero Mortimer, in *The Wild Irish Girl* that his Cromwellian ancestors had taken possession of the land of the Prince of Innismore by force, was not to be repeated in Lady Morgan's fiction.[51] Instead there was an insistence that the colonial past, despite the acts of injustice associated with it, should be accepted as an accomplished fact and a a commonplace of history. This sentiment was, appropriately, most clearly expressed by the sophisticated Europeanised descendant of the O'Donnel, who argued with a tired fatalism 'that in Ireland, as in all nations, what is won by the sword becomes legitimate property; that time sanctions usurpations, and that possessions long maintained, however gotten, are consecrated by the lapse of ages, and held by the best of all tenures, prescriptive right'. He went even further, stating 'the O'Donnels were not, *even anciently*, the original possessors of the land over which they reigned for centuries, which they won by the sword and which the sword partly won in turn from them'[52] — a sentiment in line indeed with the Gaelic tradition of pragmatic fatalism, articulated, for example, in similar language by Tadhg Dall Ó hUiginn in the late sixteenth century poem written in defence of the claims of the Anglo-Norman Mac Uilliam Burc.[53] It adds to the sense of piquancy, perhaps, that among Ó hUiginn's Gaelic patrons were the O'Donnells! While the results of conquest should be accepted, however, Morgan voiced criticism of its various stages. The main attack on the Normans came, again appropriately, from the 'true Geraldine' hero of *Florence Macarthy*, Fitzadelm, who described them as adventurers who 'took the sanction of heaven for their deeds of violence'. This was essentially a literary device, part of the process of reconciliation between the descendants of Norman and Gaelic Irish nobility, which was the main concern of the novel. Her belief that the quarrels of the thirteenth and fourteenth centuries were an enduring source of friction was articulated mainly by the seanachy O'Leary, who regularly confused events from that period with those of his own day.[54] This recognition of the importance of what Oliver MacDonagh has called 'the elision of time' in 'the Irish habit of historical thought' formed in this period,[55] persisted in all Morgan's novels. One of its main functions was to explain the sense of grievance felt by the victims of the different stages by which Ireland became, in the words of the learned chaplain to the Prince of Innismore, 'a colonised or a conquered country'.[56] Naturally, this sense of historical wrong was expressed in a manner which aided the argument in favour of Catholic emancipation as reparatory justice. Thus the Ulster O'Donnells, although 'a people unsophisticated and unrefined', had a 'hereditary fealty and attachment' to the English crown, and were driven to rebellion by the unjust persecution inflicted by new English officials like Perrott, Bagnal and Bingham, who acted against the express wishes of the Queen. Red Hugh's response therefore, was understandable, although it went too far.[57] Morgan's particular heroes, 'the descendants of the princely Geraldines'[58] were also the victims of the Tudor reconquest. In *Florence Macarthy,* for example, Walter Raleigh is attacked as a 'freebooter', and 'little better than the captain of licensed banditti' for his attacks on the Roches and the Barrys, and others

of English origin, men who still inherited from their ancestors some recollection of Magna Carta. They therefore . . . either protected or burnt their castles and were consequently 'rebels'. The persecution of the illustrious family of the Fitzgeralds, in the persons of the celebrated Earl of Kildare and the great Earl of Desmond, whose crime was being the richest subject in the empire, are too well known to need comment.[59]

In the same vein, the wars of the 1640s were described in *The O'Briens and the O'Flahertys* as being between the 'loyal Irish and English rebels', and the Cromwellian period as an unlawful tyranny. William of Orange had 'wise and benevolent intentions' towards the Irish, and was distanced carefully from the persecution of Irish Catholics under the Penal Code as he was in John Banim's major historical novel, *The Boyne Water* (1826). In a well-pitched appeal to English Whig prejudice as well as the Whig sense of justice, the worldly Gaelic Irish exile, Count O'Flaherty, reflected on the events of the seventeenth century.

I shall never dispute that the English might not have acted wisely in exterminating the Irish at the time of the revolution, and thus getting rid of a race which they looked upon as armed in the cause of despotism and bigotry . . . Having, however, permitted the Irish to live, they should not have deprived them of all the rights which give life its moral dignity.[60]

This emphasis on 'the demoralisation of the people it persecuted and brutified'[61] was central to Morgan's interpretation of the colonial process.

Her reiterated categorisation of Irish history as one of 'misrule and oppression', indeed of 'six hundred years of oppression'[62] also had a traditional Anglo-Irish focus. The villains of the piece are English governments (though not English monarchs) and even more, the corrupt, *arriviste* 'new English' adventurers who dominated Irish government from the mid-seventeenth century. She quoted as Grattan's description of them, that they were 'one of the worst of oligarchies . . . a plebeian oligarchy'[63] and also portrayed them in party terms as Irish Tories, 'advocates of their own arbitrary power', who corrupted the 'Whiggish toast' to William of Orange to mean, 'the subjection of the Catholic population, an unequal distribution of rights and the supremacy of a narrow, bigotted and impolitic intolerance'.[64] To a poor Dubliner in *Florence Macarthy* they are 'the Ascendancy, sir; only for it . . . wouldn't we be this day hand in glove, orange and green; sorrow one colour you'd know from the other, Och! but that would not do — where would the Ascendancy be? only all Irish men then'.[65] This 'banditti of dictators' came under heaviest fire in *The O'Briens and the O'Flahertys*, as 'an oligarchy, in whose members the sense of irresponsible power engendered a contempt for private morals, as fatal as their political corruption'. They are represented especially by the Knockloftys, 'dull as the Dutchmen from whom they were descended, tasteless as they were talentless', and the amoral leaders of a corrupt viceregal court, which is compared to that of Versailles, in being 'at once puerile and licentious'. These 'political vampires', were thus part of the 'proconsular despotism' against which the Anglo-Irish Whigs had to contend.[66]

The manner in which Morgan portrayed the impact of colonialism on the native Irish was also charged with moral judgment. Unlike Scott, her interest in the social dimension of the Gaelic collapse was minimal, and confined largely to answering Protestant fears about the stability of the land settlement. She concentrated instead on the psychological response, and in a way which conveyed a distinct impatience, even contempt. The hero in *Florence Macarthy* encompassed the theme in general terms when he spoke of 'that demoralisation which the misrule of centuries has impressed upon all branches of its [i.e. Ireland's] population'.[67] This was discussed in greatest detail in *The O'Briens and the O'Flahertys*, in which the hero's father, the apostate Baron Terence O'Brien, was described as a typical figure,

with thoughts ever retrospective to the glories of "ancient old Ireland", and with that religious tendency to passive obedience with which . . . Catholics are accursed, he is a rebel and a royalist on the same principles. These conflicting opinions he veils under an exterior of the most unlimited submission of the powers that be . . . In a word, he is only a "brief abstract" of a large class of his countrymen, such as six centuries of degradation had made them.[68]

Later in the novel, his idealistic son, Murrough, was urged by the heroine to leave the country, as it offered no hope for patriots. 'Here the fortitude of long endurance corrupts into obsequiousness; and the spirit of the gallant maddens into lawless intemperance'. Frustrated in his attempt to establish United Irish activity in Connaught, he was forced to agree, and he echoed the view that native demoralisation was largely self-induced, and due to the combined effects of Catholicism and a warped view of history. Thus, the Catholic gentry

slept over the degradation of their caste . . . Six hundred years of oppression were producing their moral effects. The conscientious notions of passive obedience of the Catholic were then fortified by the seared and calloused feelings of the man; while . . . pride and ambition . . . were exchanged for a silly, but too national vanity, which centred itself on the oft cited past.

Among such people he concluded, 'no political impression was feasible'.[69]

This perspective dominated the native Irish stereotype that emerges from these novels. *The Wild Irish Girl* in setting out to dispel the initial 'decided prejudice' of the hero against the 'semi-barbarous, semi-civilised Irish' developed one typical form of colonial stereotype, that of the reverse image. Thus the Irish were portrayed in this novel as heirs to a great, if destroyed civilisation, and despite their poverty were hospitable, enlightened and good-humoured. This stereotype also had its negative side; for example the explanaton as to why there were so few architectural remains of the pre-Christain era was double-edged

The ancient Irish, like the modern, had more soul, more genius, than worldly prudence, or cautious, calculating forethought . . . works of imagination seduced them from pursuing works of utility[70]

— including one can infer, uniting to resist outside aggression. In the later novels the stereotype was designed to reflect the colonial experience rather than to deny it. When the Anglo-Irish hero of *Florence Macarthy* arrived at the Dublin quays, he employed a native porter. He was 'miserably clad, disgustingly filthy, squalid, meagre and famished'. He was at the same time both 'debasingly acquiescent' and 'yet preserved the vindictiveness of conscious degradation'. Such dangerous duality was stressed several times in the novel, and was particularly threatening in the figure of Owney Rabragh, the peasant leader, who displayed 'qualities inherent in the lower Irish. Warm friends and revengeful enemies, inviolable in their secrecy, devoted in their attachments, inexorable in their resentments'. It was also emphasised, however, that the less savoury aspects of the Irish stereotype were the products of injustice, as in the explanation of Glentworth, the liberal Protestant landlord in *O'Donnel,* of the linguistic cunning of the poor as, 'the natural qualities of a people who long had nothing but address to oppose to force or to disarm oppression' — an interesting echo of Edgeworth's analysis of peasant speech.[71] A more flamboyant embodiment of the stereotype, and also an amalgam of the traditional 'wild Irish' figure with that of the fashionable 'noble savage', was Shane na Brien, the hero's foster-brother in *The O'Briens and the O'Flahertys.* He was 'a fine specimen of the mere Irish animal in its highest spiritual perfection', and an example of the degeneracy of the old native aristocracy 'to desperate outlaws'. Combining fanatical loyalty to his friends, with murderous revenge against his and their enemies, 'this last specimen of the Raparees of the earlier part of the last century, had the true Irish spirits, formed for every excitement, to madden into riotous gaiety, to sink into gloomy despondency'.[72] There were some positive elements in her portrayal of aspects of the threatening Gaelic subculture in the later novels, particularly of fosterage. There are also some surprising insights, like that into the dual loyalty of Terence Oge O'Leary, being, in his own words, 'tributory and seanachy . . . to the McCarthys' while 'servitor in the great Norman family of the Fitzadelms' — an almost uncanny echo of the position of Aogán Ó Rathaille, the great Gaelic poet of a century before, who also venerated the broken McCarthys as his hereditary lords, while depending on Anglo-Irish patronage.[73]

Lady Morgan had been fascinated by the tragedy of the dispossessed Gaelic nobility ever since meeting some real-life examples as a child. She based the Prince of Innismore partly on the McDermott of Coolavin, O'Donnel on 'the celebrated Charles O'Connor of Ballinagar', and Murrough O'Brien partly on Lord Cloncurry. Yet despite the fact that she liked to talk, even late in life, of 'my friend the O'Connor Don of Ballynagar, as legitimate a representative of the true kings of Ireland as any sovereign on or off his throne, at this moment in Europe',[74] her fictional presentation of the older generation of such people was as archaic, pathetic and obsessive figures — their ruined castles and museums full of symbols of long vanished greatness, their quarrels and ambitions rooted in an irrecoverable past.[75] The younger generation, however, were more enlightened and forward looking; made so by the tragedy of exile, the men having 'to fight on foreign grounds for foreign interests', while all her heroines after 'the purely national and natural' Glorvina[76] had been educated in Europe. Rory O'Donnell and Murrough O'Brien represented a different romantic tradition than did the Prince of Innismore, not of the broken Gaelic past, but of the adventurous European present — the former a supporter of the ancient regime in France, just as he is an apologist for the colonial system in Ireland; the latter a modern liberal and a veteran of the French revolution, who became a United Irishman. While both suffer from 'mortified pride' at their present poverty and their family's historic wrongs, they turn their backs resolutely on the past. O'Brien does so as a result of reading the 'Annals' of his family history, compiled by his anti-quarian father, and rejecting them as the 'fables' of 'a barbarous people . . . their boasted learning a tissue of monkish legends; their government, the rudest form of the worst of human institutions, feudality'.[77] While O'Brien finally despaired of changing Ireland and returned to France, Morgan's earlier young Gaelic heroes and heroines had stayed on. Their role was to be that of enlightened landlords, who had particular advantages, as will become clear, when we examine her odd treatment of one of the main worries that opponents of Catholic emancipation claimed to have, that is, the attitude of Catholics to the colonial land settlement.

In *The Wild Irish Girl,* the chaplain to the Prince dismissed 'the erroneous claim' made by the peasantry that they were 'the hereditary proprietors of the soil they cultivate', and the author in a footnote stated that the Irish of superior rank, whose ancestors had indeed been dispossessed, accepted the status quo.[78] The conformist hero of the next Irish novel, *O'Donnel,* demonstrated her contention admirably, defending the prescriptive rights of conquest, and even substantiating the claims of an English heiress to what had remained of his family's property, in court. He also repudiated the popular belief that he was, 'by the law of nature, the true heir'. And yet, at the end of the novel, by his marriage to the heiress, he *did* become, in the author's words, 'reinstated in some part of the vast possessions of his ancestors, forfeited at various periods, by the vicissitudes of property, incidental to the former unhappy state of Ireland'. In the same way, the heiress to the Macarthys repossessed their 'ancient castle and vast possessions' by her marriage to the Marquis of Dunore, while Glorvina had similarly restored to her family the land taken from them by the Cromwellian Mortimers.[79] This apparent contradiction is interesting, and reflected, in part at least, a tension between the separate aims of answering Protestant fears and of exploiting the classic symbol of reconciliation. It is also, perhaps, less of a contradiction than it seems. The alliance of the young, liberal Anglo-Irish and Gaelic nobility was an unequal one, the Gaelic partner being in a clearly subordinate position in terms of property and inheritance but still fulfilling an important role in acting as a link between the now loyal tenantry and the Anglo-Irish enlightened landlord, and thus achieving social cohesion as well as 'national unity'. Thus, for example, Florence McCarthy, after her marriage was, doubtless, able to exploit what she had earlier described as 'the prejudice which runs so strongly in favour of the representatives of [the tenants'] ancient chiefs, on my side, born and reared among them, speaking their language and assimilated to them in a thousand ways'. A similar exploitation of traditional loyalties is suggested by Maria Edgeworth at the end of *Ormond* (1817).[80]

The theme of Catholic repossession was dealt with differently in Morgan's darkest, and on the Catholic question, most confused novel, *The O'Briens and the O'Flahertys*. In this, the Catholic exile, Count O'Flaherty, recovered land at the beginning rather than at the end of the book, and he did so in accordance with stereotyped Protestant fears, by a court case over title, adding insult to injury by establishing a convent on the land! The portrayal of Catholicism throughout the novel as a sinister, Jesuit-run conspiracy also sits oddly with the declared intention of promoting the Emancipation cause, and serves as a reminder that Morgan, in the Irish Whig tradition, viewed Catholicism in itself with intense dislike, and the removal of the Penal Code as a great libertarian cause, to be achieved under the auspices of an enlightened Anglo-Irish leadership. The celebration of their time of greatest achievement and saddest defeat, the story of Ireland's lost revolution, was her real objective in what was to be, not inappropriately, her final Irish novel.

It was also appropriate that Henry Grattan should make a brief appearance, as he played a major role in the creation of the myth of the revolution achieved in 1782 and betrayed in 1800. His rhetoric echoes in her survey of the period between the 1770s, where the novel begins, and the 1790s, where much the greater part of it is set. 'America had revolted, and England, in her hour of peril, fearing Ireland as the aggressor in times of danger always fears the oppressed, reluctantly abandoned a part of that all-pervading and comprehensive system of tyranny'. The Volunteers were described in similarly extravagant and misleading rhetoric. 'Permitted to arm in their own defence, the Irish stood forth with all their ancient valour and with more than their ancient unity, to protect their native land from foreign aggression, and to realise that splendid dream of political philosophy, a national army'. Her heroes, having won 'Free Trade' and 'legislative independence', continued to fight against the corrupt Ascendancy clique, who are determined to destroy them, especially after, 'The French revolution, at its dawn so splendid and so temperate, produced in Ireland an effect the most powerful and electric'. Even thus embattled, the

Irish revolution had an instantaneous and even physical impact, as 'from the year 1782 . . . the city [Dublin] rose from its rubbish and the hovel of mud became a palace of marble'. On a different level, 'never did any country give to the world a more splendid or more intellectual generation as that which now burst forth to illustrate the benefits of political independence'.[81] The Volunteer Review in the Phoenix park, which began the second part of *The O'Briens and the O'Flahertys,* was graphically and affectionately portrayed as a great popular demonstration, led by Lord Charlemont, 'one of those men who hallow a whole people', and who had helped to establish this 'revolution without blood'. The portrayal of real historical characters in this book was simply as great public figures, looked at from a distance, very different from the brilliant psychological portraits of such people in Scott. Thus Grattan, as he marched past, was only described as 'one of the greatest men that Ireland ever produced . . . the Irish Cicero'.[82]

The most interesting aspect of Morgan's version of the 'Golden Age' of Anglo-Ireland was the inclusion of the United Irishmen, or rather the moderate aristocratic elements in that movement, firmly within the tradition. This, again, followed trends in history writing, a number of apologias by United Irish leaders having already appeared, while Moore was contemplating a life of his friend Lord Edward Fitzgerald and Madden was working on his monumental account. Her view of the early United Irish leadership as a frustrated younger generation of Irish Whigs had much validity, in terms both of their own self-perception and their ideology.[83] Its claimed aristocratic character was certainly decisive for her hero, Murrough O'Brien, proud of his descent from Brian Boru, and expelled from Trinity as 'the Irish Mirabeau', on the evidence of letters which discussed 'the separation of Ireland from England', and were believed to be his, though belonging in fact to Lord Walter Fitzwalter — clearly modelled on Lord Edward Fitzgerald. Fitzwalter, in fact, rejected separatism, which was 'as physically impossible at the moment as it would always be politically unwise', but he enthused about 'a national union, the brotherhood of affection, that community of interest, which . . . effect a regeneration by means as constitutional as they are effectual', and urged O'Brien to join the United Irishmen whose members, he assured him, came from 'the most illustrious families'. Despite some reservations, O'Brien agreed, mainly because Fitzwalter was a member, 'the descendant of the princely Geraldines, the brother of a peer of the realm'.[84]

The theme of aristocratic Anglo-Irish leadership of the movement was continued in the description of the Tailors Hall meeting that evening, presided over by Simon Butler, a descendant of 'the great Anglo-Norman Lords of the Pale'. Tone, Tandy, Drennan, Emmet and Rowan, were all described — as seen from the gallery — and their Protestantism stressed. The details and the rhetoric were based on contemporary sources, most remarkable being her echoing of an image from Tone, in her description of the rank and file at this meeting, 'the stern brow of uncompromising Presbyterianism, contrasting to the mobile, varying muscle of downtrodden Catholicism; the latter drawling forth its plaintive discontents, the former announcing its immovable resolutions'. When she described O'Brien and Fitzwalter as 'two representatives of the Norman and Milesian races of Ireland', united at 'the shrine of national independence', Morgan clearly saw such a 'national union' in terms of aristocratic leadership, just as Tone saw it in terms of the middle classes. Given her romantic view of the United Irishmen, it is not surprising that Morgan avoided the traumatic class and sectarian violence of 1798 in this novel, beyond a brief reference to 'the reign of terror which preceded the horrible epoch of the rebellion'.[85] Earlier, in *Florence Macarthy* she had given the Grattanite version of it being a reaction against ascendancy tyranny, and 'excited for the purpose of effecting a ruinous Union'. The first volume of that book gave an exaggerated account of the effect of the Union (always described as a 'betrayal') on Dublin, its trade ruined, its suburbs a sea of poverty, its magnificent centre 'still, silent and void'. It was, in the words of the Grattan-type character, Hyacinth Daly, a 'fallen capital'; its tragedy being best summed up by 'the many hotels which now succeed in the patrician streets of Dublin to the mansions of the banished nobility'. The contrast with the bustling, if vulgarised Dublin of Maria Edgeworth's, *The Absentee,* underlines their differences in political perspective as well as in literary purpose.[86]

The Union also meant an end to the Irish Whigs' shadowy dream of 'national independence' and their cause reverted to the more prosaic matter of completing the Irish revolution by emancipating the Catholics. The author herself became part of this historical phase through her roles as Whig hostess, qualified supporter of the Catholic Association, and above all, as political novelist, whose 'national tales' were intended as vivid arguments for this 'great national cause'.[87] She saw Catholic emancipation in a dual historical perspective, as both the culmination of the seventeenth-century 'revolution' in favour of civil and religious liberty, and as a necessary guarantee for the permanence of the colonial settlement, with which that revolution had a close and tension-filled relationship in Ireland. Some elements of her novels were more simply, even crudely propagandistic in the Catholic cause, like the wildly exaggerated catalogue of horrors she portrayed as the operation of the Penal Code in the 1770s, in the first part of *The O'Briens and the O'Flahertys*.[88] This was balanced, however, by the anti-Catholic tone of the novel as a whole, and its emphasis on the Anglo-Irish leadership of a passive Catholicism. The very different reality of the O'Connellite campaign, with its dynamic bourgeois Catholic leadership, its liberal Protestant auxiliaries, and its terrifyingly disciplined mass politics, had already begun to distress her, as she wrote what was to be her last Irish novel. In the aftermath of Emancipation, her diary and correspondence became strident with warnings about 'revolution' and 'terrorism', and when these subsided, querulous with disenchantment at a country she described as being 'between bedlam and a jail'. In the end, she quit 'wretched Dublin, the capital of wretched Ireland' altogether in 1837, and went to live in London, helped by a pension from the Melbourne government.[89] Her dilemma was, of course, the classic Whig one. What she believed and wanted to be the end of a revolution turned out to be the start of an entirely different one, under new auspices. The initiative having clearly passed to others within Ireland, she concentrated in her later years on urging support for the English Whigs, 'Ireland's longtime friends', and above all, for an end to agitation.[90]

While she wrote no more Irish novels after 1827, Lady Morgan did write a fictional representation of post-emancipation Irish society and politics in a play, *Manor Sackville,* published in an odd collection entitled *Dramatic Scenes of real life,* in 1833. This dark and pessimistic work featured a liberal and enlightened Englishman who, inheriting an Irish estate, tried to run it on just and humanitarian principles, only to be attacked and driven out by Orange bigots, Catholic politicians and the very peasants he had tried to help and who repaid him by an attempt on his life. Of particular significance was the connection clearly made between the activities of the agrarian secret society and the inflated rhetoric of the preposterous lower middle class catholic 'pathriots' — who disliked the hero because 'he took part with the base Whigs and talked of conciliaytion'. Safely back in London Sackville rejected the 'pathriot' argument that Ireland suffered under despotic government. 'Emancipated Ireland . . . is free . . . repose is now her most urgent necessity'. Earlier, in a key scene in the play, he had argued with the young Maynooth-trained curate for a particular form of 'repose' — that Ireland should 'forget the past'. The priest not only argued for 'the importance of keeping up the national spirit by preserving the glorious remembrance of past times', he stressed particularly that the Irish people should remember their saints and martyrs, 'who were deprived of their

liberty and their ancient, national and venerated Church'. Sackville abandoned the argument, making little impression with the assertion that
Ireland needed 'not saints, but citizens; not heroes, but peacable, industrious and calculating utilitarians'.[91] Not only had the political revolution failed to stop at Catholic emancipation, but Irish history, Morgan's
own favoured political weapon, had been hijacked by a new Catholic nationalism. She even worried that she might have been responsible for
releasing a genie, which had now run amok, and in many of her later
writings was at pains to defend the use she had made of Irish history and
legend in the interest of achieving Catholic Emancipation, while insisting
that the success of that reform meant that 'such signs and images of the
worst times in the history of humanity', which had been 'new burnished',
should 'now be returned to the old property room of Irish vanity, as no
longer applicable to the wants of the times'.

The implication that history could be so easily manipulated, and that her
version of it should prevail, tells us much about Lady Morgan's fiction as
well as her politics. She was not, of course, altogether mistaken on either
count, and we can see what she could not, that her political and her
historical perspectives were to continue as important elements in Irish constitutional and cultural nationalism. Like Liberalism in Britain a century
later, Anglo-Irish Whiggism was to become a dominant ideology even
while it declined as a political force. Lady Morgan's novels may have had
no discernible political impact, but they reflected and contributed to an increasingly popular political culture. Through such writings, at least in part,
the work of antiquarians and historians entered the arena of political
discourse, and the rhetoric of O'Connell, as well as of Young Ireland bristl-
ed with the symbolism and the shorthand that recur in all her novels —
harps and wolfhounds, 'six hundred years of oppression', the dark
despairing eighteenth century relieved by the Golden Age of Grattan's
Parliament and ending in the catastrophe of the Union. Her advocacy of a
confrontation with Ireland's colonial history as a basis for reconciliation
anticipated Davis; but her version of that history, like his, itself became a
weapon in the process of polarisation which she had aimed to reverse. In
literary terms she deserves more attention than she has received, and may
benefit from the current interest in feminist literature, as one of the first
truly professional women novelists and one whose heroines were dominant
and intellectual. She is also an important, and sometimes very good
novelist of her native Dublin, despite her normal association with the
romantic west. Her main importance as a writer, however, may lie precisely
in the area on which this paper has focused — the manner in which she

made historical sources and historical themes the raw material and the subject matter of a political fiction. While Scott's inferior in terms of both historical understanding and literary skill, she too developed a distinctive form of historical fiction, which exploited and reflected the shadowy boundary that then existed between these two related forms of literary discourse. The contrast between Morgan and Scott reflected even more the extent to which the nature of a society's historical experience shapes its literature. The Irish novel, then and since, has been haunted by history, and, with the possible exception of Joyce, has been unable to put it into the kind of perspective achieved by Scott. 'A nightmare from which I am trying to awake', as Dedalus called Irish history,[92] produced a less coherent, and in many ways more interesting fiction.

NOTES AND REFERENCES

1. Lady Morgan, *The Wild Irish Girl*, 3 vols (London, 1806); *O'Donnel. A national tale*, 3 vols (London, 1814); *Florence Macarthy. An Irish tale*, 4 vols (London, 1818); *The O'Briens and the O'Flahertys. A national tale,* 4 vols (London, 1827).
2. *O'Donnel*, i, p. vii.
3. P. Ricoeur, *Hermeneutics and the human sciences. Essays on language, action and interpretation* (Cambridge, 1981), pp 274-96.
4. F. Jameson, *The political unconscious. Narrative as a socially symbolic act* (London, 1981), p. 17.
5. cf. Leo Braudy, *Narrative form in history and fiction: Hume, Fielding and Gibbon* (Princeton, 1970), esp. Ch. 1.
6. H. Hepworth Dixon (ed.), *Lady Morgan's memoirs: autobiography, diary and correspondence,* 2 vols (London, 1863), ii, p. 324; L. Stevenson, *The Wild Irish Girl. The Life of Sydney Owenson, Lady Morgan* (London, 1936), pp 242-3; W.J. Fitzpatrick, *Lady Morgan, her career, literary and personal, with a glimpse of her friends and a word to her calumniators* (London, 1860), pp 285-6; Stevenson, *Life*, p. 237.
7. Stevenson, *Life*, pp 234, 287; *Morgan's Memoirs*, ii, pp 381-3.
8. D. McCartney, 'The writing of history in Ireland, 1800-1830', *Irish Historical Studies,* x, 1957, pp 347-62.
9. O. MacDonagh, *States of Mind. A study of Anglo-Irish conflict 1780-1980* (London, 1983), p. 6.
10. *O'Donnel*, i, pp vii-xii.
11. cf. T. Dunne, *Maria Edgeworth and the colonial mind* (O'Donnell Lecture, National University of Ireland, 1984).
12. T. Eagleton, *Literary Theory. An introduction* (Oxford, 1983), p. 73.
13. *O'Donnel* (1846 ed.), Preface.
14. *O'Donnel*, iii, p. 259.
15. *Florence Macarthy,* i, pp 133-4.
16. *Wild Irish Girl*, ii, p. 117.
17. *O'Donnel*, iii, pp 192-3, 267-8.
18. *Florence Macarthy*, iii, p. 39.

19. *The O'Briens and the O'Flahertys*, i, p. 85.
20. *O'Donnel*, i, pp vii-xii.
21. Stevenson, *Life*, p. 202.
22. G. Lukacs, *The historical novel* (English ed., 1962), pp 30-63.
23. D. Brown, *Walter Scott and the historical imagination* (London, 1979), esp. Ch. 3.
24. *Wild Irish Girl* (1846 ed.), p. xxv; *The O'Briens and the O'Flahertys,* i, p. ix.
25. *The novice of St Dominic* (1806); *The missionary, an Indian tale* (1811).
26. Brown, *op. cit.,* p. 184.
27. Stevenson, *Life,* p. 3; *Morgan's Memoirs,* i, p. 40.
28. Stevenson, *Life,* p. 159.
29. M. Butler, *Maria Edgeworth, a literary biography* (Oxford, 1972), p. 448.
30. *Morgan's Memoirs,* i, Ch. VII; ii, p. 529.
31. Miss Owenson, *The lay of the Irish harp* (London, 1807), esp. the preface; *Morgan's Memoirs,* i, pp 258-67; Stevenson, *Life,* p. 67.
32. *Morgan's Memoirs,* i, p. 164. For her misuse of Irish words, cf. ibid., pp 14, 165; *The O'Briens and the O'Flahertys*, ii, p. 293.
33. *Morgan's Memoirs,* i, pp 258-60.
34. Stevenson, *Life,* p. 1.
35. *Morgan's Memoirs,* i, Ch. 4; Stevenson, *Life,* pp 11-24.
36. *Wild Irish Girl* (1846 ed.), pp xxxiii-iv.
37. Ibid., p. xxxv, footnote.
38. *Wild Irish Girl,* ii, pp 224 ff.
39. Ibid., pp 274-319.
40. Dunne, *Edgeworth and the colonial mind;* B. Bradshaw, *The Irish constitutional revolution in the sixteenth century* (Cambridge, 1979); C. Lennon, *Richard Stanihurst, the Dubliner 1547-1618* (Dublin, 1981).
41. *O'Donnel,* i, dedication page.
42. Ibid., pp vii-xii.
43. *Morgan's Memoirs,* i, p. 519; ii, p. 5.
44. *O'Donnel,* i, pp x-xi.
45. Ibid., ii, pp 7-36; i, p. xi.
46. T. Flanagan, *The Irish novelists 1800-1850* (Connecticut, 1958), p. 133.
47. *Wild Irish Girl,* ii, pp 92-5.
48. *Florence Macarthy,* ii, p. 247; i, pp 265, 284-5.
49. *The O'Briens and the O'Flahertys,* i, pp 30, 55-6; ii, pp 211-12.
50. Sir T.C. and Lady Morgan, *The book without a name,* 2 vols (London, 1841), ii, pp 163-5, 171-2.
51. *Wild Irish Girl,* i, p. 129.
52. *O'Donnel,* iii, pp 274-5, 271-2.
53. E. Knott, *A bhfuil againn dar chum Tadhg Dall Ó hUiginn,* 2 vols (Dublin, 1921, 1926), i, No. 17.
54. *Florence Macarthy,* i, pp 312-3; iii, p. 119, 198.
55. MacDonagh, *States of Mind,* Ch. 1.
56. *Wild Irish Girl,* iii, pp 15-16.
57. *O'Donnel,* iii, pp 7-36, 333-9.
58. *The O'Briens and the O'Flahertys,* iii, p. 77.
59. *Florence Macarthy,* i, pp 321-7, 14-16.
60. *The O'Briens and the O'Flahertys,* ii, pp 273-85.

61. *Florence Macarthy*, i, pp 326-7. Cf. also ibid., iii, pp 119, 271; iv, p. 268; *The O'Briens and the O'Flahertys*, i, pp 26, 68-9; iv, pp 283-4.

62. e.g. *Florence Macarthy*, i, p. 95; ii, pp 231-2. *The O'Briens and the O'Flahertys*, i, pp 68-9; iv, pp 283-4.

63. *Wild Irish Girl* (1846 ed.), p. xxxix, footnote. The phrase was originally Edmund Burke's, in *Letter to a peer of Ireland on the Penal Laws against Irish Catholics* (1782). For a recent discussion of Burke's argument see S. Deane, *Celtic Revivals. Essays in modern Irish literature* (1985), pp 23-31.

64. *Florence Macarthy*, ii, pp 109-10.

65. Ibid., i, p. 53.

66. *The O'Briens and the O'Flahertys*, i, pp 142-5, and p. vii of preface; ii, pp 149, 154, 5.

67. *Florence Macarthy*, ii, p. 119. Also, ibid., p. 271; iv, p. 268; *O'Donnel*, i, p. 203.

68. *The O'Briens and the O'Flahertys*, i, pp 68-71.

69. Ibid., iv, pp 244-6, 283-4.

70. *Wild Irish Girl*, i, p. xxix; ii, p. 72.

71. *Florence Macarthy*, i, pp 21, 92; iii, p. 136; iv, p. 8; *O'Donnel*, i, p. 204; Dunne, *Edgeworth and the colonial mind*, pp 17-21.

72. *The O'Briens and the O'Flahertys*, i, pp 30-32; ii, pp 286 ff.

73. *Florence Macarthy*, iii, p. 62. S. Ó Tuama, *Filí faoi sceimhle* (Dublin, 1978), pp 83-184; T. Dunne, 'The Gaelic response to conquest and colonisation: the evidence of the poetry', *Studia Hibernica*, No. 20, 1980.

74. Stevenson, *Life*, p. 73; *O'Donnel*, ii, pp 317-19 (footnote); *Morgan's Memoirs*, ii, p. 195; i, p. 65.

75. e.g. *Wild Irish Girl*, i, pp 138 ff., 194-8; ii, pp 50 ff.; iii, p. 229. *The O'Briens and the O'Flahertys*, i, pp 253 ff.; ii, pp 191 ff.; 329 ff.

76. *The O'Briens and the O'Flahertys*, i, pp 71-2; Florence Macarthy, iii, p. 149; *Wild Irish Girl*, ii, p. 109.

77. *O'Donnel*, ii, p. 39; *The O'Briens and the O'Flahertys*, ii, pp 256-7.

78. *Wild Irish Girl*, iii, p. 65.

79. *O'Donnel*, iii, pp 150-61, 267-8, 304-5; *Florence Macarthy*, iv, p. 282; *Wild Irish Girl*, iii, pp 258-9.

80. *Florence Macarthy*, iii, p. 276. Cf. also *O'Donnel*, iii, pp 304-5; *Wild Irish Girl*, iii, p. 259. Cf. Dunne, *Edgeworth and the colonial mind*, pp 13-14.

81. *The O'Briens and the O'Flahertys*, i, pp 138, 140-46, 253; iii, pp 6-7.

82. Ibid., i, pp 146-7, 163.

83. e.g. T.A. Emmet et al., *Memoire, a detailed statement of the origin and progress of the Irish union . . .* (1802). T. Moore, *The life and death of Lord Edward Fitzgerald* appeared in 1831, while R.R. Madden's multi-volume series on *The United Irishmen, their lives and times* appeared between 1842 and 1846.

84. *The O'Briens and the O'Flahertys*, i, pp 161-4; iii, Ch. 2.

85. Ibid., iii, pp 112-14; iv, p. 324. Theobald Wolfe Tone, *An argument on behalf of the Catholics of Ireland* (Dublin, 1791), p. 10. T. Dunne, *Theobald Wolfe Tone: Colonial Outsider. An analysis of his political philosophy* (Cork, 1982), Ch. iv.

86. *Florence Macarthy*, i, pp 21 ff. Maria Edgeworth, *The Absentee,* 2 vols (1812), ii, Ch. 1. Cf. W.J. McCormack, *Ascendancy and Tradition in Anglo-Irish Literary History from 1789 to 1939* (Oxford, 1985), Ch. 4.

87. *O'Donnel* (1846 ed.), preface.

88. *The O'Briens and the O'Flahertys*, i, pp 22-6, 54-73, 98-102.

89. *Morgan's Memoirs*, ii, pp 313-19, 379-81. Stevenson, *Life*, p. 299.

90. *Morgan's Memoirs*, ii, pp 313-14; *Wild Irish Girl* (1846 ed.), preface; Lady Morgan, *Dramatic scenes from real life*, 2 vols (London, 1833), i, pp 244-6.

91. *Manor Sackville*, comprising Vol. i, and pp 1-30 of Vol. ii of *Dramatic scenes of real life*. Cf. especially i, pp 233-49; ii, pp 27-8; i, pp 154-63.

92. James Joyce, *Ulysses* (1922), p. 40 (Penguin ed.).

Jewish emancipation in nineteenth-century Germany and the stereotyping of the Jew in Gustav Freytag's novel *Soll und Haben* (1855)

EDA SAGARRA

Gustav Freytag's best-selling novel has frequently been the object of critical attention both in Germany and abroad, particularly since George Mosse's brief article in an early number of the Leo Baeck Yearbook drew attention to its significance as a formative influence on popular attitudes to the Jew in nineteenth-century Germany.[1] The text of *Soll und Haben* can still serve as a useful introduction to background courses for students of both German literature and history, confronting the modern reader as it does with once widely held views among the nineteenth-century German middle classes on such matters as nationalism, liberalism, the military, nobility and bourgeoisie, attitudes to women, to other races, and, in particular, to the Jews in Germany. The present paper attempts to provide a more specific location for Freytag's novel in the history of German Jews and their relations to their non-Jewish environment than has hitherto been done. It also suggests that Freytag not only exercised a formative influence on the evolution of antisemitic attitudes among his fellow countrymen, but was also widely representative of 'middle-class liberal' opinion on these and other matters in the years between the Revolution of 1848 and the founding of the Second Empire.

I. THE JEWISH COMMUNITY IN PRUSSIA AND GERMANY 1800-1900

Population

A widely held view among Germans in the nineteenth century assigned problematical character to the Jews in their midst, based on the misapprehension that Jewish numbers were 'too large' and that they were increasing out of proportion to the rest of the population. Yet at no time between 1800 and 1900 did the Jewish population in Germany — which the

160

statistics of the time and, until the 1870s, society, understood to mean unbaptised Jews — reach even 1·5% of the total population. An estimated
270,000 Jews lived in Germany in 1820, a generation later in 1848 they
numbered 410,000 or 1·23% of the total, rising to 512,153 or 1·25% in
1871 (this last figure including some 40,000 Jews from Alsace-Lorraine).
By 1910 the percentage had fallen to less than 1%, though the numbers now
stood at 615,000.[2] Lower infant mortality rates (the latter linked, it seems,
with much lower illegitimacy rates among Jews than non-Jews) and greater
longevity, did achieve higher population growth rates in the German
Jewish community between 1825 and 1861, but contrary to popular opinion, Jewish marriages were less fertile than non-Jewish over the century as
a whole, and emigration as well as conversion to Christianity took their
toll. Mass immigration into Germany was not a particularly significant
factor in Jewish demographic history at that time. Certainly received opinion thought otherwise: Treitschke's often reiterated image of the 'hordes
of trouser-selling Jewish youths streaming across the border from Poland'
had been anticipated by his friend and former associate Freytag in an essay
of 1849.[3]

Geographical distribution

Vital factors influencing the relationships between German Jews and their
Christian neighbours in the nineteenth century were population distribution and changing patterns of settlement. Here both internal migration and
emigration of Jews played a significant role.

Prussia was and remained the state with the largest population of Jews,
with some 50% of German Jews according to the 1843 census; by 1867 this
figure was 62%, including the recently annexed city of Frankfurt, 11% of
whose inhabitants were Jewish. By 1910 the percentage of Germany's Jews
living in Prussia had reached 70%. In Prussia itself the Jewish population
was concentrated mainly in the Polish provinces, approximately one half
of the total living here in 1843.[4] The Jews had not integrated with their
Polish neighbours, but continued to speak their own language, Yiddish, a
dialect of Middle High German, mixed with Hebrew and Slav words.
Pinkeles, the pedlar in Soll und Haben, is an example of this type of Jew,
and Freytag as a programmatic realist writer attempts to reproduce the
characteristic word-order and syntax of the native Yiddish speaker in German. Within the Polish provinces of Prussia, the Grand Duchy of Posen
was particularly significant in terms of its high percentage of Jews — in
some towns they actually outnumbered the Christian population: the town
where Itzig comes from, Ostrau, is on the border between Posen and

Silesia. The Austrian Empire was similar in this to Prussia, having the majority of its Jewish population in East Galicia and the Bukovina, with very high concentrations in some towns — thus 76·3% of the population of the town of Brody in Galicia in 1880 was Jewish.[5] Just as the Polish provinces of Prussia provided the bulk of the immigrant Jewish population to the big towns of Prussia in the latter half of the nineteenth century, so too Galicia and the Bukovina accounted to a large extent for the huge increase of the Jewish population in Vienna between 1800 and 1900.[6] At the time Freytag was writing his novel in the early 1850s, most Jews did not live in cities or larger towns; approximately 80% of the Jews of Central Europe lived in fact in rural areas, the bulk of them poor; many, again contrary to received opinion, in dire poverty.[7]

Occupation

However already by this time significant changes had taken place in the economic situation of the Prussian Jews. Freytag's Jewish protagonist Veitel Itzig exemplifies two important developments in Jewish life in mid-century, one being the beginning of a movement away from villages and small towns to the provincial capital, in particular to Breslau in Silesia, to Königsberg in East Prussia, and of course to Berlin. This trend was also characteristic of the Gentile population; Freytag's other protagonist, the German Anton Wohlfart, goes to the provincial capital Breslau from his home in Ostrau to seek his fortune. However, the proportion of Jews in this migratory movement was considerably greater.[8] The second development which Freytag documents in the novel is the move by Jews from their traditional occupations into those of their Gentile neighbours. Thus while Itzig's father was a *Trödler*, a secondhand dealer, legal disabilities on Jews excluding them from direct access to the markets, Itzig can aim to make his career in commerce, and indeed gets a grind in law (from a lawyer struck off the register) to equip himself for the task. This within the span of a single generation, between that of Itzig and his father, a radical redistribution in the occupation of Jews had occurred. Where before 1812 an estimated four-fifths of Jews earned their living in peddling and secondhand goods dealing, by mid-century the figure was less than one-fifth.[9]

The diversification was consolidated in subsequent decades: between 1861 and 1925 some 50% of Jews worked in commerce and banking, on average, 20% in industry and crafts and 10% as domestic servants and day labourers. Their representation in the civil service and the professions grew steadily, from 2·9% in the 1860s to 4% in 1882 and 6·7% in 1907.[10]

The prerequisite for Veitel's success must be seen to derive not alone from his more favourable legal situation, but also from the education he has enjoyed. Veitel Itzig, like his German counterpart Anton, has been to the local school. Freytag records in his novel a key feature of Jewish life in the nineteenth century: the value that Jews placed on education. From the 1850s onwards their representation in secondary and tertiary education grew rapidly, being 3-4 times higher than that of their percentage of the population as a whole in Prussia; in Berlin as many as 10% of students of grammar schools and universities at the end of the century were Jews.[11]

Legislative Reform
Internal migration and radical changes in the regional distribution and occupation of the Jewish population were associated with the rapid modernisation of the economy. This in its turn was the direct consequence of far-reaching legislative reforms in Prussia between 1780 and 1815. In Germany as a whole, the widespread regional variations in the condition of German Jews before 1871 were thus to a large extent linked with the presence or absence of similar liberalising measures.

In Prussia the most important measures affecting Jews were the Stein Municipal Ordinance of 1807, which gave civic rights to Jews in towns, and the application to them in the 1812 Ordinance of the benefits of the government legislation abolishing restraints on trade and on mobility. Although in practice, and particularly in rural areas, popular resentment of the Jews might even now prevent their entry into trades and crafts hitherto closed to them, in the long term the geographical and economic mobility of Prussian Jews, and their major contribution to the modernisation of the economy in the nineteenth century, derive to a large degree from this initiative. The 1812 Ordinance was largely the work of Wilhelm v. Humboldt, as minister of cults and public instruction: it extended civic and political rights to Jews in the Prussian provinces not annexed by Napoleon, though with certain exceptions (Jews might not be officers or be employed in the judiciary or government administration). This was the most important German emancipatory measure of the first period (i.e. 1780-1815) in the history of Jewish emancipation and represented a major breakthrough for Prussian and ultimately German Jews.

However, as so often in German Jewish history, the law was one thing, the administration of the law another. The 1812 provisions were not extended to the areas of Prussia regained or acquired in 1815, in consequence of which some twenty-one different ordinances now governed the Prussian Jewish community, a situation rightly described as 'chaotic'.[12] Particularly hurtful to educated Jews was their exclusion from the teaching profession, notably university posts in the humanities and law. A notorious case in the 1820s highlighted their position, namely that of the jurist Eduard Gans, whose appointment to the chair of law in Berlin university was blocked by a senior bureaucrat in the ministry of cults and public instruction, v. Altenstein. It was Gans's subsequent baptism and appointment to the chair which prompted Heine's celebrated remark that baptism was 'the entry ticket to European culture'.[13] Bernhard Ehrenthal, the 'good Jew' in Freytag's novel, makes this explicit in a conversation with Anton: he is forced into the solitary life of a scholar, since Jews cannot aspire to a university post.

Jewish Emancipation

In 1847 a new Ordinance relating to the Jews made the exercise of political rights independent of confessional allegiance in Prussia, and the constitutional legislation of 1848, 1849 and finally of January 1850 made all Prussians equal before the law. However, once again administrative practice blocked certain key posts, in education and the judiciary. It was not until the 1850s that the first unbaptised Jews could enter university teaching and the public service in Germany, 1871 before a Prussian university chair was filled by one. Their numbers increased rapidly thereafter in the lower ranks, but it remained very difficult for a Jew to achieve full professorial status in Prussia. (It was not easy for a Catholic either.) From the 1880s onwards discrimination against Jews in the army, civil service and judiciary became increasingly overt.[14]

Yet despite the evidence of antisemitic prejudice among government executives throughout the century, and open discrimination in the last decades, it remains a fact that Jewish emancipation both in Prussia and in Germany in general was the work of government initiative and not popular representation. The 1860s saw the ending of legal disabilities against the Jews — embodied in the legislation of 1862 for Baden, 1861-4 for Württemberg, 1867 for Austria, 1869 for the North German Confederation, and finally, by extension of the North German Confederal constitution to the Second Empire, for the whole of Germany in 1871. But such legislation did not enjoy the full support of society. Even in the so-called liberal era a supporter of emancipation, the parliamentary deputy Ludwig Häusser, could state categorically in the Baden chamber in 1862 that a plebiscite on the subject of Jewish emancipation would not win majority support.[15]

In contrast with the history of Jewish emancipation in Western European countries, proponents of emancipation in Germany favoured a gradualist approach, partly because they feared an adverse reaction among the populace, partly because German liberals believed in 'educating' the Jews for emancipation and 'educating' the population for Jewish emancipation. Whether we are talking of Prussian liberal bureaucrats in the reform era or of liberal deputies in the lower houses of the South German or Prussian chamber in the 1860s, the discussions about civic and political rights for the Jewish community exemplify the contradictions in German liberal ideology. Freytag, who always regarded himself as a liberal and was so regarded by his countrymen, is a particularly interesting example of these contradictions, both in his life and in his writings. Essentially German liberals did not accept the idea of a pluralist society. They believed that Jewish emancipation was not so much the rightful condition of all Jews, but rather a kind of prize to be gained by assimilated Jews.[16] When Freytag depicts the career of Veitel Itzig, and shows him to retain the manners and morals of the ghetto Jew, he is effectively offering a warning example, a kind of morality tale, of what must happen if the German Jews do not assimilate. Unlike the racial antisemitics of a later generation, a position he was to oppose, Freytag did not believe that Jewishness was, as it were, an 'inalienable condition' but was confident that it could be 'expunged' by the Jews assimilating to German bourgeois culture as he and his kind understood it. Emancipation from the ghetto was what Freytag strove to promote; he did not advocate, as conservatives did, conversion to Christianity, though in fact conversions were highest in the provinces which attracted Jewish migrants, East Prussia, Silesia, and Brandenburg, where Berlin is situated.[17] However Protestant liberal theology in Prussia in the mid-nineteenth century was deeply suspicious of the Judaic traditions in Christianity, and Freytag's own proud acknowledgement, expressed in his memoirs and correspondence and reminiscent of the pirate king in Gilbert and Sullivan's *HMS Pinafore*, of 'my good fortune in being born on the Polish frontier — a Prussian, a Protestant and a Silesian'[18] suggests that assimilation in his view would include the embracing of so enlightened and national a faith.

In the view of a leading authority on the subject, Reinhard Rürup, Jewish emancipation in nineteenth-century Germany suffered from the failure on the part of the German state and its population to develop and implement a coherent view of society in a time of major social, economic and political change. Ultimately the inability of government and society in Germany to accept Jewish emancipation, a fact which became increasingly evident in the years after 1878-9, was bound up, in Rürup's view, with the failure of the German middle classes to gain, or even to seek, their own emancipation in any real sense of the word.[19]

II. 'SOLL UND HABEN' IN THE CONTEXT OF FREYTAG'S LIFE AND WORK

Freytag's novel, *Soll und Haben* (English translation: *Debit and Credit,* 1857) was published in 1855, just before the final volume of Count Gobineau's seminal work on the history of antisemitism, *Essai sur l'inégalité des races humaines* (4 vols, 1853-6). The novel was an instant success. By December of that year it had been reprinted three times. Two years later three separate English translations had been made, one of them with an introduction by the then ambassador to the Court of St. James, v. Bunsen.[20] Freytag's work enjoyed considerable success in Britain subsequently, in his latter years partly through his friendship with the Crown Prince and Princess of Prussia, aftrwards Emperor Frederick III, and his English consort Empress Victoria. When Freytag died in 1895 the *Times* obituary was half a column long, and both the *Athenaeum* and the *Illustrated London News* carried a report. The success of *Soll und Haben* and many of his other works thus seems to have borne out the categorical statement of the Oxford historian J.J. Seeley, who declared in 1867 'as a rule good books are in German'.[21]

At the time of its publication, Freytag was an established writer on the eve of his fortieth birthday. He had been born the son of a doctor and mayor of the Silesian border town of Kreuzburg, had studied both in Breslau and in Berlin under the great philologist Karl Lachmann, returning as a lecturer to his home university in 1839. Here he worked under Hoffmann von Fallersleben, author of the German national anthem, *Deutschland, Deutschland über alles,* who lost his chair in 1842 for political activities. Like the majority of young German academics of his generation Freytag took an active interest in the 1848 Revolution, believing it would at last effect the transfer of political power from the feudal estates to the middle classes. The defeat of the German army in Schleswig-Holstein in the summer of 1848 and the outbreak of street violence in the autumn convinced Freytag, as it did many other middle-class German liberals, that the threat to the new political and social order in Germany came, not from the princes, but from the 'radical elements' or, as he put it in a subsequent essay, 'die Stimmführer einer wüsten Demokratie'.[22] The 'betrayal' of the Revolution by these elements was subsequently transformed by him and his kind into an abhorrence of the very idea of revolution as a force for change. In *Soll und Haben* the German settlers in the Polish provinces, professional men, artisans and farmers, aided by Prussian troops called in by them, put down an abortive revolution by the Poles: the revolution is represented by the narrator as being the work of malevolent *agents provocateurs*, its consequence chaos and suffering. The contrast between such attitudes and the emotive support given by German academics and artisans to the Polish revolution of 1830-1 is striking. Freytag had already left the academic career before the Revolution to become a journalist and writer. In 1849 he became the editor, with Julian Schmidt, of a recently founded periodical, significantly called *Die Grenzboten*. The new editors aimed at using their journal to consolidate support among the German middle class for what they understood as progressive opinion. With unconscious irony they presented the editorial position as being 'democratic' in terms of their relationship with the governments of the day, but in their resolute confrontation with the ignorance and fickleness of the masses, they declared their concern to be to promote an 'aristocracy' formed from among the educated members of German society. Here they in effect outlined the dilemma and the self-contradictions of the German right-wing liberal position in the post-revolutionary period. With initial reluctance and then growing confidence, Freytag gradually transferred in subsequent years his belief in the primacy of law to that of state power, as incorporated in the 1850 Prussian constitution. *Soll und Haben* was to contain a positive view of the Prussian army, if not of all of its aristocratic officers, as the guardian of law and order and hence of progressive commerce and an enlightened agricultural policy, based on colonisation of the East. Freytag was a founder member of the liberal organisation, the *Nationalverein* (1859) under the patronage of Prince Albert's brother, Ernst of Saxe-Coburg-Gotha, to whom the novel is dedicated. Freytag became a member of parliament of the North German Confederation, but did not seek re-election to the Reichstag after 1871. Most of his other writings went into several, even dozens of editions during his lifetime, though none was to enjoy the extraordinary success of *Soll und Haben*. He wrote two imaginative multi-volume cultural and social histories of the German people, *Bilder aus der deutschen Vergangenheit* (1859-1867) and *Die Ahnen* (1872-1880) in the form of a novel, both of which were based on his own massive collection of early modern pamphlets, now housed in Frankfurt, and on memoirs. Despite their ideological tone they still make very informative reading today, and contain a substantial body of primary material. They formed part of the 'furniture' of the self-respecting German bourgeois household from the later nineteenth century up to the Second World War. Both present German history in terms of the progressive emancipation of the German bourgeoisie. Both end, symptomatically, with the year 1848.

To those who know the text of *Soll und Haben*, or even simply its justly deserved reputation as a major document in the history of antisemitism in Germany, it may come as a surprise to learn that Freytag was on terms of warm friendship with many Jews, as for example Berthold Auerbach (1812-1882),[23] that he married a Jewess, and that he made a spirited attack on Wagner's *Über das Judenthum in der Musik* in 1869 in the very journal, *Die Grenzboten*, where twenty years earlier he had voiced such violent opinions on Jewish radicalism. Towards the end of his life he became a member of the association set up in 1890 to counter antisemitism in German public life, the *Verein zur Abwehr des Antisemitismus*.[24] To some extent it could be said in Freytag's defence on a charge of antisemitism that he was writing within a European literary tradition which had stereotyped the Jew as parasite and comic figure for centuries. After all, English literature in the age of Enlightenment included such negative stereotypes as Isaac Rapine in Smollett's *History of Peregrine Pickle* (1751) or the fool in R.B. Sheridan's *The Duenna* (1775), not to speak of the lascivious Jew in Hogarth's *The Harlot's Progress* (1731), a figure quite absent from Freytag's galaxy of Jewish rogues. But it has to be said that, as a man of wide reading and indeed erudition, Freytag was quite aware of the opposite tradition in German literature since the eighteenth century, one which was closely associated with German classical idealism and to which he himself subscribed. This was the 'counter-stereotype' of the good Jew, first recorded in Gellert's novel, *Die Geschichte der schwedischen Grafin von G.* (1747), in Lessing's comedy of 1749 *Die Juden,* and above all in the same author's great drama of religious tolerance, with a Jew at its hero, *Nathan der Weise* (1779). The existence of such radically opposite Jewish types in German literature, and their descendants, the 'good' and the 'bad' Jews in the mid- and late-nineteenth-century novels of Auerbach, Reuter, Raabe, and Fontane and others, indicates the programmatic character of the portrayal of the Jew in nineteenth-century German literature, especially in fiction. It would seem to corroborate David Landes's whimsical remark in his essay on the Jewish merchant in nineteenth-century Germany, that 'typology is in the eye of the beholder'.[25] One could add: 'stereotypology also'. One further traditional Jewish figure in European literature of the modern period should be mentioned, since it came to enjoy a renewed popularity at the time of writing of *Soll und Haben*, and because it was widely interpreted, even in the area of emancipation, as representing Jewish rootlessness as an inalienable condition. This was the legend of Ahasverus, the first known account having been published in Latin in Leyden in 1602 and immediately translated into German. In the nineteenth century such diverse figures as Goethe, Friedrich Schlegel, Shelley, H.C.

Andersen, Edgar Quinet, and most importantly, Eugène Sue, made Ahasverus or the wandering Jew the subject of a literary work.[26] Sue's novel *Le juif errant* appeared in France in 1844-5 and was very soon translated into German (1848) and widely read. Whereas the older portraits of the Jew in European literature as parasite or funny man reflected rather than promoted popular prejudice, and in terms of literature as historical evidence are less complex than later works, a programmatic character would seem to be evident in the portraits of the Jew in German literature since Lessing.[27] The self-consciousness of the author, elicited through modern methods of literary analysis, is thus a principal claim of such works to our interest in the present context. The other source of interest of Freytag's *Soll und Haben,* and a number of other similar works, such as Raabe's novel *Der Hungerpastor*, is in the incongruence between intention and effect.

The story of the 700-page long novel, *Soll und Haben*, is that of two former schoolmates, Anton, the German burgher's son, Veitel, the Jewish dealer's son from a small town on the border of Silesia, who meet again on the high road to the provincial capital Breslau (Wroclaw). Anton is on his way to a clerical post in the office of Schröter, a wholesale merchant, Veitel is hoping to find employment in some menial capacity in a Jewish businessman's household. Veitel duly finds himself work as servant and messenger to Ehrenthal, a shady dealer who hopes to ensnare a local Junker, von Rothsattel, into debt, so that he can foreclose on his estate. In this way, Ehrenthal plans, his own son, the Orientalist Bernhard, will live like a gentleman fully emancipated, both physically and morally, from the ghetto. In due course Anton gets involved in the affairs of the v. Rothsattels, goes to manage their estates in Poland, where he encounters the full horror of Polish corruption and moral laxity, and where his bourgeois integrity contrasts with the hedonism of the German aristocratic family. Meanwhile Itzig, living on his wits, gains through doubledealing and blackmail control of Ehrenthal's fortune — and many others' besides. He is finally unmasked, not least by Anton's tenacity and bravery, and meets his fate by drowning in the river Oder while trying to escape from the police through the back alleys of the Jewish quarter of the city. Anton returns from the temptations of life with the nobility to the 'authentic world' of bourgeois work. He will take no more part in politics but devote himself to commerce, rewarded with a partnership and the hand of the boss's sister.

Virtually all the Jewish figures in the book — which include, besides Veitel Itzig, the four members of the Ehrenthal family, (vulgar wife and daughter, studious son), Pinkus, the shady innkeeper and fence, Schmeie

Pinkeles, the pedlar, whose Yiddish German makes everyone laugh and whose fawning servility makes even the most minor German clerk feel superior. In every case but that of Bernhard Ehrenthal, each Jewish figure has a Gentile counterpart, who is generally represented as his or her moral superior. Unconsciously Freytag is expressing the current view, not just of conservative Christian opinion in Germany at the time, but also of the body of liberal opinion that the 'emancipators believed Jews to be morally and socially inferior' (to their Gentile counterparts).[28]

When the narrator opens his account with a description of Anton, he concentrates on parentage and home (Book I, Ch. 2); he does not describe him physically, apart from references to the cleanness and neatness of his dress. Veitel on the other hand, whom we never see in his home, is described (also Book I, Ch. 2) physically as lean, sallow, and dirty, his mien and gait associated immediately with his character. Veitel's hair is described as reddish, in conformity with the traditional notion that Judas's hair was so coloured, but also with the literary tradition of mid-nineteenth-century literary Biedermeier that the devil in human form and his associates could be recognised by their reddish hair. One of the key features of negative stereotyping of Jews in fiction and in iconography was the association of physical appearance, and in particular what were regarded as characteristic Jewish facial features, with their 'moral' character.[29] The narrator in *Soll und Haben* makes some effort to account for Veitel's character in terms of his social environment, the poverty of the schoolboy, with whom the kindly Anton occasionally shared a sandwich, and the bullying to which he was submitted — having pork stuffed into his mouth (18 f.), from which again the brave Anton is described as having attempted to save him. The narrator would also persuade the reader that the shifty Ehrenthal is not without his good side: he proves himself prepared to sacrifice his fortune for his sick son, demonstrating to the reader that paternal affection can in his case transcend money-grubbing. But it is in the figure of Bernhard that Freytag hoped to embody his 'message' to his projected Gentile *and* Jewish public: Bernhard, who anticipates in some respects George Eliot's *Daniel Deronda* (1876), self-consciously rejects Jewish business morality and seeks his ideal in the study of classical literature. He demonstrates Freytag's thesis that assimilation is possible if the Jews are prepared to abandon their religious and cultural traditions, and adopt those of their German bourgeois neighbours. In the process their knowledge of the origins of civilisation in the Oriental world can deepen and enrich German culture. That Freytag was convinced that this would come about seems clear from his later writings, at least those of the 1860s such as the essay attacking Wagner, already referred to, and in the fascinating eleventh chapter of his *Bilder aus der deutschen Vergangenheit,* entitled 'Jesuiten and Juden'. In the latter work he represents the sinister machinations of the Counter-Reformation Jesuits who attempt by fair means and foul to ensnare Jewish boys into conversion to Catholicism. But while the Jesuits continue even in the modern world to be what 'they always were', the Jews by contrast have been transformed by 'the new education', they have left fanaticism behind them, since Christians have ceased to persecute them. The chapter ends with the evocative and revealing statement: 'Und die Enkel der asiatischen Wanderstämme sind unsere Landsleute und brüderliche Mitstreiter geworden'[30] (and the grandsons of those Asiatic Nomads are now our fellow-countrymen, our brothers in the common struggle).

Was Freytag illogical or merely naive in overlooking the contradictions between his liberal philosophy and the extremely antisemitic tenor of his novel? The answer lies in the distinction he believed himself to have made between the 'Schacherjude', the huckstering or eastern Jew, and the westernised Jews of his own circle. Bernhard clearly belongs potentially to the latter, despite the recent date of his emancipation.[31] It is noteworthy that the narrator shows Anton in conversation with Bernhard over his (Bernhard's) exclusion from a university career as having a sense of shame and shared grievance (283). Veitel, on the other hand is the embodiment not just of the *Schacherjude:* he is the prototype of the rootless and feckless proletariat which Freytag as a bourgeois liberal feared, and had learned to fear during the Revolution of 1848. The 1849 essay, *Die Juden in Breslau,* conjured up a vision of chaos, which not only threatened the transfer of power from the aristocratic feudal order to the bourgeoisie, but also imperilled the prosperity of the Prussian state. The identification of the Jew with both capitalism and with the revolutionary proletariat, and thus with the pains of modernisation, was an important ingredient of antisemitic thinking in Germany as elsewhere.[32] The anachronistic as well as self-contradictory atttiude of bourgeois liberals in Germany towards the economic development of the age is well documented in *Soll und Haben,* which purports in its famous motto to represent the 'German people at work', but yet contrasts adversely the 'capitalist' methods of Jewish businessmen with the old-fashioned paternalism of the Gentile Schröter and Co. The tacit rejection, not just of capitalism, but of the industrial revolution and modern society is clearly evident in the utopian social order in this 'modern novel' and has been widely remarked on by modern critics. This feature was an important ingredient of its sustained success. A further point should be made in distinguishing intention from effect. However sincere Freytag's concern may have been — as later Jewish admirers of his work would have it[33] — to demonstrate in his novel the way forward for Jewish emancipation and assimilation, given Jewish goodwill and Gentile support, the fact that he presented the successful and 'moral' career of the 'good German' Anton in graphic opposition to the depraved and sordid life of the Jew Veitel Itzig, kept alive the tradition in Germany that the Jew was 'different'. Above all it reinforced the view that the political and social emancipation of the German bourgeoisie was something apart and distinct from the emancipation of their Jewish fellow-countrymen. Anton's steady progress through reliability and thrift to being a successful business man, who invests his gains in the firm, is contrasted with Veitel's manic pursuit of money for its own sake, a neat anticipation of the terminology coined by the antisemitic Reichstag deputy Liebermann in the 1890s of 'nützliches und schädliches Kapital' (useful and harmful capital), or 'raffendes und schaffendes Kapital' (grasping or productive capital) in Nazi parlance.[34]

The presentation of the Jewish stereotype which both reflects and reinforces antisemitic prejudice in Freytag's novel would be of interest only to a narrow literary historical public were it not for the exceptional character of the book's commercial success. While it is impossible to quantify its influence in sociological terms, the demand for a new edition every two or three years between 1855 and 1917, the fact that by 1920 over one hundred editions of the work had appeared, that it was in fact, in the words of the by no means adulatory Franz Mehring in the 1890s 'der meist gelesenste aller deutschen Romane' are indicators of its impact. (There was even an early stenography textbook of Soll und Haben.)[35] Moreover, it was a preferred confirmation present, particularly for boys, and in the latter years of the century, surprisingly, a common barmitzvah gift. So readily had emancipated Jews identified themselves with the German nationalist culture which Freytag helped to promote. Originally Jewish reception had been understandably hostile to the work, but the favourable view recorded in the Bilder and particularly the cultural and emotive distancing of themselves by liberal Jews from the orthodox 'Schacherjude' identified with the ghettos of Posen and Silesia, changed this. When Freytag celebrated his 70th birthday, the Allgemeine Zeitung des Judenthums carried a eulogy of Soll und Haben by a Breslau rabbi, although the editorial comment remained negative.[36] In fact the Jewish reception of the novel, which space does not permit elaboration here, is an illuminating example of the contradictions and problems of identity of the German Jewish community in the last decades of the Wilhelmine Empire.

In attempting to correlate the reception of Freytag's novel and developing prejudice against 'the Jew' in late nineteenth- and early twentieth-century German society, the key element was Freytag's persuasive promotion of the Jewish stereotype. The association in the novel between 'German' and 'patriotic, national, moral' values, and the labelling of the Jew as the antagonist of the German, morally inferior, unpatriotic, hedonistic; the fact that Anton is a rounded (if not very convincing) character, whereas Veitel is a clever caricature, all this influenced the adolescent reader and surely helped shape his perceptions in later life. That it should have been written and have established its reputation at a time when the legal emancipation of German Jews was at last being attained, is one of the many tragic ironies of German Jewish history. Rürup has rightly observed that in order 'to assure a lasting settlement of the "Jewish Question" in the spirit of emancipation it would have been essential — indeed one of the most important prerequisites — to break down the traditional negative stereotypes among the Christian population'.[37] Freytag's most popular work achieved the reverse. The novel *Soll und Haben*, and its reception in Germany up to the time of the Holocaust thus exemplify with particular force Landes's comment that, while the Jewish type constantly changed and adapted in the course of nineteenth-century history, the stereotype in contrast 'clinging like a shadow, inconstant like a shadow, never really died'.[38]

NOTES AND REFERENCES

The text of *Soll und Haben* used is that of Deutscher Taschenbuch Verlag, edited by Hans Mayer (Munich, 1977).

1. G.E. Mosse, 'The image of the Jew in German popular culture' in *Leo Baeck Yearbook* (= *LBYB*), 2 (1957), pp 218-227.
2. Heinrich Silbergleit, *Die Bevölkerungs- und Berufsverhältnisse im deutschen Reich* i (Berlin, 1930), cited in Jakob Toury, *Soziale und politische Geschichte der Juden in Deutschland 1848-1871. Zwischen Revolution, Reaktion and Emanzipation* (Schriftenreihe des Instituts für Deutsche Geschichte, Universität Tel Aviv 2) (Dusseldorf, 1977), p. 9; cf. also his 'Der Eintritt der Juden ins deutsche Bürgertum' in *Juden in der deutschen Umwelt 1800-1850. Studien zur Frühgeschichte der Emanzipation,* ed. Hans Liebeschütz and Arnold Paucker (Tübingen, 1977), p. 139 ff.; for Austria see 'Die Völker des Reiches' in *Die Habsburger Monarchie 1848-1918,* ed. Adam Wandruszka and Peter Urbanitsch. (Kommission fur die Geschichte der österreich-ungarischen Monarchie 1848-1918) (Vienna, 1980), vol. III/2, p. 881.
3. Treitschke: (*Unsere Aussichten*) 'Über unsere Ostgrenze aber dringt Jahr für Jahr aus der unerschöpflichen polnischen Wiege eine Schar strebsamer hosenverkaufender

jüdischer Jünglinge', quoted in W. Boehlich, *Der Antisemitismusstreit* (Frankfurt, 1975), p. 3. Freytag's essay was published anonymously in the *Grenzboten*, 3 (1849); here he speaks of 'the Jewish element' as 'a disease in the life of the Eastern portion of Prussia which can only be cured by rigorous means'. Earlier in the essay he outlined the problem as he saw it: 'The position of Silesia on the frontier of Poland and Galicia favours a continual influx of Polish huckstering Jews, and this Jewish element that comes from the East begins the process of development in the first generation with us. The second generation goes to Berlin, the third to Frankfurt. Since it is here that the distillation begins, it follows that most of the filth remains with us'. I quote here Bramsted's translation from his pioneering study, originally published as his doctoral dissertation under Karl Mannheim in the London School of Economics, cited in Ernst Kohn-Bramstedt, *Aristocracy and the middle classes in Germany; social types in German literature 1830-1890* (London, 1937), pp 135 and 134. (2nd ed., 1964 under Kohn Bramsted).

4.   Ernest Hamburger, *Juden im öffentlichen Leben Deutschlands. Regierungsmitglieder, Beamte und Parlamentarier in der monarchischen Zeit 1848-1918* (Tübingen, 1968), p. 7.

5.   Gerald Stourzh, 'Galten die Juden als Nationalität Altösterreichs?' in *Prag-Czernowitz-Jerusalem. Der österreichische Staat und die Juden vom Zeitalter des Absolutismus bis zum Ende der Monarchie* (Studia Judaica Austriaca X), ed. Anna M. Drabek, Mordechai Eliav and G.S., (Eisenstadt, 1984), p. 74.

6.   Toury, *Geschichte,*, p. 37. Where in 1840 40% of Prussian Jews lived in Posen, by 1910 43% lived in the Greater Berlin area: cf. Hamburger, *Juden*, p. 29 and Julian Barty's, 'Grand Duchy of Poznan under Prussian rule. Changes in the economic position of the Jewish population 1815-1848', *LBYB*, 17 (1972), p. 202. The increase in Vienna's Jewish population was even more significant; it grew by some 2800%, from under 0·3% to c. 10% of the total population, between 1800 and 1900, Wandruszka, *Habsburger Monarchie*, vol. II/1, p. 47.

7.   Cf. R. Rürup in discussion of: Werner J. Cahnman, 'Village and Small-town Jews in Germany. A typology', *LBYD*, 19 (1974), p. 133.

8.   D.S. Landes, 'The Jewish Merchant. Typology and Stereotypology in Germany', *LBYB*, 19 (1974), p. 15; also Hamburger, p. 19.

9.   R. Rürup, 'Judenemanzipation und bürgerliche Gesellschaft in Deutschland' in *Emanzipation und Antisemitismus. Studien zur 'Judenfrage' der bürgerlichen Gesellschaft* (Kritische Studien zur Geschichtswissenschaft 15) (Göttingen, 1975), pp 14, 26 f.

10. Landes, op. cit., p. 15.

11. Hamburger, op. cit., p. 30 and his note 14.

12. Marjorie Lamberti, 'The Prussian government and the Jews. Official behaviour and policy-making in the Wilhelmine era', *LBYD*, 17 (1972), p. 6.

13. Cf. Carl Cohn, 'The Road to Conversion', *LBYD*, 6 (1961), pp 259 ff.

14. Peter Pulzer, 'Religious and Judicial Appointments in Germany 1869-1918', *LBYB*, 28 (1983), pp 185 and 201 f.; cf. also Rürup, 'Emancipation and Crisis — The "Jewish Question" in Germany 1850-1890', ibid., p. 25.

15. Rürup, 'German Liberalism and the Emancipation of the Jews', *LBYD*, 20 (1975), p. 59.

16. Rürup, *Emancipation und Antisemitismus*, p. 18.

17. Jakob Katz, 'The German-Jewish Utopia of Emancipation' in *Emancipation and Assimilation. Studies in Modern Jewish History* (Farnborough, 1972), pp 92 and 102-110.

18. *Reminiscences of my life*, transl. by Katherine Chetwynd, vol. i (London, 1890), p. 3.

19. Rürup, *Emanzipation und Antisemitismus,* p. 36; Rürup also draws attention in the same volume to Marx's point in his *Zur Kritik der hegelschen Rechtsphilosophie* that the German bourgeoisie failed to see their own emancipation in terms of the universal emancipation of man, in 'Anhang: Emanzipation — Anmerkungen zur Begriffs-geschichte', p. 130.

20. *Debit and Credit.* A novel, transl. by Mrs Malcolm (London, 1857); *Debtor and Creditor. A Romance from the German of Gustav Freytag* by William Stewart (London, Blackwood's London Library, 1857); *Debit and Credit,* transl. by Lucy Caroline Cumming, with a preface by C.C.J. Bunsen, 2 vols (Edinburgh, 1857).

21. Quoted in: Paul M. Kennedy, *The rise of the Anglo-German antagonism 1860-1914* (London, 1980), p. 114 (ch. 6 of Kennedy's book, *Religious and Cultural Connections,* provides useful background to Freytag's reception in Britain in the nineteenth century).

22. 'Der Streit über das Judentum in der Musik' (*Grenzboten*, 22, 1869) in *Gesammelte Werke*, 16 (Leipzig, 2nd ed., 1897), p. 321. Ironically *Die Grenzboten* was founded by a Jew, Ignaz Kuranda (in 1841).

23. Auerbach refers to Freytag as a man 'den ich sehr liebe' (1851), 'der mir ein wirklicher Freund ist' (1859), *B.A. Briefe an seinen Freund Jakob Auerbach. Ein biographisches Denkmal* (Frankfurt, 1884), vol. I, pp 84, and 115.

24. On the association cf. Barbara Suchy, 'Verein zur Abwehr des Antisemitismus (I). From its Beginning to the First World War', *LBYB*, 28 (1983), p. 202 f.; Landes, op. cit., p. 11.

25. Landes, op. cit., p. 11.

26. Leon Poliakov, *The History of Anti-Semitism* (London, 1966), vol. i, p. 242. Useful introductions to the stereotyping of the Jew in literature: Edgar Rosenberg, *From Shylock to Svengali* (Stanford, California, 1960) and Pierre Angel, *Le personnage juif dans le roman allemand 1855-1915. La racine littéraire de l'antisémitisme de l'Outre Rhin* (Montreal, 1973), which also treats of Freytag.

27. It would be interesting to make a comparative study of genres in the presentation of the Jew in nineteenth-century German literature. Popular comedy — including Nestroy — tended to retain the traditional notion of the Jew as funny man in the mid-century at a time when prose fiction was already consciously striving to promote a positive counter stereotype. Kauffmann, *Der Dorfjude,* 1841, Auerbach, etc.

28. Fritz Stern in the discussion of papers by L. Cecil, Reinhard Rürup and Monika Richarz in *LBYB*, 20 (1975), p. 80.

29. Cf. Henry Wassermann, 'The Fliegende Blätter as a Source for the Social History of German Jews', *LBYB*, 28 (1983), pp 93 ff.

30. *Gustav Freytags Werke* (Hamburg, n.d.), vol. 7, p. 60. Compare his statement in *Der Streit über das Judentum in der Musik* (op. cit., p. 321): 'wir halten einen ernsten Angriff auf die jüdischen Menschen unter uns nach keiner Richtung für zeitgemäss, nicht in Politik, nicht in Geschichte, nicht in Wissenschaft und Kunst, denn auf allen diesen Gebieten sind unsere Mitbürger israelitischen Glaubens werthe Bundesgenossen', though he adds 'es hat Jahre gegeben, in denen die Stimmführer einer wüsten Demokratie zum grossten Teile junge Männer jüdischen Glaubens waren'. The different values implicitly ascribed to 'israelitisch' as against 'jüdisch' are perhaps worthy of note.

31. But of course Bernhard is a physical cripple and dies, symbolically, in the course of the story.

32. Bernard Lazare, *Antisemitism. Its history and causes* (London, 1967), p. 162. Lazare points to the currency of 'an exaggerated conception of the role which Jews have played in the development and organization of industrial society, a conception in which the Jews appear as the representatives of the revolutionary spirit against the spirit of established order'.

33. Hans Otto Horch has drawn attention to the anomalies of Jewish reception of the novel, as documented in the columns of the liberal Jewish paper, the *Allgemeine Zeitung des Judenthums*, edited from 1837-1889 by Ludwig Phillipson. I am grateful to Dr Horch for allowing me to see part of the manuscript of his Habilitationsschrift: *Conditio Judaica. Juden und Judentum im Spiegel liberaler Erzählliteratur und liberaler jüdischer Literaturkritik* (Aachen, 1984), p. 392 f. (to be published shortly).

34. Bartys, op. cit., p. 202.

35. The 8th edition of the stenography text appeared in 1920. For details of editions cf. Heinsius, *Allgemeiner Bücherlexikon,* Leipzig, 1852 ff., vols 12-19; Hinrichs, *Fünfjahrs-Katalog*, Leipzig, 1891 ff., vols 9-13; *Deutsches Bücherverzeichnis*, Leipzig, 1916 ff., vols 1-4; cf. also Michael Kienzle's study, *Der Erfolgsroman. Zur Kritik seiner politischen Oekonomie bei Gustav Freytag und Eugenie Marlitt* (Stuttgart, 1975).

36. *Allgemeine Zeitung des Judenthums,* 50 (1886), pp 547-50. ('Die Juden in Gustav. Freytags Dichtungen', zu seinem 70. Geburtstag von G. Deutsch).

37. Rürup, 'Emancipation and Crisis', op. cit., *LBYB*, 28 (1983), p. 17.

38. Landes, op. cit., p. 23.

Popular Religion and Irreligion in Victorian Fiction

DAVID HEMPTON

Victorian novels, because of their quantity and quality, have been irresistable quarries of information for social historians, especially those who, like the Victorians, are interested in religion. Quarrying is, of course, rough work and is generally more concerned with extracting raw materials than in appreciating the landscape within which they are found. Literary critics have therefore been rightly suspicious of a certain kind of historical approach to literature which has been described by E.M. Forster as a kind of pseudo scholarship.[1] Conversely, empirically minded historians have often had their nerves set on edge by the amateurish historical methods employed by some literary critics. Interdisciplinary study, to coin Michael Wolff's phrase, seems to teeter on the brink of becoming anti-disciplinary study.[2] Problems emerge most commonly when literature is made to yield more fruit than it can reasonably bear, or when historians bring to it a lack of imagination and critical sophistication. The more difficult the source, therefore, the sharper ought to be the historian's tools.[3]

As with all writers of fiction, Victorian novelists, both consciously and unconsciously, have left pictures of their society. They are not meant to be exact reproductions of reality, even supposing that such a thing were possible with any kind of literature, and they all use distorting lenses, both deliberately and unintentionally. These may include the sex and social class of the novelists, their artistic purposes, their family backgrounds and regional preoccupations, their use of fiction for deliberate propaganda or for material rewards, their ignorance and personal grudges, and the intellectual limitations imposed by their lack of information and acceptance of current ideologies. These 'distortions', most of which are shared by historians in any case, are not necessarily a disadvantage from an historical point of view. Novelists' misconceptions are themselves revealing, as are the features of their society which they take for granted. Novelists can, moreover, tell us what it felt like to live under certain conditions in a way that historians cannot rival. Few would disagree with J.J. Massingham's comment on *Lark Rise to Candleford* the 'Flora Thompson does not reconstruct the shattered fabric like an historian nor illustrate and analyse it like a sociologist: she reanimates it.'[4]

Nevertheless, using novels to shed light on Victorian religion has particular dangers, because the novelists' own personal experiences count for so much. The stakes are therefore high in this kind of enquiry, but so too are the potential benefits, especially at the popular level where alternative sources are thinnest. Indeed it is surprising that popular religion has attracted so little attention from nineteenth-century historians and literary critics by comparison with the exhaustive treatment of novels of faith and doubt, and of those representing specific theological traditions.[5] The aim of this essay then is to look at Victorian religion in *town* and *country* through the eyes of some of the period's most eminent novelists and autobiographers. Their perceptions may help revise some of the traditional historical assumptions about the religious life of the period, though by definition these are merely suggestive and not conclusive.

I.   URBAN POPULAR RELIGION

First, the perplexing mystery of the place was, who belonged to the eighteen denominations? Because whoever did, the labouring people did not. It was very strange to walk through the streets on a Sunday morning, and note how few of *them* the barbarous jangling of bells that was driving the sick and nervous mad, called away from their own close rooms, from the corners of their own streets, where they lounged listlessly, gazing at all the church and chapel going, as at a thing with which they had no manner of concern.

Charles Dickens, *Hard Times* (1854)

The essential value and truth of Dickens's writings have been unwisely lost sight of by many thoughtful persons, merely because he presents his truth with some colour of caricature. Unwisely, because Dickens's caricature, though often gross, is never mistaken. Allowing for his manner of telling them, the things he tells us are always true. I wish that he could think it right to limit his brilliant exaggeration to works written only for public amusement; and when he takes up a subject of high national importance, such as that which he handled in *Hard Times*, that he would use severer and more accurate analysis . . . But let us not lose the use of Dickens's wit and insight, because he chooses to speak in a circle of stage fire.

John Ruskin, 'Unto This Last' (1860)

Whatever the value of Dickens's fiction for social historians in general, informed critics are highly sceptical of the evidential value of his treatment of religion. His own presuppositions and biases are generally too near the surface.[6] He admired instinctive goodness and a capacity for fancy and fun. He valued tolerance, human solidarity and good-natured charity. Above all he approved of a humanitarian form of religion which connected with the daily concerns of ordinary people. By contrast, he hated hypocrisy, dogma, enthusiasm, ritualism, nostalgic medievalism, Roman Catholicism and mysticism. He particularly disliked the revivalist/fundamentalist wing of dissent with its uneducated preachers, grimy chapels and rampant sectarianism. His novels are full of 'little Bethels' and dissenting preachers with greasy complexions, bulbous eyes, lank hair, squints and physical deformities. In speech they bawl, snivel and mutilate the English language. Even the names are revealing: Melchisedech Howler, Jabez Fireworks and Mr Glib. So clever was Dickens's language, and this is where literature is at its most pernicious from the historian's viewpoint, that his anti-dissenting rhetoric, which was itself built on an eighteenth-century dramatic tradition, has been enormously successful in convincing posterity of the religious hypocrisy of Victorian England. As Horace Walpole's writings have so lamentably proved, the better and more quotable the writer, the more damage he may cause in falsyifying the past. Why then start with Dickens on religion? Ruskin's footnote in 'Unto This Last' is suggestive.[7] Although echoing the wish of many historians that Dickens would use 'severer and more accurate analysis' in his treatment of serious subjects, Ruskin sees, as with a Von Gogh painting, that his bold brush strokes are curiously effective in highlighting the truth of his social observation. In the passage on Coketown religion quoted earlier, Dickens identified two issues which have subsequently occasioned much debate among social historians. First, he drew attention to the apparent apathy of the labouring poor towards denominational religion and, in addition, the inadequacy of contemporary utilitarian and statistical diagnoses of that problem. Second, he pointed to the proliferation of sects as one aspect of a much broader lack of social cohesion.

There was, of course, nothing new about the observation that the labouring poor were less than avid church attenders. The rapid growth of towns, methodism, and radical politics at the end of the eighteenth century had provoked a good deal of heart searching among concerned bishops and clergy.[8] The core of the problem was perceived to be working-class infidelity in the manufacturing towns. Faced with the problem of religious competition in an apparently depressed market, the denominations responded, understandably, by trying to improve the efficiency of their ecclesiastical institutions in a fairly crude utilitarian way. There were demands for more churches, more educated clergy, more services, more frequent observation of the sacraments, more daily and Sunday schools, and more rigorous visitation returns.[9] This approach is satirised by Disraeli in *Coningsby* when Rigby states that 'want of religious faith was solely occasioned by want of churches'. According to Rigby, Peel's ecclesiastical commission had the problem of infidelity under control, and the real question of the day was the architectural style of the new churches.[10]

Early Victorian novelists, for all their prejudices, selectivity and artistic colouring were, on the whole, more astute observers of the causes of urban popular infidelity than were religious and political leaders. The latter after all had to arrive at practical solutions for practical problems whereas the novelists were relatively independent of institutional controls and allegiances. Insights into popular infidelity from early Victorian literature may be conveniently grouped under three headings: the differences between urban and rural religion; the distinction between belief and practice; and the poverty of the religion of the poor.

In *Silas Marner* George Eliot creatively inverts the conventional pattern of a relatively religious countryside contrasted with irreligious towns which seemed to have been irrefutably demonstrated by the census of religous worship in 1851.[11] What is hinted at through Silas, however, is that the religion of the countryside was a rather pale mixture of deference, dependency, custom and community solidarity whereas popular urban dissent was based more on voluntary commitment to religious associations.[12] Social historians have indeed confirmed that English rural migrants and Irish catholic peasants were not as religious, at least in a conventional sense, as rural romantics would have it.[13] It took time to create alternative church and chapel cultures in towns, and many passed through the net untouched. But urban living was not necessarily the cause of popular infidelity: it simply forced the issue more than rural living had done.

Moreover, the novels of Mrs Gaskell and Charles Kingsley suggest that the relative absence of formal religious observances did not necessarily mean a lack of christian belief and practice in early Victorian cities. *Mary Barton* and *North and South* in particular are suffused with religious values in facing death and disaster, in establishing a rudimentary moral code, in neighbourly concern in times of economic hardship and depression, and in developing a sturdy respectability in family life. How far these were the preoccupations of a Unitarian minister's wife on domestic visitation duty and how far they accurately reflect the views of the non-dissolute

Manchester poor is for the social historian to unravel. But the novels, supported by oral evidence relating to the late nineteenth century, suggest that denominational adherence may not be the best guide to the religion and morality of the Victorian working class.[14] Such a view in no way undermines the importance of sectarian allegiances for those who did attend church.

That these were a minority in Victorian cities has never been challenged, and the novels show why. The sheer grind of poverty and disappointment, a concern for tangible objectives rather than after-life speculations, the dowdiness of religion compared with popular recreations and public houses,[15] and the distrust of fervent religion among male workers because it introduced unnecessary tensions in a culture seeking a convivial consensus, all played their part. In addition, through admittedly untypical characters like John Barton and Alton Locke, the novelists portray a nascent class consciousness fuelled by dislike of bourgeois christian morality and hypocrisy.[16] This chimes in with both Susan Budd's work on working class biographies and with E.P. Thompson's view that religion's most serious disadvantage was that it did not offer working men practical solutions to problems of everyday life, with the possible exceptions of Sunday schools and religious welfare agencies like the St. Vincent de Paul societies.[17] The novels of William Hale White are the best literary expression of the view that religion, to be of any use to working people, had to have a clear social function. For those who gathered in Drury Lane 'their trouble was not the forgiveness of sins, the fallacies of Arianism, the personality of the Holy Ghost, or the doctrine of the Eucharist. They all *wanted* something distinctly. They had great gaping needs which they longed to satisfy, intensely practical and special.'[18]

Less grandiosely, Dickens acknowledged that the drabness of urban life required tangible compensations like fun, liquor and opium which the churches could not be expected to provide. What they could do was build more churches, but they found, as with the British soccer and film industries in more recent times, that institutions cannot stem the tide of indifference caused by complex social changes merely by improving their facilities. The acuteness of Dickens's observation of early Victorian religion is marred by a paradox in his own writing which is worthy of wider application. The so-called sympathiser with the poor disliked the enthusiastic and credulous religious behaviour of the poor. Here indeed is a recurrent theme in Victorian literature. Leslie Stephen, for example, in 'Religion as a Fine Art' wrote that 'a religion to be of any value must retain a grasp upon the great mass of mankind and the mass are hopelessly vulgar and prosaic'.[19] Kingsley's solution to this dilemma was to show that the crudity of the religion of the poor was due mainly to inadequate leadership. In *Two Years Ago* Kingsley described a Bryanite methodist meeting in which an ignorant preacher exploited the psychological weakness of women and teenage girls by cultivating an excessive fear of hell. He was on the verge of creating mass hysteria when an Anglican major of aristocratic bearing saved the little congregation from disaster by appealing to manliness, reason and love.[20] Kingsley's mixture of anglican, male and racial chauvinism has not worn well, but he does point up a profound tension in both Victorian literature and the religious denominations themselves. Almost all of the early Victoian novelists and churchmen wanted to reclaim the poor for some form of religion, if only for purposes of social control, but none of them liked the messiness of the religion of the poor. One interesting sidelight on this issue is the way in which John Wesley and early methodism, after a century of abusive criticism, came to be admired by the early Victorians, Kingsley included, as a shining example of well-controlled plebeian religion.[21] Victorian methodism, however, was scarcely of the same standard and by the end of the period it took someone of Samuel Butler's cynical hedonism to conclude that the poor were both irredeemably vulgar and perfectly able to get along without any kind of religious paternalism.[22]

A second aspect of Victorian religion identified by Dickens in *Hard Times* was the proliferation of religious denominations. This was not a new phenomenon, but by the time of the religious census in 1851 its urban manifestations had become more obvious. The roots of the problem went back to the period 1780-1830 when a complex set of circumstances and crises resulted in the emergence of a new class society. In England this was accompanied first of all by an explosion of non-denominational renewal and then inexorably by a drive for denominational discipline.[23] By 1830 the old denominational order, which had been solidified by the Act of Toleration, had given way to a new one. This process was facilitated by the weakness of the English state and church. The period 1828-51 was therefore accompanied by bitter sectarian conflicts which in large measure gave the character to the politics of the period. What Disraeli described in *Tancred* as 'an anarchy of creeds' had by 1890 resulted in 244 officially registered denominations, though even that was probably an underassessment.[24] Thus Samuel Wilberforce's comment that 'the tendency of all things round us is to break our people into separate and unsympathising classes' applied also to religion which many had hoped would act as social cement in the class divisions of mid-nineteenth-century England.[25]

Early Victorian novelists were therefore writing in a period of social and religious fragmentation, three results of which are evident in their fiction. First, there is a reduction in the number of genuinely historical novels after the fashion of Scott.[26] These give way to novels searching out the background to the early Victorian epoch. Charlotte Brontë, George Eliot, Hale White and Mrs Gaskell all used this technique quite deliberately. Second, many of the 'condition of England' novels show a desire for social cohesion accompanied by dislike of class-conscious organizations and religious sectarianism. Trade unionism, chartism and evangelical dissent are therefore almost universally vilified, even at the expense of factual accuracy.[27] Disraeli's description of Wodgate (Willenhall) in *Sybil*, for example, is based on Blue Books, but he deliberately (and inconsistently) exaggerated the irreligion of Wodgate because dissenting efforts did not fit his ideological scheme.[28] Similarly, though less dishonestly, Dickens, for artistic purposes, emphasised the divisiveness of trade unionism in *Hard Times* while writing a more favourable eyewitness account of the Preston strike for his magazine *Household Words*.[29] Dickens's aim in *Hard Times* was to highlight the inhumanity of exclusive and intolerant organizations, however worthwhile their cause, and the same idea is at the root of much fictional criticism of dissenting religion. 'These cramping cults', wrote H.G. Wells from bitter experience, 'do indeed take an enormous toll of human love and happiness . . . they make frightful breaches in human solidarity'.[30] In a period of apparent social fragmentation it is not surprising that the novelists should pinpoint the divisiveness of dissent as its most serious evil. Victorian fiction emphasises therefore the Calvinism of dissent (though most nineteenth-century nonconformists were not Calvinists), its detrimental effect on family cohesion, as in *Alton Locke* and *The New Machiavelli,* and its contribution to the ugliness and disorder of the urban landscape by building 'low-pitched gables up dingy streets'[31] and riding roughshod over ancient parish boundaries. In a society nervous about its culture and stability dissenting religion, especially of a crudely populist variety, was castigated for being both vulgar and divisive. Such attacks from the Victorian intelligentsia were in part a self-fulfilling prophecy as the popular dissenting press railed against the evils of fiction and gloried in their own lack of worldly wisdom.[32] Literature is itself a vibrant historical agent.

A third characteristic of early Victorian fiction was an attempt to recover an organic society in which religion would once again act as a cohesive force. For Disraeli this ideal was to be realised through a national church fulfillings its holy mission to the poor accompanied by England's ancient community rituals.[33] Such medieval nostalgia was dismissed by Marx and Engels in the *Communist Manifesto* as being 'always ludicrous in its effect, through total incapacity to comprehend the march of modern history'.[34] For Kingsley the ideal was a marriage of the cooperative spirit of socialism with the moral goodness of christianity. Inevitably this mixture contained too much christianity for doctrinaire socialists and too much socialism for Kingsley's anglican colleagues.[35] One unfortunate by-product of history's unfavourable judgement on the practicality of Disraeli's and Kingsley's organic ideas has been the relative neglect of serious research on the role of the Church of England in Victorian towns and cities.

In contrast to Disraeli and Kingsley, Dicken's concern for human solidarity, tolerance, disinterested charity and fun was an attempt to develop an older English consensus on the social function of religion. As with Flora Thompson's treatment of religion in a village community, Dickens unselfconsciously draws attention to a greater degree of religio-moral homogeneity in English society than is immediately obvious from historians' concentration on the bitter sectarian conflicts of the Victorian period. According to sensitive writers of fiction, including Mrs Gaskell, the unchurched were not necessarily the ungodly, denominational hagiographers notwithstanding.

II.   RURAL POPULAR RELIGION

Observing these people narrowly, even when the iron hand of misfortune has shaken them from their unquestioning hold on the world, one sees little trace of religion, still less of a distinctively Christian creed. Their belief in the Unseen, so far as it manifests itself at all, seems to be rather of a pagan kind; their moral notions, though held with strong tenacity, seem to have no standard beyond hereditary custom.

George Eliot, *The Mill on the Floss* (1860)

It is hard to avoid the conclusion that paganism was dominant and Christianity recessive in popular religion. Paganism was rarely christianized, but Christianity was often paganized.

James Obelkevich, *Religion and Rural Society* (1976)

The serious study of popular religion, defined helpfully by Natalie Davis as that which is practised and experienced as distinct from that which is defined and prescribed, has been pioneered by Reformation and early modern European historians.[36] By comparison with the modern period their inferior denominational, institutional and statistical information combined with their superior ritualistic, legal and devotional material, has

led to more creative, if inevitably tenuous, reconstructions of sixteenth-
and seventeenth-century popular religion.

One important result of this work has been to show that Victorians, by
exaggerating the religiosity of the medieval past, over-reacted to the
popular infidelity of their own day. This distortion was reinforced by the
Gothic revival and by the renewed interest in the visible past. Thus, by
isolating a problem they in fact created one. Moreover, this Victorian
misconception has bedevilled twentieth-century attempts to reconstruct
Victorian religion. Our preoccupations have been largely theirs. Consequently, until the timely appearance of James Obelkevich's fine study of
rural religion in Lincolnshire, nineteenth-century religious historians have
been more concerned with the *changes* occasioned by urban, nonconformist, and catholic growth than with the massive *continuities* of
anglicanism, popular religion, and rural society.[37] There is also a problem
of evidence, because ecclesiastical records, in the main, deal with clergy,
buildings, services, schools and discipline, whereas those at the bottom of
the social pyramid are conspicuously silent. As a result, Obelkevich was
driven, rather more frequently than he wished one suspects, to the use of
folklore, impressionistic literature and Victorian fiction to illuminate the
dark corners of rural religion. With this kind of evidence the social
historian has to take the risk of being misled in the effort to understand the
nuances of popular religious belief and practice. This is particularly true of
rural religion, because the most helpful novelists, George Eliot and
Thomas Hardy, are also on occasions the most misleading. If properly used, however, literature is of use to the historian in three main areas. First,
Victorian novels suggest that the conventional boundaries constructed by
empirical historians between religion and irreligion, christianity and superstition, 'traditional' and 'modern' attitudes, and even between the
denominations and the sexes have been too rigid. Second, the novels offer
subtle and otherwise unobtainable insights into the social function of
religion in rural communities. Third, they introduce new, and sometimes
surprising, dimensions to the debate about the nature and pace of
'secularization' in rural England.

On the question of boundaries Obelkevich has clearly established that
there was an enormous gulf between the world of popular religion and the
worlds of church and chapel, but this is not to say that the same people
could not find themselves on different sides of this gulf at different times
without any apparent sense of incongruity.[38] Flora Thompson, for example, estimates that nine out of ten Lark Rise inhabitants would have
declared themselves members of the Church of England having been

christened and married in the parish church.[39] In addition, they buried their dead at church, attended festivals at Christmas, Easter, and harvest time, visited the rectory on May Day, qualified themselves for the valuable charities dispensed by clerical families, paraded their finery and singing voices on Sundays, and could be roused at particular times to exhibit half-hearted displays of anti-catholic sentiment. The majority, of course, never darkened the church's door outside festival time unless closely bound by deference to squire or clergyman, and most of them, especially the men, resented clerical visits, particularly if the subject of religion was mentioned. According to Flora Thompson most Lark Rise residents were also perfectly at home in the world of folk tales, ghosts, haunted places and devil's stories, but rather from the point of view of rural entertainment than from dread of unfriendly supernatural visitations. Lark Rise morality was similarly ambivalent. Illegitimacy was looked upon with a mixture of sympathy and disapproval, with the latter giving way to the former after the birth of a child, but adultery was subject to community hostility expressed in rough music and skimmington rides, while lying and stealing were repudiated without benefit of ceremony. Social utility and social consensus were therefore more important determinants of Lark Rise religion and morality than were church dogmas or popular superstitions. This is at the root of the suggestion made by both Flora Thompson and George Eliot in *Silas Marner* that too much religious enthusiasm by way of church-going and religious devotion was regarded as antisocial behaviour by those who wished not to be placed at a disadvantage in their dealings with the Almighty.[40] Popular rural religion was therefore predominantly syncretistic in belief and inextricably bound up with community morality in practice. The traditional labels of christianity and paganism are thus insufficiently flexible to describe historical reality.

Another boundary highlighted by Victorian fiction is that between anglicanism and nonconformity, church and chapel. The sharpness of this division and the degree of hostility occasioned by it depended largely on local social and economic circumstances. The tensions of an emerging class society were commonly translated into religious forms, which accounts, for example, for the close links between agricultural trade unionism and Primitive Methodism in Lincolnshire and East Anglia where anti-anglican sentiment and the political objectives of farm labourers were two sides of the same coin.[41] With regionality and chronology all important in assessing the relationship between church and chapel in rural communities, there is little value in broad generalisations from fictional fragments. Nevertheless, literature, especially of an autobiographical kind, suggests that denominational allegiances and conflicts were more complex than mere tables of membership statistics would allow. Edmund Gosse's *Father and Son*, for example, shows how the little Devonshire Plymouth Brethren assembly was built on the foundations of earlier Wesleyan Methodist and Bible Christian evangelism. In such small communities the denominational label counted for less than the simplicity of the religious forms and the social bonds of the membership. What is particularly valuable about Gosse's portrait is that it restores a sense of the dignity, albeit tinged with comic absurdity, of humble rural religion, which is all too rare in ideologically committed histories. 'I wish I could paint', he writes, 'in colours so vivid, that my readers could perceive what their little society consisted of, this quaint collection of humble, conscientious, ignorant and gentle persons. In chronicle or fiction I have never been fortunate enough to meet with anything which resembled them. The caricatures of enmity and worldly scorn are as crude to my memory, as the unction of religious conventionality is featureless.' [42]

This is in the same spirit as Flora Thompson's treatment of Lark Rise methodists, or 'Devil dodgers' as they were called for their practice of attending parish church on Sunday morning and their own cottage meetings in the evening. The author shows how the methodists, and the catholics for that matter, drove a thin wedge into the anglican uniformity of village religion, but they were relatively easily accommodated so long as they refrained from overtly attempting conversions. Similarly the methodists accepted the centrality of the parish church in village religion until a ritualistic vicar offended their evangelical sensibilities. Flora Thompson's account of methodist meetings rings with the authenticity of mingled sympathy and gentle criticism. She captures the warmth of religious enthusiasm transmitted through extempore prayer, lively singing, fervent preaching and mutual confession. The weekday reserve and godly discipline of the methodists gave way on Sunday evenings to shining eyes and loving expressions. On the other hand, she pokes fun at the exaggerated and highly coloured testimonies of the methodist faithful, the religious equivalents of public house yarns, and at the uneducated preachers basking so self-consciously in their religious limelight. The exemplary lives of the methodists in Lark Rise earned community respect, but there is evidence to suggest that methodists were singled out for harsh treatment if their moral pretensions failed to match their moral practice. [43] Hypocrisy was therefore more resented than religious enthusiasm.

Other boundary areas of rural religion still awaiting proper historical treatment are those of age and sex. Several surveys of religion in town and country have shown that women were more faithful in performing their religious duties than men and that changes in the forms of worship during the century were partly responsible for this pattern.[44] For example, the great upheaval caused by the replacement of the village band's rough music by the more polished tones of Miss Day's organ in *Under the Greenwood Tree* was a frequent occurrence in anglican parish churches. The organists who succeeded the parish clerks and village bands were chiefly the wives and daughters of parsons, squires and farmers and 'were much less independent than their predecessors and far more likely to be subservient to the clergyman'. Paradoxically therefore, the 'improvements' in religious worship instigated by reforming anglican clergy, especially from the High Church wing, inexorably separated the Church of England from male village culture. 'Whatever the wishes of the villagers', Obelkevich concludes, 'anglican services became more dignified, more feminine, and more clerical.'[45] The most insightful account of this transformation is in Samuel Butler's *The Way of all Flesh,* which, although not published until 1903 is based on the author's acute social and religious observations of the early and mid Victorian periods. In particular, Butler gives his impression of the changes in worship in the parish of Battersby-on-the-Hill (really Langar in Nottinghamshire where Butler's father, Thomas, was rector), a small village of 500 inhabitants. At the beginning of the period the old Norman church was falling apart, but it was reasonably well attended by the village faithful, including the agricultural craftsmen and labourers. The worship was accompanied by a doleful gallery choir with rudimentary musical instruments. Butler described their efforts as 'discordant, but infinitely pathetic', and he detected a wild and haunting strain which reminded him of pre-Reformation litanies, psalm singing on emigrant ships, and Welsh Methodist camp meetings. Some of this is mere nostalgia for primitive rural religion which seemed to take hold of the mid-Victorian intelligentsia in reaction to cities, ritualism and red-brick conventicles. Butler's opinions, moreover, need careful handling because many of them are filtered through hatred of his father's religion.[46] Nevertheless, Butler's account of Battersby parish church half a century later is revealing. The church had been carefully restored, which, according to Butler was the most distinctive and characteristic feature of the Victorian age, and in it

there was a harmonium played by a sweet-looking girl with a choir of school children around her, and they chanted the canticles to the most correct of chants, and they sang Hymns Ancient and Modern; the high pews were gone, nay, the very gallery in which the old choir had sung was removed as an accursed thing which might remind the people of the high places . . .

But in the evening later on I saw three very old men come chuckling out of a dissenting chapel. There was a look of content upon their faces which made me feel certain they had been singing; not doubtless with the old glory of the violoncello, the clarinet and the trombone, but still songs of Sion and no new-fangled papistry.[47]

The social supporters of this effete worship were of a higher level than their predecessors, but otherwise not much had changed. Butler describes them as good sensible folk whose ideal was the maintenance of the status quo and who 'would have been equally horrified at hearing the Christian religion doubted, and at seeing it practised'.[48]

Another dimension to the inequality of the sexes was the way in which clergymen were perceived by men and women in small communities. The fragmentary literary evidence suggests that women accepted the refinements of the clergy, both anglican and Wesleyan, as an attractive expression of cultivated gentlemanly values, whereas men with an emerging, if still inchoate class consciousness, were more resentful. In Thomas Hardy's short story, *The Distracted Preacher,* Stockdale, the young Wesleyan fresh out of theological college, is interestingly called 'an old woman' by the village smugglers,[49] and similar tensions of class, age and manliness are evident in the confrontation between the new vicar and the village band in *Under the Greenwood Tree.*[50] Flora Thompson is explicit in *Lark Rise to Candleford*, as is D.H. Lawrence in his autobiographical novel *Sons and Lovers*, that men resented clerical interference in their households much more than women.[51]

These isolated references, of course, prove nothing, but they do raise interesting questions about anglican attempts to put its own house in order after 1835 by building and restoring churches and parsonages, increasing the percentage of university trained clergy and having more cultivated services. These reforms, laudable though they were in terms of energy and zeal, showed little genuine understanding of the role of religion in rural culture. Ironically the Church's most successful innovation, the harvest thanksgiving service, was in reality a symbolic concession to popular paganism.[52] Nonconformist denominations were not immune from the complex cultural problems faced by the Church of England, but their more enthusiastic religious atmosphere and, crucially, the wider number of acceptable religious (and political) jobs for men to do, delayed the seemingly inexorable processes that were confining religion to the young, the old and the female.

In measuring religious adherence age is yet another flexible boundary which does not show up well in churchgoing statistics. It is now well known that the christian churches, at least in an institutional sense, exercised more influence over the young, through Sunday and day schools, than over any other age group in Victorian England.[53] Moreover, research on a narrow selection of working class biographies has shown that definite conversions to christianity were most common among the age group fourteen to seventeen, and were most prevalent in the context of a revival meeting.[54] A high proportion subsequently lost their faith in mature adulthood, possibly to return to it in old age. The point is that a single life could consist of various phases of faith and doubt, and that the common division between the religious and the irreligious is far too rigid. This is well illustrated in the heroine of George Moore's *Esther Waters* who experiences a Plymouth Brethren upbringing, gives birth to an illegitimate child, marries the owner of a public house cum-gambling den (though she very nearly married a Brethren preacher), is on the receiving end of religious disapproval most of her life, yet still manages to return to a simple faith in older age as much out of nostalgia and consolation as conviction. Esther's life has parallels with her Brethren mistress and companion in old age who likewise found the pressures of life difficult to square with the simplicities of faith. Esther's mistress, Mrs Barfield,

loved to hear Esther tell of her father and the little shop in Barnstaple, of the prayer-meetings and the simple earnestness and narrowness of the faith of those good brethren. Circumstances had effaced, though they had not obliterated, the once sharply marked confines of her religious habits. Her religion was like a garden — a little less sedulously tended than of yore, but no whit less fondly loved.[55]

Moore's fiction, indirectly supported by recent oral evidence, suggests that for the old the influence of nostalgia for their religious past, the need for companionship in the present, and fear of a bleak future all coalesced to revive the dying embers of personal religion.[56] Thus, the early Victorian churches' herculean efforts with the young probably bore unexpected fruit in the aged up to half a century later.

Victorian literature shows, therefore, that the categories constructed by historians to make sense of the period need to be sufficiently flexible to incorporate the complexities of popular religion, but fiction must never be allowed to determine typicality or causality.

A second feature of rural religion illuminated by literature is the complicated relationship between social and religious changes, and in particular, to what historians have called, for want of a better word, 'secularization'.[57] The question is secularization from what, because historians, for obvious evidential reasons, have concentrated more on the external expressions of religious cultures than on the internal psychology of religious beliefs. They have, of course, creatively extrapolated from rituals, festivals and observances, but this folklorish method contains its own biases towards the colourful life of the community as distinct from the mundane life of the individual. Of all the Victorian novelists George Eliot tried harder than anyone before Hardy to uncover the psychological and sociological roots of popular religion, but with limited success. Intuitively she believed that religious views, as with Nancy Lammeter's, in *Silas Marner* were a mixture of 'narrow social traditions, fragments of church doctrine imperfectly understood, and girlish reasonings on her small experience'.[58] But even this triad of social determinism, rudimentary ecclesiastical penetration, and personal experience was overlaid in Nancy's case by subconscious fears of providential hostility against practices such as the adoption of a child. All this is plausible enough, for George Eliot was at home in the world of the provincial English squirearchy, but she was also prepared to dig deeper into the religious mentality of the Raveloe peasantry.

Such strange lingering echoes of the old demon-worship might perhaps even now be caught by the diligent listener among the grey-haired peasantry; for the rude mind with difficulty associates the idea of power and benignity. A shadowy conception of power that by much persuasion can be induced to refrain from inflicting harm, is the shape most easily taken by the sense of the Invincible in the minds of men who have have always been pressed close by primitive wants, and to whom a life of hard toil has never been illuminated by any enthusiastic faith. To them pain and mishap present a far wider range of possibilities than gladness and enjoyment.[59]

This is strikingly similar to Obelkevich's conclusion that popular religion was overwhelmingly pessimistic whereas christianity's soteriology was, at least in theory, relatively optimistic. This also has echoes in *Silas Marner*. Dolly Winthrop, the Raveloe 'good liver' whose theological ignorance was matched by a simple faith in the goodness of God — despite the repeated triumphs of evil in the world — plays an important part in restoring Silas Marner's faith after his unpleasant experiences of popular urban dissent. Despite Dolly's dialect and homely language, however, one can never quite forget George Eliot's own struggle to find meaning and morality in a godless universe.[60] It is in the translation of elite attitudes and concepts into popular consciousness that the interface between history and literature is at its most dangerous for the historian. Moreover, the better the novelist, the greater is the danger of being misled. Everyone knows, for example that Warner, Disraeli's handloom weaver in *Sybil*, is simply mouthing Blue

Book reports in his long soliloquy on working conditions,[61] but Dolly Winthrop's religious views are etched in with considerbly more conviction. This is no mere abstract point, because George Eliot claims that her popular reconstructions are based on personal experiences, and she is often prepared to generalise from particulars, yet the rigid social structure she presents in isolated Raveloe is grossly misleading.[62] Raymond Williams is therefore right to state that 'though George Eliot restored the real inhabitants of rural England to their places in what had been a socially selective landscape, she does not get much further than restoring them *as a landscape*'.[63] Nevertheless, one only has to compare her rural scenes with Trollope's mannered descriptions to see how profoundly she succeeded.

Whatever her weaknesses, George Eliot's treatment of rural religion is unsurpassed until the writings of Thomas Hardy, though Hardy's feel for the English rural landscape and its historical roots is probably more reliable than his rural characterization. Hardy is nevertheless particularly illuminating because he is both 'the educated observer and the passionate participator' in a period of profound social change.[64] He may have exaggerated, as Flora Thompson suggests, the 'social and mental restlessness' at the heart of Jude's tragedy,[65] but he was aware that rural England was not only being changed from the outside by railways, reaping machines, education, the press, and a creeping bureaucracy, but was also changing itself from within by the voluntary capitalization of agriculture to meet new marketing opportunities. Religion, and superstition for that matter, could not survive these changes unchanged.

Religion was itself, moreover, an instrument of change through the evangelical and ritualistic revivals which eventually poked their way into most rural corners. Late Victorian novelists are not only immensely skilful in showing how these changes affected older religious practices, but, more revealingly, they suggest that English local communities were increasingly brought under the umbrella of national religious movements resulting in both greater denominational self-consciousness and in a wider gap between the religious and the irreligious. This paradox of national religious integration combined with increased local differentiation parallels the arguments of early modern British historians about the effects of puritanism and literacy in local communities.[66]

It is hard to resist the conclusion, therefore, that by helping to disrupt the primitive rural consensus upon which a genuinely popular religion depended, fervent religion was the unwitting bearer of secularization. This is not to deny that secularization is a profoundly complex process involving as it must community fragmentation, changes in the security of life, the growth of non-religious popular recreation, and a rudimentary scientism conveyed through education and the media.[67] Thus, a host of incidental comments in Hardy's fiction, from the decline of witches to the phasing out of thees and thous, chimes in with Obelkevich's conclusion that the most important step in the secularization of rural culture was the depersonification of the forces good and evil.[68] To a limited extent therefore, rationality and notions of luck triumphed over personal familiarity with supernatural forces, whether benign or malevolent, in the profound transformation of English rural society at the end of the Victorian age.

Near the end of *Father and Son* Edmund Gosse makes a plea to the reader to imaginatively re-create the kind of religion practised by his father, which had become, according to the author, virtually extinct in the twentieth-century world.[69] Whatever the validity of Gosse's particular point, his plea for a leap of the imagination is central to a proper historical understanding of nineteenth-century religion. Victorian fiction not only facilitates that leap, but in the process shows that the history of popular religion is rather more complicated, and dare one say, important than many ecclesiastical and social historians have supposed.[7]

NOTES AND REFERENCES

1. Valentine Cunningham, *Everywhere spoken against, Dissent in the Victorian novel* (Oxford, 1975), pp 1-7.
2. Michael Wolff, 'Victorian study: an interdisciplinary essay', in *Victorian Studies,* 8, no. 1 (Sept. 1964), pp 59-70.
3. Good recent examples include R.F. Foster, 'Political novels and nineteenth-century history', in *Winchester research papers in the humanities* (Winchester, 1981), and John Lucas, *The literature of change* (Sussex, 1980), especially ch. 2.
4. Flora Thompson, *Lark Rise to Candleford* (with intro. by H.J. Massingham, Penguin edn., 1973), p. 9.
5. See Donald Stone, *Novelists in a changing world* (Harvard, 1972), R.L. Wolff, *Gains and losses, novels of faith and doubt in Victorian England* (London, 1977), pp 513-6, and J.W. Burrow, 'Faith, doubt and unbelief', in Laurence Lerner (ed.), *The Victorians* (London, 1978), pp 153-73.
6. Cunningham, *Everywhere spoken against,* pp 190-230, and Humphry House, *The Dickens world* (Oxford paperback edn., 1961), pp 106-32.
7. John Ruskin, 'Unto this last', ed. by P.M. Yarker (London, 1970), pp 32-3.
8. R.A. Soloway, *Prelates and People, ecclesiastical social thought in England 1783-1852* (London, 1969), pp 55-84.
9. G.F.A. Best, *Temporal Pillars* (Cambridge, 1964), Owen Chadwick, *The Victorian Church,* pt. 1 (London, 1966), and D.N. Hempton, 'Bickersteth, Bishop of Ripon: the episcopate of a mid-Victorian evangelical', in *Northern History,* xvii (1981), pp 183-202.

10. *Coningsby*, Bk. 3, Ch. 2.

11. D.M. Thompson, *Nonconformity in the nineteenth century* (London, 1972), pp 147-55, K.S. Inglis, 'Patterns of religious worship in 1851', *Journal of Ecclesiastical History*, 11 (1960), pp 74-86, and Robert Currie, Alan Gilbert and Lee Horsley (ed.), *Churches and church-goers: patterns of church growth in the British Isles since 1700* (Oxford, 1977).

12. *Silas Marner*, Chs. 1, 2 and 10.

13. D.M. Thompson, 'The churches and society in nineteenth-century England: a rural perspective', in *Studies in Church History*, 8 (1972), pp 267-76, and S.J. Connolly, *Priests and people in pre-famine Ireland 1780-1845* (Dublin, 1982).

14. Hugh McLeod, *Religion and the working class in nineteenth-century Britain* (London, 1984). I am indebted to Dr McLeod for showing me his paper 'New perspectives on Victorian working class religion: the oral evidence', to be published in *Oral History* (1986).

15. Brian Harrison, 'Religion and recreation in nineteenth-century England', in *Past and Present*, 38 (Dec., 1967), pp 98-125. See also *Esther Waters*, Ch. 3 where the heroine's stepfather refers to the Plymouth Brethren as 'your hymn-and-misery lot'.

16. *Mary Barton*, Ch. 35 and *Alton Locke*, Chs. 1, 4 and 5.

17. Susan Budd, *Varieties of Unbelief: atheists and agnostics in English society 1850-1960* (London, 1977), pp 104-23; E.P. Thompson, 'Anthropology and the discipline of historical context', in *Midland History*, 1 no. 3 (1972), pp 41-55; and T.W. Laqueur, *Religion and respectability: Sunday schools and working class culture, 1780-1850* (London and New Haven, 1976).

18. *The Deliverance of Mark Rutherford*, Ch. 6.

19. Leslie Stephen, *Essays in free thinking and plain speaking* (London, 1873). For a recent interpretation see A.D. Gilbert, *The making of post-Christian Britain* (London, 1980), pp 47-67.

20. *Two Years Ago*, Ch. 17.

21. *Alton Locke,* Ch. 24 and *Two Years Ago*, Ch. 17. See also *Adam Bede*, Ch. 3.

22. *The Way of All Flesh*, Chs. 57-60.

23. See W.R. Ward, *Religion and Society in England 1790-1850* (London, 1972); Ward, 'The religion of the people and the problem of control, 1790-1830', *Studies in Church history,* 8 (1972), pp 237-57; and David Hempton, *Methodism and politics in British society 1750-1850* (London, 1984).

24. *Tancred*, Bk. 2, Ch. 1; Cunningham, *Everywhere spoken against*, pp 25-47.

25. John Kent, 'Feelings and festivals, an interpretation of some working-class religious attitudes', in H.J. Dyos and Michael Wolff (ed.), *The Victorian city*, 2 vols. (London, 1973), 2, pp 855-71.

26. Raymond Williams, *The English novel from Dickens to Lawrence* (paperback edn. London, 1984), pp 9-27.

27. Geoffrey Carnall, 'Dickens, Mrs Gaskell, and the Preston Strike', in *Victorian Studies,* 8, no. 1 (Sept., 1964), pp 31-48; Patrick Brantlinger, 'The case against trade unions in early Victorian fiction', in *Victorian Studies*, 13, no. 1 (Sept., 1969), pp 37-52; and Brantlinger, *The spirit of reform* (Harvard, 1977), pp 81-149.

28. Cunningham, *Everywhere spoken against,* pp 103-4. See also S.M. Smith, 'Willenhall and Wodgate: Disraeli's use of Blue Book evidence', in *Review of English Studies*, N.S. 13 (1962), pp 368-84.

29. Compare, for example, *Hard Times,* Bk. 2, Ch. 4 with 'On Strike', in *Household Words*, 8 (Feb., 1854), pp 553-9.

30. *The New Machiavelli*, Bk. 1, Ch. 3.

31. *Adam Bede*, Bk. 1, Ch. 3. George Eliot is here describing anti-Methodist caricatures. For dissenting architecture, and its responses to charges of philistinism see Clyde Binfield, *So down to prayers: studies in English nonconformity 1780-1920* (London, 1977), pp 145-85.

32. For a vareity of dissenting views on the novel see Cunningham, *Everywhere spoken against*, pp 48-62.

33. Robert Blake, *Disraeli* (London, 1966), pp 167-220; D.R. Schwarz, *Disraeli's fiction* (London, 1979), pp 78-124.

34. Karl Marx and Friedrich Engels, *Manifesto of the Communist Party* (orig. ed. 1848, reprinted by Progress publishers, Moscow, 1969), pp 78-80.

35. Chadwick, *Victorian church*, 1, pp 346-63; and Troben Christenson, *Origin and history of Christian Socialism 1848-54* (Aarhus, 1962).

36. N.Z. Davis, 'Some tasks and themes in the study of popular religion', in Charles Trinkaus and H.A. Oberman (ed.), *The pursuit of holiness in late medieval and renaissance religion* (Leiden, 1974), pp 307-36; and Davis, 'From "popular religion" to religious cultures', in Steven Ozment (ed.), *Reformation Europe: a guide to research* (St. Louis, 1982), pp 321-41.

37. James Obelkevich, *Religion and rural society: South Lindsey 1825-1875* (Oxford, 1976).

38. Hugh McLeod, 'Recent studies in Victorian religious history', in *Victorian Studies*, 21, no. 2 (1978), pp 245-55.

39. *Lark Rise to Candleford*, Ch. 14.

40. *Silas Marner*, Ch. 10.

41. Nigel Scotland, *Methodism and the Revolt of the Field* (Gloucester, 1981).

42. *Father and Son*, ch. 6.

43. McLeod, 'Recent studies', n. 10.

44. Pamela Horn, *The rural world 1780-1850* (London, 1980), p. 156; Hempton, *Methodism and politics*, p. 13; Hempton, 'Bickersteth', p. 187; McLeod, *Religion and the working class*, p. 14; and *Alton Locke*, Ch. 5.

45. Obelkevich, *Religion and rural society*, pp 149-50.

46. See Arnold Sier (ed.), *The family letters of Samuel Butler 1841-1886* (London, 1962), and Samuel Butler, *Ernest Pontifex or The way of All Flesh* (ed. with intro. and notes by D.F. Howard, London, 1964).

47. *The Way of All Flesh*, Ch. 14.

48. *The Way of All Flesh*, Ch. 15.

49 *The Distracted Preacher*, Ch. 6.

50 *Under the Greenwood Tree*, Pt. 2, Ch. 4.

51. *Lark Rise to Candleford*, Ch. 14 and *Sons and Lovers*, Ch. 2.

52. Obelkevich, *Religion and rural society*, pp 158-61.

53. See Laqueur, *Religion and respectability*, and Hempton, *Methodism and politics*, pp 86-92.

54. Budd, *Varieties of unbelief*, pp 105-6. For the impact of revivalism on Victorian society see Richard Carwardine, *Trans-atlantic revivalism: popular evangelicalism in Britain and America, 1790-1865* (London, 1978) and John Kent, *Holding the fort: studies in Victorian revivalism* (London, 1978).

55. *Esther Waters*, Ch. 4.

56. *Esther Waters*, Chs. 44-8; McLeod, *Religion and the working class*; and McLeod, 'New perspectives'.

57. See McLeod, *Religion and the working class* and Gilbert, *The making of post-Christian Britain* for differing interpretations of the pace and characteristics of secularization.

58. *Silas Marner*, Ch. 17.

59. *Silas Marner*, Ch. 1.

60. Basil Willey, *Nineteenth-century studies* (London, 1949), Ch. 8; B.J. Paris, 'George Eliot's religion of humanity', *English Literary History*, 29 (Dec., 1962), pp 418-43.

61. *Sybil*, Bk. 1, Ch. 13.

62. Quite why this should be so is by no means clear since George Eliot was usually meticulous about this sort of thing. Some have suggested that she may have been influenced by a contemporaneous Polish novel by J.I. Kraszewski called *Jermola the Potter*. See Mathilde Blind, *George Eliot* (London, 1883), pp 139-42 and Marghanita Laski, *George Eliot and her world* (London, 1973), p. 79. The most likely explanation, however, is that it suited her artistic purposes to portray Raveloe as a closed and static community.

63. Williams, *The English novel*, p. 77.

64. Williams, *The English novel*, p. 106.

65. This is Jude's own phrase, *Jude the Obscure*, Pt. 6, Ch. 1. *Lark Rise to Candleford*, Ch. 2.

66. Keith Wrightson, *English Society 1580-1680* (London, 1982), pp 222-28 is a useful summary of this literature.

67. Gilbert, *The making of post-Christian Britain*, Chs. 3 and 4.

68. Obelkevich, *Religion and rural society*, pp 329-31.

69. *Father and Son*, Epilogue.

70. A similar conclusion is reached through a different route by McLeod, *Religion and the working class*, p. 16.

Mark Twain:
historian of a lost world[1]

OWEN DUDLEY EDWARDS

The historian must go to Twain with the knowledge of facing an extreme case of common reputation in conflict with reality. It is not only a matter of an author profoundly challenging the intellectual orthodoxy of his times being reduced to the paternity of pretty stories for children. This is what faces the reader of Swift or Melville. Huge chasms yawn between the Swift or the Melville of reality, and the emasculated versions of *Gulliver's Travels* and *Moby Dick* which make acceptable Christmas gifts for children, but the reality can be opened up quickly enough if the full texts are examined. In Twain's case it is the full texts themselves, of *Tom Sawyer* and *Huckleberry Finn*, that most children meet — the pap or picture-comic versions do not yet dominate the market. It is a matter of looking at the familiar pages to discover the witness Twain is giving, but is not being commonly perceived to give, and going on from there to a vast sprawling corpus of work.

Twain's witness in *Tom Sawyer* and *Huckleberry Finn* again differs from those of Swift and Melville in that for most of the time he is testifying to his child audience about the world he saw as a child. This greatly strengthens his value for the historian. To a surprising extent the popular writer for children is not autobiographical. Success seems often to turn on a capacity to observe consciously. A.A. Milne may have known little enough about his son Christopher Robin, but insofar as he made any observations, it was the child of the next generation, not of his own, that he observed. Richmal Crompton Lamburn (one of the most successful students of *Tom Sawyer* among writers for children) observed younger relatives to create her William. Frequently, writing for children owes its success to an adult's translation of adult experience to child terms: Stevenson used his mature experience of conflict between the respectable and the reprobate, the Highland and the Lowland, to produce Silver *versus* Smollett, or Allan Breck *versus* David Crawford's minister and lawyer. And when there is directly autobiographical material, its usual effects are introvertive, as with Dickens's *David Copperfield,* Joyce's *A Portrait of the Artist as a Young Man* and the most bitterly anti-parent passages in Enid Blyton's early 'Five' books. Where we do find an author bringing to life her childhood world as well as herself, as with Louisa M. Alcott's *Little Women,* it is usually a very small and ordered world.[2]

Twain therefore excites particular remark and respect. He was an astoundingly wide-eyed child observer, and his breadth of observation is strikingly unaccompanied by any desire to thrust himself forward. Dickens's blacking factory, Joyce's artistic musings, Blyton's experience of adult betrayal, demand that the reader make good the lack of sympathy they remember having needed: the classic case here is probably Kipling's 'Baa, Baa, Black Sheep'. Alcott asks for some identification also, but in a far less self-pitying or self-admiring way: and perhaps altruism and unquestioning self-sacrifice account for this dignity. But while Tom Sawyer's 'St Petersburg' makes good use of Samuel Clemens's Hannibal, Missouri, Tom is much more than the boy Clemens.[3]

Most of the adventures recorded in this book really occurred; one or two were experiences of my own, the rest those of boys who were schoolmates of mine. Huck Finn is drawn from life; Tom Sawyer also, but not from an individual — he is a combination of the characteristics of three boys whom I knew, and therefore belongs to the composite order of architecture.

This kind of architecture greatly increases the author's range of vision. It brings problems with it, though these may be of the kind that invite more disquiet from the literary critic than from the historian. Tom Sawyer, however composite, achieves a unitary character in the book which bears his name; but thereafter he becomes a different character. Critics are generally unhappy about the 'Tom' passages in *Huckleberry Finn,* and with reason. There is a box-office element in his presence — Twain was both satirist and victim of the box-office but his status as both in part derives from his own sense and use of it. The public wanted more Tom as well as more Huck, probably more Tom than Huck before the appearance of *Adventures of Huckleberry Finn,* and so Tom had to be brought back. It was against Twain's initial better judgment:[4]

So endeth this chronicle. It being strictly a history of a *boy,* it must stop here; the story could not go much further without becoming the history of a *man.* When one writes a novel about grown people, he knows exactly where to stop — that is, with a marriage; but when he writes of juveniles, he must stop where he best can.

Most of the characters that perform in this book still live, and are prosperous and happy. Some day it may seem worth while to take up the story of the younger ones again and see what sort of men and women they turned out to be; therefore it will be wisest not to reveal any of that part of their lives at present.

But Tom has at the end of the book gone through certain rites of passage. After his great flirtations of the past — poor Amy Lawrence! — he has settled into a relationship with Becky Thatcher that is to be taken as permanent, sanctified by 'our wedding-cake' eaten by them in the cave when it is all that stands between them and starvation (apart from the bats, candle-ends and stalagmites which would give Injun Joe the last food he ever ate). Twain the observer would know that a flirt in the past could prove a flirt again; but by the end of this story Tom is largely ceasing to reflect Twain's sources. Again the title *The Adventures of Tom Sawyer* speak a finality in the definite article suspiciously lacking in *Adventures of Huckleberry Finn*. But Huck, by nature and circumstances, lives a life of adventures; Tom lives a life in which adventures end. Huck is metaphor for the endless frontier; Tom for the frontier in the process of settlement, luxuriating in its frontier memory when settlement is already firmly secured. No doubt Twain wished to make the point that romanticism is pleasing in a boy, dangerous in an adult, and so Tom's enthusiasm for fantasy, delightful in *Tom Sawyer*, is cruel and dangerous in the adult problems at stake in *Huckleberry Finn*. But it won't do. The first hero has been brought back to ride hobby-horses. The Tom who odiously tricks and manipulates Nigger Jim (in many ways akin, as Dr John Whitley has argued,[5] to that other Tom who gets his — and the *Huckleberry Finn* Tom Sawyer's — deserts, in being sold the river at the end of *Pudd'nhead Wilson*) is simply not the Tom who faces the horror of revenge by Injun Joe but has the terrific and lonely courage to save Muff Potter. As the attractions of box-office increased, matters became worse. The fortunately discarded 'Huck Finn and Tom Sawyer among the Indians' credits Tom with a voracious consumption of the writings of James Fenimore Cooper, in order to carry on Twain's literary war with Cooper and his anxiety to testify to the need for genocidal hatred of the Indians instead of their gentle popular romanticisation. The intent was evil, and it is pleasing to think that his own characters rebelled — although in fact the cause of abandoning the story was that the heroine had so obviously been raped by Indians that there was no way to satisfy the box-office insistence that she could not be — but what concerns us here is that Twain's social purposes had come so violently between him and his own creation that his efforts to manipulate Tom Sawyer had finally pushed him totally out of control. The Tom of *Tom Sawyer* reads a child's version of Robin Hood; but where would he get the time or the patience to survive a volume by Cooper?[6]

The example of Tom Sawyer is a reminder to the historian that Twain could do violence to his source-material with a remarkably free hand when he liked, but that the heaviness of that hand conveys its warnings. The historian is called on to test the evidence of Twain's observation presented; unity of character is less likely to concern him. The student of literature is faced by the pitfall of the orignal Tom being followed by subsequent other Toms, supposedly the same but actually different, and many critics have been caught in that trap. *Huckleberry Finn* itself gives significant warnings that Twain is not going to be able to call back Tom Sawyer, for all of his success in finding fresh adventures for Huck. Becky Thatcher is a very flesh-and-blood heroine in *Tom Sawyer*, but in *Huckleberry Finn* she becomes 'Bessie Thatcher'! We can argue that Huck, as the narrator, is testifying to resentment against his friend Tom's involvement with Becky, and the world of bourgeois advancement which she and her judicial father represent, or that while to respectable persons names like Rebecca and Elizabeth are demonstrably different a drunkard's son may find little to distinguish Becky from Bessie. These things may be true enough. *Tom Sawyer* is very anxious to assert the fact that the scapegrace Tom will ultimately follow the path of respecable advancement laid out with all the precision of the small-town streets of post-frontier settlement, the work of settling being indeed carried out by sawyers and thatchers. But the historian can hardly avoid the obvious conclusion that Twain had forgotten the girl's name, and if there is symbolism it consists in his having so far lost his interest in, and hence his hold on, Tom that he could not name the recipient of that love which nearly brought him to his death.[7]

But in his true identity, Tom Sawyer and his world brilliantly encapsulate what Mark Twain had seen and heard in his native Hannibal. He was clearly proud of his capacity for recall from his childhood, and significantly makes something of it by endowing the young Satan with the same quality in the discarded 'Schoolhouse Hill' draft of *The Mysterious Stranger*. The difficulty about this extraordinary hold on memories of that childhood world, memories perhaps all the stronger because of the several schools attended by the young Clemens, is that where applied in adult contexts they could prove misleading. The most graphic illustration of Twain's limits in this respect is provided by his early novel *The Gilded Age*, written with Charles Dudley Warner and published in 1873. On the surface, it would seem to be the ideal example for the historian in quest of the writer's value as historical witness. To define an age in history and still more to give a name to it is, as Professor MacDonagh stresses, a particular gift of the creative writer to the historian. And the title has won widespread acceptance as the appropriate label for the age of expansion, greed, corruption and falsehood after the Civil War. The problem is that the novel's attractions resemble those of the age it seeks to define, and in the way it uses to define it: gilded. Twain and Warner seem to be anatomising the early 1870s. In fact, much of the material is drawn from Twain's youth. What we are seeing, at its most authentic, is not the United States after the civil war, but before it. It is not truly from the same stable as the outstanding critiques of the period such as Henry Adams's *Democracy*, Henry George's *Progress and Poverty*, Edward Bellamy's *Looking Backward 2000-1887*, the social novels of William Dean Howells and, above all, that remorseless exposure of contemporary England which so well applied to the United States, Anthony Trollope's *The Way We Live Now*.[8] It derives from the swindles and speculations of the world which also produced Charles Dickens's *American Notes* and *Martin Chuzzlewit*, Herman Melville's *The Confidence Man* and *The American Democrat* of Twain's detested James Fenimore Cooper. If *The Gilded Age* does perform a service to the historian, it is to remind us that however revolutionary the impact of the civil war, corruption was nothing new, and much that horrified Henry Adams could have been recognised as a continuity from an earlier era had he given himself the eyes with which to see it. Much of what change there was reflected the enormous expansion in territory, in technology, in population, in bureaucracy, in communications and in human knowledge, but for all the great growth, much of the character of the period could be found in embryo in the America of the 1840s. As for the character of the age, does 'gilded' really convey the achievements of Carnegie in steel or Rockefeller in oil? They deserve rude epithets, no doubt, but this is hardly the *mot juste*. Not even the appearance they gave themselves with their new wealth is captured by it: Carnegie never sought to seem anything other than a canny Scotsman, or Rockefeller other than a hard-shell Baptist. Vanderbilts and Stanfords might seem more 'gilded', and their offspring more still, but the term remains misleading and unsatisfactory. There was enough gold around to provide a profusion of ostentation; it was much more the decade that ended with the 'fortyniners', which lusted for gold and so often found and offered only gilding. Here Twain's prowess in recall has actually made him a danger to historical scholarship and, like himself, we must return to the 1840s.[9]

And here in *Tom Sawyer* we find gilding with — in all senses of the term — a vengeance. The relevant episode triumphantly closes chapter XXI. The chapter itself ('Youthful Eloquence — Compositions by the Young Ladies — A Lengthy Vision — The Boys' Vengeance Satisfied') is instructively irrelevant to the main business of the book, however broad a construction is placed on what that might be. Specifically, Tom hardly appears, save to make a mess of reciting Patrick Henry's 'Give me liberty or give me death'; otherwise he is simply anonymously present as one of the boys and it is not intended that we should think him the ruling spirit in what follows. Especially in its early stages *Tom Sawyer* rambles, and the main plot after its introduction with the murder in chapter IX, the Huck-Tom oath of silence in chapter X and the arrest of Muff Potter in chapter XI, does not resurface until chapter XXIII when it carries the story to its end in chapter XXXV; but all the intervening material is thrown around Tom. Even a set-piece such as the church service in chapter V exists to be disrupted by Tom's 'pinch-bug'. What is happening, and why is this chapter XXI in the book? Perhaps the breakdown on the Henry speech may serve to remind us that Tom loves liberty but will not be able to sustain his commitment to it: he is intended to be a part of an ordered society and will not in the end evade the destiny carved out for him by his aunt and his surname. But the whole chapter cannot exist to bear this brief symbol. I want to suggest that when Twain appears to be doing violence to the structure of his creative writing, this is the moment for particular vigilance on the part of the historian. It means that Twain has work to do which urgently impels him to break his logical course of action, and that means either that he has some particular message to impart, or that memory is forcing him to produce an episode whose importance he cannot evade.

The chapter is not entirely based on memory, certainly. Twain adds a note at its conclusion pointing out that the 'pretended "compositions" quoted in this chapter' to illustrate the recitations at the school prizegiving 'are taken without alteration from a volume entitled 'Prose and Poetry, by a Western Lady' — but they are exactly and precisely after the school-girl pattern and hence are much happier than any mere imitations could be'. But this is no more than a frank exposition of an *aide-mémoire*. Twain quotes from three of them 'Is this, then, Life', 'A Missouri Maiden's Farewell to Alabama' (a 'poem'), and 'A Vision' (which after quotation Twain sums up: 'This nightmare occupied some ten pages of manuscript and wound up with a sermon so destructive of all hope to non-Presbyterians that it took the first prize. This composition was considered to be the very finest effort of the evening. The mayor of the village, in delivering the prize to the author of it, made a warm speech in which he said that it was by far the most "eloquent" thing he had ever listened to, and that Daniel Webster himself might well be proud of it.') Of the compositions at large Twain had already given a general account:

Each in her turn stepped forward to the edge of the platform, cleared her throat, held up her manuscript (tied with dainty ribbon), and proceeded to read, with laboured attention to "expression" and punctuation. The themes were the same that had been illuminated upon similar occasions by their mothers before them, their grandmothers, and doubtless all their ancestors in the female line clear back to the Crusades. "Friendship" was one; "Memories of Other Days"; "Religion in History"; "Dream land"; "The Advantages of Culture"; "Forms of Political Government Compared and Contrasted"; "Melancholy"; "Filial Love"; "Heart Longings"; etc., etc.

A prevalent feature in these compositions was a nursed and petted melancholy; another was a wasteful and opulent gush of "fine language"; another was a tendency to lug in by the ears particularly prized words and phrases until they were worn entirely out; and a peculiarity that conspicuously marked and marred them was the inveterate and intolerable sermon that wagged its crippled tail at the end of each and every one of them. No matter what the subject might be, a brain-racking effort was made to squirm it into some aspect or other that the moral and religious mind could contemplate with edification. The glaring insincerity of these sermons was not sufficient to compass the banishment of the fashion from the schools, and it is not sufficient to-day; it never will be sufficient while the world stands, perhaps. There is no school in all our land where the young ladies do not feel obliged to close their compositions with a sermon; and you will find that the sermon of the most frivolous and least religious girl in the school is always the longest and the most relentlessly pious.

0836The rest of the chapter swirls around the schoolteacher, Mr Dobbins, identified as being based on J.D. Dawson, the Hannibal schoolmaster with whom young Sam Clemens had most to do. Mr Dobbins makes a vigorous, if anonymous, appearance early in *Tom Sawyer* when he falls into Tom's trap by forcing him to sit with the girls (which Tom, anxious to make the acquaintance of Becky Thatcher, is delighted to do) after having first whipped him for the crime of admitting he was late because he stopped to talk with Huckleberry Finn ('Thomas Sawyer, this is the most astounding confession I have ever listened to. No mere ferule will answer for this offense. Take off your jacket.').[10] Later Mr Dobbins separates them, and later still takes some satisfaction while unseen in watching Tom and Joe Harper playing with a tick which each has to prevent, with a pin, from crossing to the other's side of a drawn line. (This last was an episode in Dawson's academy, but decorum required that in Twain's version he substitute a tick for his own original playmate, a louse.)[11] Further corporal punishment follows. But it is not until Tom returns to school after his pirate episode with Huck and Joe, culminating in their attendance at their own funeral, that Dobbins really comes into his own. The incident is that in which Becky tears the schoolmaster's book, for which Tom later takes the blame, but Twain goes to some lengths to explain the book:[12]

The master, Mr Dobbins, had reached middle age with an unsatisfied ambition. The darling of his desires was, to be a doctor, but poverty had decreed that he should be nothing higher than a village schoolmaster. Every day he took a mysterious book out of his desk and absorbed himself in it at times when no classes were reciting.

It proves to be a volume entitled *Anatomy* by an unnamed professor. In this chapter the antecedents of the torn volume are all that is in question, but in the next, the problematic chapter XXI, the lost medical career achieves a different importance, and it begins:

Vacation was approaching. The schoolmaster, always severe, grew severer and more exacting than ever, for he wanted the school to make a good showing on "Examination" day. His rod and his ferule were seldom idle now — at least among the smaller pupils. Only the biggest boys, and young ladies of eighteen and twenty escaped lashing. Mr Dobbins's lashings were very vigorous ones, too; for although he carried, under his wig, a perfectly bald and shiny head, he had only reached middle age and there was no sign of feebleness in his muscle. As the great day approached, all the tyranny that was in him came to the surface; he seemed to take a vindictive pleasure in punishing the least shortcomings . . . the boys . . . swore-in the sign-painter's boy, told him the scheme, and asked his help. He had his own reasons for being delighted, for the master boarded in his father's family and had given the boy ample cause to hate him. The master's wife would go on a visit to the country in a few days, and there would be nothing to interfere with the plan; the master always prepared himself for great occasions by getting pretty well fuddled, and the sign-painter's boy said that when the dominie had reached the proper condition on Examination Evening he would "manage the thing" while he napped in his chair; then he would have him awakened at the right time and hurried away to school.

And the rest of the chapter follows, describing the ill-success of Tom, the girls' compositions, and the rest, and culminates:

Now the master, mellow almost to the verge of geniality, put his chair aside, turned his back to the audience, and began to draw a map of America on the blackboard, to exercise the geography class upon. But he made a sad business of it with his unsteady hand, and a smothered titter rippled over the house. He knew what the matter was, and set himself to right it. He sponged out lines and re-made them; but he only distorted them more than ever, and the tittering was more pronounced. He threw his entire attention upon his work, now, that all eyes were fastened upon him; he imagined he was succeeding, and yet the tittering continued; it even manifestly increased. And well it might. There was a garret above, pierced with a scuttle over his head; down through this scuttle came a cat, suspended around the haunches by a string; she had a rag tied about her head and jaws to keep her from mewing; as she slowly descended she curved upward and clawed at the string, she swung downward and clawed at the intangible air. The tittering rose higher and higher — the cat was within six inches of the absorbed teacher's head — down, down, a little lower, and she grabbed his wig with her desperate claws, clung to it and was snatched up into the garret in an instant with her trophy still in her possession! And how the light did blaze abroad from the master's bald pate — for the sign-painter's boy had *gilded* it!

There is no particular reason to assume the incident itself goes beyond wish-fulfilment. But its symbolism, taken in conjunction with the title of the earlier novel written with Warner, opens up satisfactory fields for investigation by critic and historian alike. Firstly, the total picture of Mr Dobbins is formidable, but balanced with remarkable economy. He is frustrated, brutal, insecure, ruthless, hungry for applause, given to drink, and Twain gets all of these points across — including the very nasty one of the punishment of girls up to the age of 17 — effectively but without any Dickensian labouring of the point. He knows how to rule by terror — the inquisition as to the torn book ('the slow torture of these proceedings') is handled with the effectivness that Tom has anticipated and only Tom's sudden self-accusation saves Becky, 'white with terror', from giving herself away; on the other hand he is fundamentally stupid, and indeed his system requires a victim rather than the truth. But Twain has quietly laid his ground for an understanding of Dobbins, stemming from a career in medicine aborted by poverty, and kept before him by the continued self-infliction of pain, shame and resentment in poring over the *Anatomy*, once an activity denoting hope, now a symbol of hopelessness. There is no pride in a home — he and his wife are boarders — and no attempt to cultivate good relations in lodgings — the sign-painter's boy hates him so much as to invite fairly spectacular retribution when the logical chain of deduction will prove him the culprit. Dobbins may get satisfaction by his sarcasms, his inquisitions, and his floggings, but it all amounts to a severe case of self-hatred. All of this is established where to the normal writer, especially the normal autobiographical writer, a drunken and brutal schoolmaster is *sui generis*, an occasion for sympathy with his victims, a plague requiring no explanation. Yet having given the motives for Mr Dobbins's nature Twain remorselessly sums up the education he is putting forward. It is, simply, gilding, and worthless and inappropriate gilding. The insincere and absurd compositions are as egregious and tawdry as the master's gilded dome. The educational gilding is pernicious and alien: St Petersburg is a real world, and Becky Thatcher a very real little girl, with her interest in Tom growing into love for him, her anger at his flirtations, her betrayal of him in her anger, her disastrous curiosity about the master's book, her gentleness and her weakness in the cave. She shows a startling absence of snobbery from the first, despite the absurd deference lavished on her father. Yet although she is not assumed to be one of the composition-readers, to such dishonour of the female intellect will the system reduce her. And Dobbins because of rather than in spite of his poverty and his lost vocational idealism is fitted for nothing more than gilding the lily of her natural virtues with tawdry, insincere, moralistic nonsense, by means of fairly horrible physical and psychological barbarities. In place of the real decency which she, like Tom, obtains from her environment there is gilded upon her this dreadful mishmash of genteel culture assumed to embody the virtues of the New England heritage. Twain said his source for the compositions was 'Western': in fact it was a 'Georgia' lady, published in Tennessee,[13] and the alteration was probably made to stress that it embodied what obtained in his youthful Missouri, but the culture touchstone being New England is asserted by the mayor's citation of Daniel Webster. Twain was living in Hartford, Connecticut, when he wrote *Tom Sawyer* and he clearly wished the cultural curse on his Missouri to be sent home to roost. In the context, it could not be more appropriate that Tom is punished by Dobbins for admitting talking to Huckleberry Finn: the false alien culture cannot permit any expression of respect for the true, indigenous one.

This offers us an entirely new meaning for Twain's original term 'gilded age', and it places the protest not in terms of the nexus of American government and society, where Twain's authority was weak, but in a cultural sphere, where he was strong. In this he does invite a comparison with Trollope's *The Way We Live Now*, and this time it does not leave him looking threadbare and anachronistic. Trollope began his attack on what had become of his era by assailing the corruption which had reduced reviewing to the furtherance of cultural rubbish, and this supplies a keynote for his book as a whole. Twain was now able to attack his own times not by a spurious chronological transposition of phenomena of his boyhood, but by a direct examination of the potential social evils of cultural falsification by education in that boyhood, whence it could be deduced why America had corrupted itself by the time he was writing. And this time his evidence was eminently judiciously presented in its own historical context.

In cultural terms, Twain's philosophy grew to argue a corrupting of genuine settler values by an absurd aping of Eastern genteelism, and while this became a very deep preoccupation and conviction, he largely kept his fine powers of observation in play to document his argument. It is a position both idealistic and nostalgic, and it logically ended, in *The Mysterious Stranger* with going to war against God and man in their entirety. He asserted the values of the unrespectabilised and ungilded West through

Huckleberry Finn, boy and book, and he took to the vernacular the better to make that betrayed and increasingly rejected world speak for itself.[14] The polite world was not grateful to him for 'stopping to talk with Huckleberry Finn' himself, to the extent of a novel consisting of Huck's side of the talk, and whether he meant it or not his later attempts on the same lines reduced Huck to a tame and imprisoned animal, a box-office device, absurdly the narrator for a society more literate than himself. *Huckleberry Finn*, by contrast to things like 'Tom Sawyer Abroad' and 'Tom Sawyer Detective', is Huck in his own world, speaking for and about figures without voices in the respectable, genteeling society — his dreadful father, his companion Nigger Jim, his acquaintances made *en route*, unable to perceive themselves as he can, even the King and the Duke, above all the river itself voiceless but speaking through him. It is the great work asserting the power, dignity and integrity of the environment, and doing so with much clearer assertion of its firm basis in historical and cultural fact than Turner's frontier thesis articulated a few years later; and it, like Turner, speaks the language of a doomed society, not only in the disappearance of the land frontier but in the vanishing of the water frontier. The United States up to 1830 assumed itself to be destined for a waterway economy: the railroad destroyed that, as it would also destroy the western wilderness. Twain enabled us to hear the language and logic of the water culture before it died, and in the process argued for its vitalisation of American culture as well as playing a part in that vitalisation. This is in itself a great achievement: one of the greatest services the writer can give to history is to enable it to come to terms with the culture of a society whose meaning has passed away.

Much else of Twain's literary career involved a passionate attack on the sources of cultural destruction of the western frontier and water worlds and their reduction to subservience to what he saw as cheap Eastern genteelisms. These in their turn he sought to pursue to their roots, and hence his attack on Europe, and its vaunted culture, as seen in *The Innocents Abroad,* or *A Tramp Abroad,* an attack all the stronger in its easygoing humorous iconoclasm. The attack is turned on the most insidious danger posed by Europe, its past, and the beguiling mystification which the romantic portrayal of that past uses to mislead the modern world, above all is asserted in *A Connecticut Yankee At King Arthur's Court.* The catholic church, organised and surviving means of perpetuating what Twain saw as a pernicious version of that past, receives particular attention. Central throughout is the argument of the profit-motive, so that the corruption of *The Gilded Age*, with whose novelty he had so much difficulty, is now the descendant of something very old and the power with which that longevity is attended continues to flesh itself at the expense of new and innocent societies. 'The Man That Corrupted Hadleyburg' is the clearest expression of this last process. Finally Twain sees the whole christian ethos as a means by which the corruption and tyranny of the past is perpetuated, and the logic of his attack on that takes him into the nihilism of *The Mysterious Stranger*. For all of its flaws — and Twain is all the more instructive as being a frequently flawed writer — the whole is a philosophy remarkably developed and impressively asserting its various dimensions, the more so as the acute observation so often proves the groundwork of what he is asserting. The historian must be on his guard against the ideologue, and Twain certainly was that. But continually in his exposure of his reader to the process of observation Twain enables his vigilant student to test his conclusions and hypotheses, and separate theory from fact. Moreover, the historian gains immeasurably by being given a fresh view of humanity from so unusual a perspective, asserted in such uncompromising terms. Twain's war against the genteel tradition makes him an object of historical scrutiny in his own right: the historian should remember that his own entire technique is in itself a product of the genteel tradition. In certain ways Twain is one of the healthiest challenges to a dehumanising, prettifying, self-admiring scientificism since Herodotus. We hear the voices of lost peoples in Herodotus; we hear them in Twain; how often do we otherwise hear them in historiography, without the dangerous and insidious emasculations with which they are set in a context of genteel writing?

Huckleberry Finn constantly plays with astonishing brilliance and versatility on the theme of the attempts by the American East, the European past, the mythologies of genteelism, to undermine and corrupt the innocence of the boy on the river. The Duke and the King, frauds themselves, but battening on a tradition which at bottom is nothing but fraud, constitute perhaps the most formal expression of this. There is a major contrast in the two novels from this point of view. *Tom Sawyer* assails the process of Western settlement where it becomes false to itself, as in education, but there is much in it which deserves and receives affection and respect. It does not give the frontier all its own way as the ideal. Tom's embrace of the frontier, at its most extreme, is evident in the pirates' escapade, but at its conclusion our sympathies are turned against his selfishness and towards the suffering of Aunt Polly. And Aunt Polly is the embodiment of small gentility imported to the west and imposed on it as part of the process of settlement. Twain is of outstanding value in showing the extent to which settlement, so far from remaking its population in the light of the frontier, goes to great lengths to try to reproduce in miniature what it holds dear and righteous in the more firmly settled world whence it has come. The community as a whole, led by the now ennobled minister,[15] has the greatness to thank God that it has been hoaxed, and the boys are safe. This followed the most beautiful gesture of Aunt Polly's life, one which conflicts absolutely with her respectable demeanour. The reader's heart goes out to her, however unwilling the recipient of her generosity:

Aunt Polly, Mary and the Harpers threw themselves upon their restored ones, smothered them with kisses and poured out thanksgivings, while poor Huck stood abashed and uncomfortable, not knowing exactly what to do or where to hide from so many unwelcoming eyes. He wavered, and started to slink away, but Tom seized him and said:
    'Aunt Polly, it ain't fair. Somebody's got to be glad to see Huck'.
    'And so they shall. *I'm* glad to see him, poor motherless thing!' And the loving attentions Aunt Polly lavished upon him were the one thing capable of making him more uncomfortable than he was before.

Aunt Polly, therefore, reaches her crown at the moment when she literally embraces the frontier symbol, and does so with no other motive than her innate goodness.

    The kindness Huck receives later, from the Welshman and the Widow Douglas, is different: it is recompense for his having saved the Widow from an appalling fate, very bluntly described by Injun Joe:[16]

'Give it up, and I just leaving this country forever! Give it up and maybe never have another chance. I tell you again, as I've told you before, I don't care for her swag — you may have it. But her husband was rough on me — many times he was rough on me — and mainly he was the justice of the peace that jugged me for a vagrant. And that ain't all. It ain't the millionth part of it! He had me *horsewhipped!* — horsewhipped in front of the jail, like a nigger! — with all the town looking on! HORSEWHIPPED! — do you understand? He took advantage of me and died. But I'll take it out of *her*.'
    'Oh, don't kill her! Don't do that!'
    'Kill? Who said anything about killing? I would kill *him* if he was here; but not her. When you want to get revenge on a woman you don't kill her — bosh! you go for her looks. You slit her nostrils — you notch her ears, like a sow's!'

    Twain is playing it like it is, in more ways than one. Huck saves the widow from the revenge of Injun Joe, formerly convicted of being a vagrant; and he is himself a vagrant. And it was Injun Joe who gave greatest offence to reviewers: the voice of the frontier, admittedly in what was to Twain the unacceptable form of it, the transgression of the racial frontier, proved a precursor as an object of genteel reviewer dislike much as would Huck himself in the novel that bore his name.[16] *Tom Sawyer* is a book about the mind of new settlement facing both the charm of the frontier, represented by Huck Finn, and the fear of it, represented by Injun Joe. As a metaphor Injun Joe dominates St Petersburg, and significantly he is pressed into use by Dr Robinson when the needs of medical science, harbinger of the advancement of civilization, demands the recruitment of someone partly within and partly beyond civilization's pale. As reportage Injun Joe's value is as testimony to the need for newly settled areas to invoke, however unwillingly, the dangerously untamed frontier representative. The actual original of Injun Joe was a much more harmless figure, amusing in drink, tedious when Clemens's father reformed him into temporary sobriety, and believed by the young Sam Clemens to be damned.[17] In his *Autobiography* Twain discusses him under the same head as the originals for Huck's father, also drunks. And in fact old Finn in *Huckleberry Finn* performs something of the same service as Injun Joe in *Tom Sawyer* — the savage, misanthropic, drunken sadist, the ugliest face of the frontier, priding himself in his beastliness on his superiority to blacks (again like Injun Joe).[18] Twain made no bones about the racism of the lowest whites, or part-Indian half-breeds. The greatness of *Huckleberry Finn* is nowhere more evident than in the pains Twain took to show the slow, difficult evolution of Huck to an acceptance of Nigger Jim as his loved comrade. In so doing he testified once again to the world which had vanished by the time he wrote. Segregation and racial hatred there was, and perhaps more of it than there had been, but the peculiar sense of racial distinctions in the non-segregated world of slavery was recorded here with delicacy, precision and detail, and for this reason the book is perhaps the most valuable source on black-white relations under slavery that has ever been written. *Uncle Tom's Cabin* is a valuable work in explaining how slavery operated; but *Huckleberry Finn* enters the mind of the slavery-dominated society, all the more effectively because it is doing so through its most basic vernacular in the mouth of an individual embodying the most extreme form of self-created freedom. The growth of Huck's love for Jim is in itself both a testimony and an incitement to the extension of freedom.

Huck is free; but it is a freedom that flourishes and can extend itself partly because of his ignorance. Not only Dobbin's genteel derivative education, but the whole accumulation of past knowledge, breaks and fragments when it falls upon Huck. Consider his great discourse on history to Jim. It is founded on what Twain believed to be the essential truth of the wrongness of European monarchy, tyranny, class distinction, oppressive tradition and privilege, and all the rest. But Huck sustains this knowledge by the most magnificent Mississippi of nonsense in which history has ever been served up.[19]

'But, Huck, dese kings o' ourn is regular repscallions; dat's what dey is; dey's reglar rapscallions.'

'Well, that's what I'm a-saying; all kings is mostly rapscallions, as fur as I can make out.'

'Is dat so?'

'You read about them once — you'll see. Look at Henry the Eight; this'n 's a Sunday-School Superintendent to *him*. And look at Charles Second, and Louis Fourteen, and Louis Fifteen, and James Second, and Edward Second, and Richard Third, and forty more; besides all them Saxon heptarchies that used to rip around so in old times and raise Cain. My, you ought to see old Henry the Eight when he was in bloom. He *was* a blossom. He used to marry a new wife every day, and chop off her head next morning. And he would do it just as indifferent as if he was ordering up eggs. "Fetch up Nell Gwynn", he says. They fetch her up. Next morning, "Chop off her head!" And they chop it off. "Fetch up Jane Shore", he says; and up she comes. Next morning "Chop off her head" — and they chop it off. "Ring up Fair Rosamun." Fair Rosamun answers the bell. Next morning, "Chop off her head". And he made every one of them tell him a tale every night, and he kept that up till he had hogged a thousand and one tales that way, and then he put them all in a book, and called it Domesday Book — which was a good name and stated the case. You don't know kings, Jim, but I know them; and this old rip of ourn is one of the cleanest I've struck in history. Well, Henry he takes a notion he wants to get up some trouble with this country. How does he go at it — give notice? — give the country a show? No. All of a sudden he heaves all the tea in Boston Harbor overboard, and whacks out a declaration of independence, and dares them to come on. That was *his* style — he never give anybody a chance. He had suspicions of his father, the Duke of Wellington. Well, what did he do? — ask him to show up? No — drownded him in a butt of mamsey, like a cat. Spose people left money laying around where he was — what did he do? He collared it. Spose he contracted to do a thing; and you paid him, and didn't set down there and see that he done it — what did he do? He always done the other thing. Spose he opened his mouth — what then? If he didn't shut it up powerful quick, he'd lose a lie, every time. That's the kind of bug Henry was; and if we'd had him along 'stead of our kings, he'd a fooled that town a heap worse than ourn done. I don't say that ourn is lambs, because they ain't, when you come right down to the cold facts; but they ain't nothing to *that* old ram, anyway. All I say is, kings is kings, and you got to make allowances. Take them all around, they're a mighty ornery lot. It's the way they're raised.'

But dis one do *smell* so like de nation, Huck.'

'Well, they all do, Jim. *We* can't help the way a king smells; history don't tell no way.'

This is not merely rejection, in the scientific sense as well as the intellectual, of European history; it also rejects Eastern history, including the American Revolution and Tom Paine's *Common Sense* which it lampoons along with all else. Europe, the American east, the past and the genteel tradition fail with Huck, and Twain has anticipated Yeats in the effect of that failure: [20]

> Fail, and that history turns into rubbish,
> All that great past to a trouble of fools.

But Huck, if not Twain, does not need to anticipate another Irish author, Joyce. History may be a nightmare; but it is not Huck's nightmare, so he does not need to try to wake from it. Twain was trying to awaken his audience from it, but Huck is free. [21] The success of this passage, its dual function in denouncing the European and American Eastern past and reducing it to nonsense, arises from that quality in Twain which renders him so valuable as a historical insight — its free flow. It proceeds unforced, strong and free like the river, and Twain trusts to it like a swimmer floating on the river. The contrast, when made, is excruciating with similar passages in 'Tom Sawyer Abroad', where Huck and Jim are merely stupid and ignorant and the genteel audience is being invited to laugh at their ignorance, partly in a larger design of satirising Jules Verne. [22] Here Twain is forcing his reluctant material into an alien setting and design; his creatures themselves resent it and are obviously forced, with worthless results.

Leacock's stress on Twain's urgent need to write of things as they were, something he carried so spectacularly into the use of the vernacular, brings him to his fine statement on *Huckleberry Finn*: [23]

. . . it is the epic of a vanished America . . . there are those, there must be, who consider the *Adventures of Huckleberry Finn* the greatest book ever written in America.

An outstanding feature of the book is that it is American literature. Whatever the works of Washington Irving and Fenimore Cooper and Longfellow were, there is no doubt about *Huckleberry Finn*. Every now and then the dispute breaks out in the colleges and spills over into the press as to what *American* literature was and is, and when it began. Like all controversies, the dispute is bottomless and involves a hopeless number of definitions of terms. But by American literature in the proper sense we ought to mean literature written in an American way, with an American turn of language and an American cast of thought. The test is that it couldn't have been written anywhere else.

Modern scholarship would go very far in support of this judgment, articulated in 1932 but probably conceived about twenty years earlier. [24] The failure to protect British copyright in nineteenth-century America saturated the market with British writers whom American publishers did not pay, and hence any domestic production that might win an audience had to be conceived in the fashionable terms of British convention. Twain was fighting his century single-handed. Coming as he did from humour — so much so that he was condescendingly referred to in public life habitually as 'Mark', an acceptably genteel mode of allusion to one who was an entertainer rather than a serious writer — he learned his craft in a market where 'dialect' was permissible and even desirable in the eyes of the editorial entrepreneur. Hence his method of seeking the language as well as the narrative of reality was able to serve its apprenticeship uninterrupted by restraints other than those of his wife, William Dean Howells, and either selected private censors. But a novel was another matter, and Twain lacked either the outside encouragement or the inward confidence to return to the method with success after *Huckleberry Finn*. It was natural, then, that his crusade for a genuine American literature — only to be crowned by success in the aftermath of his death [25] — should have led him to a state of permanent vigilance against what he saw as the imposition of a bogus European culture in place of the real thing. This presents few problems to Leacock, fighting his own struggle against the genteel English tradition which he saw stifling the birth of Canadian literature. Twain's perceptions of Europe — when not bogged down in private cults of Joan of Arc — speak eloquently for him. On the other hand he sees Twain's private unorthodoxies as apparently unrelated, but this seems to be because they were so little perceived. In fact they were all related to Twain's fight for American self-perception. So, did Twain's crusade against the omnipresence of the artificial European-dominated genteelism come between his witness and its veracity?

The question of Twain's mission distorting his vision is most urgent when we confront his assessment of Europe's place in American culture on a grand scale. And here the classic example, one which has demanded and received very serious attention from historians, is his charge that Sir Walter Scott caused the American Civil War. This is not the outgrowth of an unworthy petty jealousy tricked out in chauvinism, such as was his irritation because Verne could write better adventure stories and Conan Doyle better detective ones, while ignoring the fact that in *Huckleberry Finn* he had produced literature greater than either. This is a serious historical thesis, for all of its *opéra bouffe* character. Indeed the slapstick nature of the charge carries its own strength. Because Twain is being funny, wildly funny, in launching a piece of grand-design historical causation, it has to be taken very seriously. For, as Leacock saw, the stronger the humour, the clearer the vision. It is black humour, as *Pudd'nhead Wilson* is — too black for Leacock, that — but it is humour clear enough.[26]

Against the crimes of the French Revoluton and of Bonaparte may be set two compensating benefactions: the Revolution broke the chains of the *ancien regime* and of the Church, and made of a nation of abject slaves a nation of freemen; and Bonaparte instituted the setting of merit above birth . . . Such benefactions as these compensate the temporary harm which Bonaparte and the Revolution did, and leave the world in debt to them for these great and permanent services to liberty, humanity, and progress.

Then comes Sir Walter Scott with his enchantments, and by his single might checks this wave of progress, and even turns it back; sets the world in love with dreams and phantoms; with decayed and swinish forms of religion; with decayed and degraded systems of government; with the sillinesses and emptinesses, sham grandeurs, sham gauds, and sham chivalries of a brainless and worthless long-vanished society. He did measureless harm; more real and lasting harm, perhaps, than any other individual that ever wrote. Most of the world has now outlived a good part of these harms, though by no means all of them; but in our South they flourish pretty forcefully still. Not so forcefully as half a generation ago, perhaps, but still forcefully. There, the genuine and wholesome civilization of the nineteenth century is curiously confused and commingled with the Walter Scott Middle-Age sham civilization and so you have practical, common-sense, progressive ideas, and progressive works, mixed up with the duel, the inflated speech, and the jejune romanticism of an absurd past that is dead, and out of charity ought to be buried. But for the Sir Walter disease, the character of the Southerner — or Southron, according to Sir Walter's starchier way of phrasing it — would be wholly modern, in place of modern and mediaeval mixed, and the South would be fully a generation further advanced than it is. It was Sir Walter that made every gentleman in the south a Major or a Colonel, or a General or a Judge, before the war; and it was he, also, that made these gentlemen value these bogus decorations. For it was he that created rank and caste down there, and also reverence for rank and caste, and pride and pleasure in them. Enough is laid on slavery, without fathering upon it these creations and contributions of Sir Walter.

Sir Walter had so large a hand in making Southern character, as it existed before the war, that he is in great measure responsible for the war. It seems a little harsh toward a dead man to say that we never should have had any war but for Sir Walter; and yet something of a plausible argument might, perhaps, be made in support of that wild proposition. The Southerner of the American revolution owned slaves; so did the Southerner of the Civil War; but the former resembles the latter as an Englishman resembles a Frenchman. The change of character can be traced rather more easily to Sir Walter's influence than to that of any other thing or person. . . .

A curious exemplification of the power of a single book for good or harm is shown in the effects wrought by Don Quixote and those wrought by Ivanhoe. The first swept the world's admiration for the mediaeval chivalry-silliness out of existence; and the other restored it. As far as our South is concerned, the good work done by Cervantes is pretty nearly a dead letter, so effectually has Scott's pernicious work undermined it.

Now, the point about Twain to which we must always return, is that he was his own man, and as Leacock has argued, exceptionally so given his background and isolation. Shaw, in his preface to *Saint Joan*, points out that he had no medieval sense, and says that *The Innocents Abroad* and *A Connecticut Yankee at King Arthur's Court* shows that he looked on medieval saints and Arthurian knights with the eye of a 'street-arab',[27] but the term is much too parochial. A street-arab has the cultural equipment of a Pirenne at his disposal compared to the Mississippi river-boy and Nevada frontier vagrant that Twain was. We have to go to him, not for what he lacked, but for what he possessed. His Joan and his Edward VI, above all his King Arthur, have to be considered as the pictures drawn by a writer who did possess a historical mind, but whose historical technique was entirely limited to his own observation. His idea of the past as he had viewed it, or as he might deduce it from conversation with seniors, was subjected to observation and analyses. He lived through an era incredible in its change. He was acutely aware of what that change would lose, and while this passage singled out things it could well lose, much of his work actually resembled that of Scott in seeking to preserve the traditions and folklore of the countryside of his youth. *Life on the Mississippi* is a magnificent attempt at cultural conservation, and supremely valuable on this account. This paper has stressed his creative writing, if only because the claims of his more directly observant prose assert themselves clearly enough, but its richness, its clarity, its vividness, its common sense make him in many respects an ideal reporter. But in this work, and certain others, he is being more than the simple observer; like Scott, he wanted to capture for posterity a dying world. *Tom Sawyer* is particularly rich in its emphasis on superstition, and he is witness to the degree to which a life peculiarly dependent on the environment is thrown even more forcefully into the arms of the supernatural, based on immediate folk tradition, than might be found in a society less at the whim of Nature. The codes of honour exhibited in *Huckleberry Finn* through Colonel Sherburn, or through the Grangerford-Shepherdson feud, give us the phenomena which presented themselves to Twain. So the passage we have just quoted is at its most noteworthy a statement of a general condition in the ante-bellum South of which these things are vivid illustrations. Twain is therefore inviting the historian to consider a highly artificial romanticism as one of the conditions leading to war, and, rightly, he notes it as present on both sides of the future war divide. He also argues that it continued in the south after the war. He naturally sees its operation most clearly in literary terms, but it is a general post-bellum Southern *malaise*. His theses suggest a society fumbling desperately for a culture, indeed an identity. His great sense of the potentially lethal character of false values is of outstanding help to him here. He does not deduce that the ease with which the so-called Scott romanticism caught on in the South, and indeed in the North, indicates how vulnerable was the young United States to artificial impregnation by parasite cultures, but he leaves the deduction easy to make. What we cannot expect from him is fairness to Scott, a sense of the realism of his approach as opposed to the romanticism of his readers, and above all a satisfactory yardstick with which to judge the medieval actuality as against Scott's version. He was even correct in noting that the infection of Scott and of Cooper erupted in essentially juvenile minds, though he botched it in trying to stick his own creation, Tom Sawyer, with the propensity: it lay for Hugh Walpole to bring out exactly the appeal *The Talisman* might have to a not over-bookish schoolboy.[28] What Twain did succeed in doing was to show how once a schoolboy had shown the potential rewards of his romantic obsessions in sheer greed, as happens with Tom's discovery of the treasure, it could prove an obsession to very sober citizens.[29] The problem about Sir Walter Scott was that the principal determinable impact of his literary influence on Southern society was, as Rollin G. Osterweis has shown, in Virginia, a part of the country Twain knew much less well than his native old South-west, or even the new South-west.[30] Nor could Twain be expected to realise that what Virginia made of Scott was what many other parts of the North Atlantic were making of him, Dublin for instance. Scott had furnished materials for the romantic movement; his own work was much more restrained, and contained much stronger guards, than was to be found in his degenerate followers whether in Ireland, America or elsewhere.[31] Twain had, then, appreciated and forced attention on the significance of irrational romanticism; his diagnosis of its origin was weak. But the sensationalism of that diagnosis had the merit of forcing attention on his conclusions, and he did history a service thereby. It may also be said that his demand for a new Southern literature, while unduly optimistic and generous in its view of his friends George Washington Cable and Joel Chandler Harris, asserted an agenda which would be taken up by the development of realistic Southern literature after his death, and with some sense of his influence.[32] Twain has to be seen as some Quixotic enunciator of the absurd, in such contexts as this, but the historian must be initially impressed by the sheer pygmy resolution of his attempts to prove the impossible, and subsequently drawn along his trajectory to the extent of surveying the new and unperceived terrain encountered on the way. In the case of his Scott thesis, what Twain above all leads the historian to do is to consider the force of culture in modern history — and thus, ironically, performing for American historiography the same service that Scott performed for British, that of driving narrow historians to broader fields if only to look to their laurels when popular novelists seem to shape public taste on the past.[33] The value of Twain as a writer remains undiminished for the historian despite the fact that he himself was at his creative weakest in writing historical fiction. *The Prince and the Pauper*, his fable of Edward VI and his double, has the merit of trying to produce flesh-and-blood boys amid a historical context, and as a friendly critic remarked, it is in fact Scott that he resembles in his sense of human beings and his belief in his interpretation.

Twain as a writer is witness to much which might otherwise elude the historian, or have eluded historians. He is in certain respects a hostile witness. If in commencing his evidence we think of him as being sworn, it is wise to remember that he will not swear by history. He is much more likely to swear at it. His own life and casual writing abounds in evidence not considered here which makes him an outstanding case-study, of particular importance to European historians because he stood outside so much of the European experience in the early life on which he drew to such literary (and historical) advantage, and because he warred against the European heritage so much. Europeans are naturally ready to make more of their links with the American past than Americans do, and the European historian of the United States does a service in stressing what Americans — still so much in Twain's long shadow — are apt to undervalue. But Europeans in their turn need to remind themselves that there is in the United States something really quite alien to Europe as well as much that descends from it, and Twain's hard-hitting testimony as well as his cultural crusades force us to come to terms with it. He is all the more valuable as a witness in being so accessible. His world is alien to the European, yet he draws his readers to it, and makes them respond to its dynamics. Halley's comet returned and he was born; it returned again when he died; it is with us once more today. He is, like the Hank Morgan he so much resembled, a dangerous Chief. He is impulsive and anachronistic; he is given to ferocious enthusiasms; he may follow out obsessions to insane lengths; his impatience with history may result in grand illumination or in grand electrocution. His logic may appear as mad to us as Hank Morgan's to the knights; and yet we may discover that what seems to be nonsense and is often presented as nonsense takes us farther into sense than we have any hope of going. We are overwhelmingly remote from him; and we are, if we will be, among the closest of his Gang, his friends, his followers.

He will not be easily typified, and if I have given some clues to his value to the historian as a witness here, it is only beginning to open up the subject. He wrote in magnificent protest against racial injustice. His earliest work included attacks on the Californian persecution of the Chinese. He denounced the persecution of the Jews, the war against the Filipinos, the lynching of Blacks, the reprisals after the Boxer Rising. Yet his record in literary judgment of the ethnic group whose sufferings at the hands of white Americans were most quantitatively destructive, the Amerindians, is one of bitter hostility. It is an instructive witness on the contours of prejudice and the limits of humanitarianism. It may owe something to the fact that Twain responded to Europe as the extremest of Americans, and yet knew there to be a group of Americans to whom he was but irredeemably European himself. The frontier superstitions and small-town shibboleths he chronicles so well had a half-believed terror of a spirit world behind them, as *Tom Sawyer* indicates so well, and this spirit world even seems to have some common features with the Amerindians' own ideas of spirits, or at least with such of them as were known, rightly or wrongly, to the white frontier community. It is part of the strength of Injun Joe that he first is taken by Tom and Huck to be a devil — admittedly, so are his companions, but he then murders one and frames the other — and he retains much spirit-like quality for the rest of his career, as he reappears without warning again and again, as the 'deaf-and-dumb' Spaniard in the haunted house, on the floor of Temperance Tavern room, above all in the cave. And Injun Joe retains the other aspect also, that of a recognizable *alter ego*, not only for Muff Potter, or old Finn, but even for Tom himself once he suffers the fate which Tom and Becky so narrowly escaped. But it is a chilling thought that Injun Joe only elicits sympathy and identification as a fellow-human when he is dead. It was, after all, the paradigm of the White attitude so widely expressed in nineteenth-century America.

The case of Injun Joe suggests that there was more in Twain's witness, as man and writer, than he realised he was revealing. But even when he is in control of his material, he is remarkable in his delicate propensity for being at once within the mind of the boy he describes and outside it, just as he can move with convincing difference through the minds of several child protagonists — Tom, Huck, Becky Thatcher, Amy Lawrence. The tension within Twain's own mind between the process of white civilization and the call of the frontier means that both Tom and Huck are logically justified in their different responses to specific symbols. The law in particular is the yardstick here. Insofar as Judge Thatcher represents the law, one might conclude there is little difference in their reactions to him: both of them pull the wool over his eyes at different times, Tom over Sunday-school proficiency, Huck over his own intentions as to his share of the treasure.[35] If anything Huck seems to have more respect for him than Tom. But when the crisis comes in *Tom Sawyer*, it is Tom who places the demands of the law before a private oath, whereas both in *Tom Sawyer* and *Huckleberry Finn* Huck will place no faith in the law at all. There is also an implication that the same difference extends to divine law, at any rate by the end of *Huckleberry Finn* (though there, as stated above, Tom is no longer to be regarded as consistent with his character in the earlier work). On the human law point, Twain is very helpful in enabling the historian to see the different patterns of settler response to a thinly-administered law. The scapegrace among the settlers will, for all of his rascality, acknowledge the magnetism of the legal edifice; the nomad will not, although he may use the law to accomplish specific ends. As to the ease with which Twain moves in and out of his subjects' minds, there is a classic example in *Tom Sawyer* when the question is under debate between Huck and Tom as to the identity of the howling dog. Is it a stray dog — and hence a harbinger of bad luck to them — or, harmlessly, their old acquaintance Bull Harbison? Twain then footnotes:[36]

If Mr Harbison had owned a slave named Bull, Tom would have spoken of him as 'Harbison's Bull'; but a son or a dog of that name was 'Bull Harbison'.

The gradations of prejudice are very finely observed here. There is no degradation in the animal nickname, as a general point — the corpse Dr Robinson wished to resurrect is that of Horse Williams, who is so called even by the legal authorities — but the placing of a slave's status below child or dog is eloquently asserted by use of the possessive case, Twain certainly intended his audience to savour to the full the degradation involved, all the more by his quiet, didactic manner, as well as the footnote's seeming irrelevance to the business in hand (which has been sensational enough to prohibit any normal wandering of the reader's attention).

This paper of mine complicates the issue of Twain as witness in one serious respect: I have been so far in sympathy with my subject's Protean quality as a witness that I have paid very little attention to one of the most important considerations for the historian — change over the passage of time in a writer's life. In part this has been dictated by Twain's own hold over memory. *Tom Sawyer, Huckleberry Finn* and other of his writing concerned with the Mississippi really exist in two different time-frames: the date of composition, and the date being recollected. The composition itself extends over different periods, separated by a short interval in the case of *Tom Sawyer,* a much longer in that of *Huckleberry Finn.* It is agreed that various events altered Twain profoundly: marriage and children, domicile in the East, literary success, financial disaster, long residence in Europe. Optimism is believed to have dominated his early writing life, a deepening despair his later. The last years are a 'dark period' which requires evaluation in its own right as is required also for, say, Anthony Trollope. The evidence of the writing, reflecting a movement towards despair, is to some extent offset by the rise to social pre-eminence which in the view of Orwell, for one, involved a treason on Twain's part to the ideals he had initially expressed.[37] Without prejudice to this argument, Twain often seems self-contradictory: the man who gave his age the label of 'the gilded age' charging it with corruption, artificiality, falseness and dissimulation was the friend and admirer of General Ulysses S. Grant, who had presided over the most corrupt administration of the nineteenth century, and the panegyrical obituarist of Speaker of the House 'Czar' Thomas B. Reed, iron defender of the political *status quo.*[38] The bitter and seminal critic and artist who led all his fellow-countrymen in opposing British cultural domination of the United States crowned his honours by the acceptance of an honorary doctorate from Oxford University in recognition of the great name he had achieved in the English literary scene.[39] Yet I would argue that memory forced a unity on his witness as a writer, and that the very act of perpetually returning to the past for what constitutes his most significant evidence to the historian, invites us to consider his work as a totality at least in the initial activity of assessing his services to us. It was true that the lapse of time meant that first Tom, and then Huck, lost the power they once possessed to unlock the key to memory for him. Even where in a late and failed effort, 'Tom Sawyer, Detective', there are moments in which the wellspring of the old inspiration seems to be gushing with useful new material, refined and processed with his old skill, it is weakened by Huck's narrative which in its prime, in *Adventures of Huckleberry Finn*, had been the main conduit of the greatness pervading the whole. But *Pudd'nhead Wilson*, neglected in this paper, is a triumphant proof of how much Twain could still draw from the same source.

It is a darker work, and it conveys a grim commentary on the smallmindedness of the Hannibal-type river town where he had been critical but kindly and indulgent to so many of its foibles in *Tom Sawyer.* Yet it is not inconsistent with *Tom Sawyer,* some of whose perceptions of darkness and Jeremiac analyses have been noted above. Twain always possessed an ambiguous response to so many of his favourite themes: the pattern of small-town settlement, the types of frontier freedom, even the European past. *The Prince and the Pauper* may be a literary failure, but it reflects a love of English history however small its understanding of it. The oscillations in the texts of *The Mysterious Stranger* between St Petersburg and Europe convey the unity of Twain's area of inspiration, even at the moment of snuffing it out. These ambiguities greatly strengthen Twain as witness. In a sense they testify to an unconscious search for balance, even objectivity, however partisan his mode of expression usually appeared to be. Similarly his failure to think historically was balanced by his brilliant mastery of topography, a compensation in which he was followed by his disciple, Robert Louis Stevenson. (And the same may be said for the work of another disciple, Rudyard Kipling.) [40] We are in the West, or on the river, with Twain, as we are in the Highlands, or in Edinburgh, with Stevenson, although the exact point of association may sometimes be hard to determine. As Bernard DeVoto pointed out, constructively if pedantically, even the ages of Tom and Huck vary from incident to incident on any sensible reading. [41] But equally it does not matter. His creations say what they have to say, and we are left to make the most of them, and Huck's *caveat* at the beginning of *Huckleberry Finn* retains its force: [42]

You don't know about me, without you have read a book by the name of 'The Adventures of Tom Sawyer', but that ain't no matter. That book was made by Mr Mark Twain, and he told the truth, mainly. There was things which he stretched, but mainly he told the truth. That is nothing. I never seen anybody but lied, one time or another, without it was Aunt Polly, or the widow, or maybe Mary. Aunt Polly — Tom's Aunt Polly, she is — and Mary, and the Widow Douglas, is all told about in that book — which is mostly a true book; with some stretchers, as I said before.

And in the absence of history as written by Aunt Polly, or Mary, or the Widow Douglas, the historian may remain well content with Mark Twain as witness.

NOTES AND REFERENCES

1. This paper was to have been delivered in the presence of my mother, Sheila Dudley Edwards (Síle Ní Shúilleabháin), who had first introduced me to Mark Twain, whose ideas on literary witness to history are partly reflected in this paper, and who was a native of Cork: and this would have been the greatest thing of all for me in a Conference whose invitation was one of the greatest honours I have ever received. But Mother died, suddenly

and painlessly, on 20 April 1985, a few hours before the 75th anniversary of Mark Twain's death. I know how grateful she is (my views on immortality are not Twain's) for the kindness of so many friends to me on her behalf, at the Conference: I want to thank especially Joseph Lee, John A. Murphy, Denis Kennedy and the editor. The paper was greatly assisted by the ideas of Professor Thomas Kilroy, who spoke on Twain at the North American Studies Conference at Edinburgh University in February 1969, and by a conversation I had with Professor Henry Nash Smith, the greatest authority on Twain of his time, when he visited Edinburgh in the early 1970s. I dedicate it to my mother's memory.

2. These references are obvious, apart from that to Enid Blyton: see her *Five on a Treasure Island* (London, 1942), and Barbara Stoney, *Enid Blyton* (London, 1971). R.C. Lamburn wrote as 'Richmal Crompton'. On nostalgic American juvenile fiction the most perceptive essay I know is George Orwell (Eric Blair), 'Riding Down from Bangor', in Sonia Orwell and Ian Angus (eds), *The Collected Essays, Journalism and Letters of George Orwell*, IV (2nd ed., Harmondsworth, 1970, pp 281-87).

3. Mark Twain, *Mississippi Writings* (New York, 1982), p. 3; D. Wecter, *Sam Clemens of Hannibal* (Boston, 1952). Cf. also Mark Twain's preface to *The Adventures of Tom Sawyer* (1876). I have used the Library of America reprints of *The Adventures of Tom Sawyer, Life on the Mississippi* (1883), *Adventures of Huckleberry Finn* (1884), *Pudd'nhead Wilson* (1894).

4. Twain, *Mississippi Writings*, p. 215. See also Twain to William Dean Howells, 5 July 1875, and 18 Jan. 1876, in Charles Neider (ed.), *The Selected Letters of Mark Twain* (New York, 1982), pp 86-89.

5. John S. Whitley, 'Kids' Stuff: Mark Twain's Boys' in Robert Giddings (ed.), *Mark Twain: A Sumptuous Variety* (London, 1985), pp 72-75. I dissent, however, from Dr Whitley's 'To the end Tom remains resolutely himself', believing that at best he is but a thin thread of himself. I am most grateful to Professor Dennis Welland for his discussion of this point with me.

6. 'Huck Finn and Tom Sawyer among the Indians', in Walter Blair (ed.), *Mark Twain's Hannibal, Huck & Tom* (Berkeley and Los Angeles, 1969), pp 92-140, with introductory matter pp 81-91. For Twain's famous demolition of Cooper see his 'Fenimore Cooper's Literary Offenses' reprinted from *North American Review* (July 1895), in George Dekker and John P. McWilliams (eds), *Fenimore Cooper — The Critical Heritage* (London, 1973), pp 276-87. The indictment charges Cooper with unreal depiction of Indians but did not argue for their innate savagery as this fragment does. Presumably this is what Twain meant when he said 'I am quite sure that (bar one) I have no race prejudices'. 'Concerning the Jews', 1899, in Charles Neider (ed.), *The Complete Essays of Mark Twain* (Garden City, N.Y., 1963), p. 236. Blair tentatively ascribed the fragment of 'Huck and Tom among the Indians' to 1884, after Twain had finished *Huckleberry Finn*.

7. Twain, *Mississippi Writings*, pp 661 and (editorial note by Guy Cardwell) 1079. B. De Voto, *Mark Twain at work* (Cambridge, Mass., 1942), pp 9-10, 73-74, 78-79.

8. W.S. Gibson (ed.), *Mark Twain's Mysterious Stranger Manuscripts* (Berkeley and Los Angeles, 1969); Mark Twain and C.D. Warner, *The Gilded Age* (1873). For a contemporary American acknowledgement that 'the vices which Mr Trollope so effectually uncovers are not only common, but in their thin disguise, get ready admission and not infrequent respect in the society of both England and America' see the unsigned notice in New York *Harper's Magazine* (Oct. 1875), reprinted in Donald Smalley (ed.), *Anthony*

Trollope — The Critical Heritage (London, 1969), p. 414.

9. Obviously there is some contemporary material: for instance Twain was very briefly the secretary to Senator William M. Stewart of Nevada in Washington, D.C., in 1867-8. But the strongest inspiration is pre-war: Colonel Sellers, for instance, was based on Twain's mother's cousin James Lampton, as known to him in the 1840s and 1850s (*Autobiography*, pp 19-20).

10. Twain, *Mississippi Writings*, p. 49.

11. Wecter, *Sam Clemens of Hannibal*, pp 134, 296. De Voto, *Twain at Work*, pp 37-39.

12. Twain, *Mississipi Writings*, p. 128. De Voto, *Twain at Work*, 14-16, becomes excited about the exclusion of sexual implications from the episode. I am rather more concerned about the inclusion of social ones.

13. The author in question was Mary Ann Harris Gay whose *Prose and Poetry* (afterwards *The Pastor's Story and Other Pieces; or, Prose and Poetry*) went through 'at least eleven editions, under three or more imprints' following its publication in Nashville, Tennessee, for the author ('a Georgia lady') in 1858 (Twain, *Mississippi Writings*, p. 1074 (Cardwell's note)).

14. Henry Nash Smith, *Mark Twain — The Development of a Writer* (Cambridge, Mass., 1962), p. vii *et passim*.

15. Twain, *Mississippi Writings*, p. 115.

16. *Ibid.*, pp 175-76. De Voto, *Twain at Work*, pp 19-20, asserts that 'belief grows reluctant' at this passage: not mine. Similarly he draws attention (p. 13) to Twain's alteration of Joe's original notion of the revenge proprieties toward women ('you cut her nose off — and her ears') to the present form. 'Perhaps Olivia Clemens or Mark's children had shrunk from these expressions, though more likely it was Mark's own nerves that flinched'. The ultimate effect of the original form of revenge would be more hideous, but there is a hissing sadism about the later form which makes it far more chilling to me than the businesslike brutality of its predecessor. Twain's emendation seems more likely to be artistry than nerves. In passing, the patronising use of the name 'Mark' in speaking of an adult writer seems in its way more offensive than Injun Joe's various modes of expression.

17. Mark Twain, *Autobiography* (3rd ed., London, 1960, ed. C. Neider), pp 68-69; Wecter, *Sam Clemens of Hannibal*, pp 151, 158.

18. 'It is interesting to discover that Injun Joe's companion in the grave-robbing was originally Old Man Finn. He became Muff Potter, no doubt to prevent Huck's oath from putting his father's life in jeopardy' (De Voto, *Twain at Work*, p. 17). De Voto's information is important, even if his comment is fatuous — the oath would have been less important or non-existent, had that plan been followed, and the burden of vindication would have fallen not on Tom, but Huck, which was a sufficient reason for abandoning the idea. The point indicates that Twain intended from a very early stage to make something of old Finn, and his original coupling with Injun Joe is significant given that old Finn's Negrophobia (*Mississippi Writings*, pp 650-51) is a nastier echo of Joe's. Finn bears little enough resemblance, apart from his alcoholism, to the pathetically good-natured Muff Potter. On the other hand, the notion expressed in Kenneth S. Lynn, *Mark Twain and Southwestern Humor* (Boston, 1959), p. 197, that *Jim* is 'hauntingly foretold' in the death of Injun Joe, is nonsense, although the material in the same book on the precursors of Twain in Southwestern humour is very useful.

19. Twain, *Mississippi Writings*, pp 775-76. It was Twain's literary antagonist Matthew Arnold who once referred to history as 'that huge Mississippi of falsehood' (*Essays in*

Criticism. First Series (London, 1865): 'Literary Influence of Academies', quoted in John Barlett, *Familiar Quotations* (13th ed., Boston, 1955, p. 622)). Could this have inspired Twain? The word 'Mississippi' would certainly have caught his attention, had he encountered the passage. The humour of the thing would have appealed to him, and he met Arnold in Hartford on 14 November 1883, when *Huckeberry Finn* was nearing completion. Although his attacks on Arnold still lay in the future, he would have seen him as the representative of elitist culture imposing itself on the world. Cf. Henry Nash Smith and William M. Gibson (eds), *Mark Twain — Howells Letters — The Correspondence of Samuel L. Clemens and William D. Howells 1872-1910* (Cambridge, Mass., 1960), I, pp 449-50, fn.

20. W.B. Yeats, 'Three Songs to the Same Tune', and 'Three Marching Songs', *Collected Poems of W.B. Yeats* (2nd ed., London, 1950), pp 322, 378, the versions being identical.

21. James Joyce, *Ulysses* (Paris, 1922). Roger B. Salomon, *Mark Twain and the Image of History* (New Haven, 1961), p. 210 actually concludes its entire text 'For the Twain of *The Mysterious Stranger*, as for so many later writers, history (to paraphrase Stephen Dedalus) had become a nightmare from which one must — somehow — awake to live and write'. I have certain reservations about this valuable book — among other things it fails to allow for Twain's sectionalism, to the extent of being highly critical of the American East rather than simply defensive about a Jeffersonian past — but this final argument rather neatly underscores the freedom of Huck from history.

22. 'The story was heavily indebted to "that French idiot", Jules Verne just as its sequel, *Tom Sawyer, detective*, was an attempt to cash in on the rage for Sherlock Holmes', J. Kaplan, *Mark Twain and his World* (London, 1974), p. 155.

23. S. Leacock, *Mark Twain* (2nd ed., London, 1938), pp 90-91.

24. It is my assumption that Leacock's view of Twain was largely established abut 1910-14 when most of his own best work was done, and Twain's influence on him was freshest.
  A late work by Professor Henry Nash Smith (anything by whom is indispensable on Twain), quotes Ernest Hemingway's remark 'all modern American literature comes from one book by Mark Twain called *Huckleberry Finn'*, [Hemingway, *The Green Hills of Africa* (New York, 1935), p. 22 — the date is noteworthy as three years after Leacock's analysis], as well as some apposite comments from George Santayana. Professor Smith concludes his analysis of *Huckleberry Finn* here (p. 119):

It now appears that Huck's transcendence of this dominant value system has been implicit from the outset in Mark Twain's choice of Huck's vernacular speech as the narrative medium of the entire story. Academically correct speech, especially if it is in the slightest degree exalted, has been systematically linked in this book with hypocrisy, self-dramatization, fraudulent claims to status, cynicism, and cruelty, all radiating outward (so to speak) from the institution of slavery. Huck's perspective escapes the control of the dominant popular culture by virtue of the fact that his vocabulary lacks the high-sounding abstract terms (such as property, sin, and Providence) in which it is incorporated and without which its values cease to exist. Thus his vernacular speech not merely expresses a state of mind characterized by inner freedom, it embodies that state of mind, indeed it *is* that state of mind. The primary achievement of *Adventures of Huckleberry Finn* is its language; through Huck Finn, Mark Twain made available to the next generation of writers a literary prose freed from the associations and connotations of the decadent high culture of the nineteenth century. This prose (and the cultural revolution it embodies) is what the successors of the native humorists . . . had to put in place of the genteel tradition. Smith, *Democracy and the Novel* (New York, 1978), pp 107-27.

25. Professor Henry F. May, *The End of American Innocence* (London, 1960), has made the definitive case for dating the success of American culture in breaking free form its British provincial status as between 1912 and 1917.

26. Twain, *Mississippi Writings*, pp 500-02. Professor Dennis Welland (*Mark Twain in England*(London, 1978)), has shown how little reconcilable humour and seriousness of purpose seemed to the Victorian English who encountered Mark Twain's work; it remains one of the legacies of the genteel tradition against which he protested that the one quality or the other will be given excessive pre-eminence in any common analysis of passages such as this.

27. Dan H. Laurence (ed.), *The Bodley Head Bernard Shaw. Collected Plays with their Prefaces* (London, 1973), IV, p. 44 (Preface to *Saint Joan* dated May 1924). Salomon, *Twain and the Image of History*, p. 20 n. lists thirty historians read by Twain, and omits Herodotus. I would feel that this simply shows he filled, but did not build, his mind in studying history.

28. Walpole, 'Saladin and the Black Bishop', *Jeremy and Hamlet* (London, 1923).

29. Twain, *Mississippi Writings*, p. 210.

30. Ostwerweis, *Romanticism and Nationalism in the Old South* (New Haven, 1949).

31. See G.S.R. Kitson-Clark, 'The Romantic Element 1830 to 1850' in J.H. Plumb (ed.), *Studies in Social History* (London, 1955).

32. William Faulkner seems to me the obvious case of a natural literary influence here; Robert Penn Warren seems one of more consciously assumed intellectual influence. William Van O'Connor, 'Why *Huckleberry Finn* Is Not the Great American Novel', *College English* (Oct. 1955), reprinted in Barry A. Marks (ed.), *Mark Twain's Huckleberry Finn* (Boston, 1959), p. 105, announces that 'Writers like . . . Faulkner do not derive from Twain'. Faulkner (are there really any writers like him?), was very enthusiastic about Huck and Jim, although not Tom, which, not surprisingly, indicates that we should to to *Huckleberry Finn* and not *Tom Sawyer* to find points of inspiration for his work (Lynn, *Mark Twain and Southwestern Humor*, p. 137), beginning possibly with Huck on Henry VIII and stream-of-consciousness in *The Hamlet* to which Lynn (p. 221) would add the Benjy section of *The Sound and the Fury*. Admittedly, Faulkner was rude about Twain in 1922 (Willand, *Twain in England*, p. 230 and n.).

33. Scott's achievement in cultural history and the lacuna it thereby revealed in conventional history are eloquently expounded by T.B. Macaulay in his essay 'History', *Edinburgh Review*, XLVII (May 1828). I have discussed the importance of his folklore conservation in fiction in my 'Scott as a contemporary Historian' in Alan Bold (ed.), *Sir Walter Scott — The Long-Forgotten Melody* (London, 1983), pp 65-90. The most interesting recent discussion of Southern cultural attitudes is Bertram Wyatt-Brown, *Southern Honor — Ethics and Behavior in the Old South* (New York, 1982). Professor Wyatt-Brown finds interesting responses to *The Heart of Midlothian* in the South (p. 235), which certainly argues for a much more reputable choice of Scott on the part of some Southerners than Twain, who was evidently thinking of *Ivanhoe* and *The Talisman*, would suggest. On the other hand the continued popularity of the last two, at least in plot-outline, is indicated by their being taken up by Hollywood (1953 and 1954, respectively, *The Talisman* as *King Richard and the Crusaders*).

34. Mark Twain, *The Prince and the Pauper* (1881). Hjalmar Hjorth Boyesen, unsigned review of *The Prince and the Pauper*, *Atlantic* XLVIII (Dec. 1881), reprinted in

Anderson and Sanderson, *Twain - Critical Heritage,* pp. 87-88. Boyesen, Norwegian-born Professor of German at Cornell University, was, like Twain, a friend and protégé of William Dean Howells.

35. Twain, *Mississippi writings,* pp. 35-36, 639-40. Judge Thatcher is believed to have been based on Twain's father (Charles A. Norton, *Writing Tom Sawyer* (Jefferson, N.C., 1983), p. 80), but his legal symbolism is vital.

36. Twain, *Mississippi Writings,* p. 72,n.

37. Orwell, 'Mark Twain — the Licensed Jester', *Collected Essays, Journalism and Letters,* II, pp. 369-74. The essay originally appeared in *Tribune,* 26 Nov. 1943.

38. Kaplan, *Mark Twain and His World,* pp. 120-21, 128-30. C. Neider, *Completed Essays of Mark Twain* (New York, 1963), pp. 311-12.

39. Welland, *Twain in England,* pp. 224-25.

40. *Autobiography,* 268-90, gives modest accounts of his meetings with them. Stevenson does not include Twain among his three literary forbears in the poem dedicatory to *Treasure Island* (though he does mention Cooper), but then *Tom Sawyer* is not about pirates but about playing pirates, which would give the game away. But Injun Joe is an obvious precursor to Pew, and to Silver at his most murderous; and his unexpected appearances prefigure the pirates' unexpected presence in the stockade. And *Kim* is clearly a child of *Huckleberry Finn.* See Rudyard Kipling, *From Sea to Sea* (London, 1900), II, pp. 182-98.

41. De Voto, *Twain at Work,* pp. 18-21.

42. Twain, *Mississippi Writings,* p. 625.

Fictional Images of Irish-America

LAWRENCE J. McCAFFREY

Tugged up from their home roots, taken and going willingly from the
sea smell and the peat smells ... Shoved into a boat and with sweating
and cursing and stinking and praying, with deaths and births, with old
age and youth, they landed and a shovel was placed in their hands or a
hammer or a spade and they built Boston and New York and Chicago
and Philadelphia. And in the evening they walked home in the leaning
shadows of the gray stone to their one room or two rooms and fell into
bewildered sleep.[1]

Waves of Irish Catholics began battering the American shore in the
1820s. While less educated, skilled, or sophisticated than Irish Protestant,
English, Scots or Germans who left Europe for the United States, Irish
Catholic emigrants had the means to purchase passage and food for the sea
voyage and for an early survival stake in America. They also possessed the
courage and determination to leave familiar surroundings, families, and
friends, and to set out on a long and dangerous journey to a land almost
beyond their comprehension.[2] Lacking agricultural and other economic
skills, prohibited by their Catholic communal personalities from settling in
lonely rural spaces, the Irish became the unskilled proletarian pioneers of
the American urban ghetto.[3]

Despite life difficulties, early Irish Catholic immigrants managed to
build and buy churches and homes, beginning a slow climb toward respectability. Then the 1840s tide of wretched Famine refugees pulled Irish-
America back down to poverty depths. In many American cities the Irish
huddled in suffocating attics, damp basements, or tarpaper shacks without
basic washing or sewage facilities. Still, they made a contribution. Unskilled Irish men and women speeded the American industrial and
transportation revolutions. Irish women domestic servants gave comfort
and leisure to middle-class Anglo-Protestants by cleaning their houses and
minding their children. And Irish soldiers died for America in the Mexican
and Civil Wars and on the Western Frontier.

227

The transition from rural Ireland to urban America traumatized immigrants. That and poverty nurtured physical and mental disorders, alcoholism, crime, brutality, and family breakups. The Irish social problem and, more importantly, their religion made them the first large scale victims of American nativism. According to one American newspaper: 'Scratch a convict or a pauper and you are certain to tickle the skin of an Irish Catholic.'⁴ Struggles for survival and acceptance, frequent failures, and Anglo-American prejudice added to the paranoia and defeatism that many brought from Ireland.

Cultural and economic poverty, a lack of self-esteem, and concentrations on survival, then mobility, delayed an Irish-American literature. Appropriately it emerged from journalism. Immigrants educated in nationality by Thomas Davis of the *Nation* and Charles Kickham of *The Irish People* formed the personality of Irish-America. Starting in the 1870s, John Boyle O'Reilly and his protégés at *The Boston Pilot* authored a large quantity of prose and poetry. However their work was flawed by imitations of the romanticism of the *Nation* and the idealism of the New England literary establishment.⁵

A truly Irish dimension of American literature began in the 1890s with Finley Peter Dunne's Mr Dooley essays in *The Chicago Evening Post*. Experiences as a sports, police, and political reporter gave his writing a direct and realistic impact. More than a clever satirist using an Irish brogue to comment on local and national foibles, Dunne was a social historian who also created the first authentic urban ethnic community in American fiction.⁶ In conversations with McKenna and Hennessey, patrons of his Archey Road (Archer Avenue) saloon, Martin Dooley, Roscommon expatriate, described and analyzed Bridgeport's unskilled workers, firemen, policemen, housewives, widows, priests, criminals, and Clan-na-Gael nationalists.

Empathizing with the Irish survival effort in America, Dunne understood how it calloused their personalities and pragmatized their virtue. He also explained how ambitious mothers insisting on schooling and Americanization for their children, educated sons and daughters growing apart from greenhorn parents, and how new immigrants pushing the Irish up the occupation ladder and out to new sections of the city, dissolved an Irish neighbourhood.

Changing fashions have diminished the artistic reputation of another Chicagoan, James T. Farrell, Irish-America's first literary star. Although he attended the University of Chicago, to Catholics a centre of pagan materialism, Farrell remained self-consciously Irish with a Joycean determination to travel a lonely road, telling the truth about his own kind. Mostly written in the 1930s and early 1940s about the 1920s, the Studs Lonigan and Danny O'Neill novels are Farrell's best work.[7] His Washington Park subjects are the children and grandchildren of Dunne's Bridgeport Irish. Reaching the skilled labour and lower middle-classes, they have moved from coldwater to steamheated flats. Impressive looking Catholic churches and schools are neighbourhood focal points and monuments to their increasing affluence. Prosperity brought physical comforts, but urban tensions and competitiveness introverted their emotions. Internalizing aspirations, emotions, and feelings, expressing them in fantasies and daydreams, they are unable to physically or verbally express affection, frustration, or loss. So they explode in anger. Although seeming to be doing well in urban America, Farrell's Irish are insecure. Like their immigrant forbears they are refugees, pushing farther and farther south in the city to avoid an expanding black ghetto.[8]

Overcoming Anglo-Protestant intolerance and its own insecurities, Irish-America continued the journey to social respectability. Common suffering during the 1930s economic depression, followed by World War II common cause reduced inter-religious and ethnic frictions in the United States. When such cinema notables as Spencer Tracy, Pat O'Brien, and Bing Crosby in the late 1930s and early 1940s played Irish-American priests as masculine social workers in Roman collars, they integrated catholicism into American popular culture. After 1945, many Irish-Americans took advantage of G.I. Bill educational opportunities, increasing their membership in business and the professions. Middle-class incomes and status financed and motivated Irish flight from urban racial tension spots to the suburbs.

Literature was slow to record Irish-American occupational, social, and geographic changes and the resulting transformation in attitudes. While more didactic than literary, Harry Sylvester's 1947 novel, *Moon Gaffney*, had a tremendous impact on Irish-Americans, intent on shedding ethnic provinciality. His presentation of middle-class 1930s New York Irish-Americans is negative. Catholic college or university education, Democratic Party politics, conscientious religious practices did not mean intellectualism, social justice concerns, or christian charity. Generally Sylvester's characters are so obsessed with respectability and conformity that they exude mediocrity. Despising blacks as animals and Jews as Bolsheviks they think of Irish-Americans as the chosen people, the only real catholics and patriots. Their charm and wit is frivolous and often cruel. Alcohol, a substitute for sex, fuels their socializing. They prefer

crowded places with drinks in their hands to intimate situations with someone in their arms. [9]

Intellectual and literary links are difficult to establish but there seems to
be connections between the works of Sylvester and more talented writers
who followed him. Tom McHale's *Farragan's Retreat* paints late 1960s
middle-class Irish-America with more satiric strokes but in theme he
resembles Sylvester. Jim, Anna, and Arthur Farragan manage a
Philadelphia construction-trucking company started by their immigrant
parents. Jedda, their mother, discovered that their brother Stephen was a
homosexual and sent him off to die in World War II. Another brother, Edmund, was too simple-minded for the family business. So the Farragan's
bought his way into a small retreat order, the Tirungians, and later its
Father Generalship.

Jim and Anna are flag-waving patriots and racists. At her daily firearm
practice Anna shoots at targets resembling black males, fervently hoping
for an occasion to kill a real one as burglar, mugger, or rapist. Arthur is
kind and sensitive, but an Irish Catholic prude. He turns holy pictures and
statues to the wall while making love to Muriel, his wife. But that was in the
past. Muriel has told Arthur that since the painful birth of twin daughters
sex has become repugnant. Now she is preoccupied with efforts to canonize
murdered Italian rape victims. Blessed Elizabeth La Voci is her present
cause. Continuing to worship Muriel as a preciously beautiful, demented
saint, Arthur turns to Marie Glennis, the daughter of a former college
sweetheart, for companionship and physical gratification. Muriel,
however, only pretends madness and frigidity to escape Farragan in-
volvements. She is having an affair with Binky Applebaum, a Jewish
lifeguard, who told Arthur that he was emasculated in Korean combat.

Because Anna's Malcolm was killed and Jim's Edward wounded in Vietnam while Arthur's Simon opposed the war and fled to Canada to avoid
the draft, Jim and Anna insist that Arthur must avenge family and country
by executing his own son. Pretending to assent, he slips out of his alibi
retreat at Edmund's monastery not to kill but to warn Simon of Farragan
vengence. However, the violent deaths of all of the family, except his
father, free Simon from danger. When Arthur discovers that Muriel and
demolitions expert, Binky, have terminated his siblings and are lovers he
shoots himself. [10]

Jimmy Breslin, Joe Flaherty, and Pete Hammill have written about
mostly working or lower middle-class New York Irish who share Farragan
values and prejudices. In Breslin's *World Without End, Amen*, Dermot
Davey's father has deserted his family and returned to Ulster. Dermot, a

bribe taking, alcoholic policeman, is shackled to Phyllis in a double-fault, cold marriage. Despite his character faults, Davey considers himself a patriot defending his country from 'commies, niggers, and liberals'. He and other cops work in Alabama Governor George Wallace's presidential primary campaign. In their favourite bar they accompany Kate Smith's jukebox records, 'God Bless America' and 'The Star Spangled Banner', insisting that other patrons stand and join them in the National Anthem.

One night, Dermot and his partner, Sergeant Johno O'Donnell, use and abuse a black trans-sexual. Pleading the old Irish excuse, drink, they are suspended for only two weeks on the understanding that they will join other alcoholic policemen on an Irish tour conducted by the department chaplain, Monsignor Carrigan. Dermot's Irish journey becomes a family search. He visits his mother's Belfast relatives and locates his father tending bar in a Derry pub. Dermot is shocked to discover that Catholics are the blacks of Northern Ireland. This and love for civil rights activist, Deirdre O'Doherty, a Bernadette Devlin clone, force him to reconsider his prejudices and to become involved in the Northern Ireland civil rights movement. After Deirdre is killed by a bullet intended for Bernadette, Dermot returns to New York sadder but only temporarily wiser than when he left. Soon he is again boozing and intimidating blacks.[11]

Joe Flaherty's *Tin Wife* is a more complex examination of New York Irish cops. Like Dermot's, Eddie Sullivan's original idealism has been corrupted by the shady side of police work. His racist remarks, however, are something more than blind prejudice. He and his comrades are at war in city streets against mostly black and Hispanic enemies. Eddie also realizes that Irish and other catholics once were urban outcasts. He and others in the force are defending their present respectability from their past. Most of Eddie's work associates, including blacks and Hispanics, are contemptuous of liberal, middle-class reformers who claim to love the poor but live apart from and imprison them in patronizing welfarism.[12] Both Breslin's and Flaherty's policemen express a negative working-class opinion of higher education for their children. What was good enough for fathers and mothers is appropriate for sons and daughters. College is for Jews; the 'economic Holy Trinity' of civil service security, benefits, and pensions for the Irish.

Literature has concentrated on the two most important aspects of Irish-America, religion and politics, with fluid borders between the two. Politics defended against nativism, provided social services, and gave access to power and through power to economic opportunities. Historian Patrick O'Farrell has described Irish catholicism as more than dogma and liturgy:

'it is a set of values, a culture, a historical tradition, a view on the world, a disposition of mind and heart, a loyalty, an emotion, a psychology — and a nationalism'.[13] Anglo-American protestant prejudice forced Irish leaders of American catholicism to construct alternative institutions featuring schools, hospitals, orphanages, and asylums. Politicians and priests shared Irish-American leadership. Similar instincts and talents guided men who managed wards and parishes, cities and dioceses. Political machines and the Catholic institutional alternative incorporated catholic into Irish-America, strengthening both.

Some writers have highlighted the positive qualities of Irish catholicism. For immigrant generations it bridged Ireland and America, offering the familiar in a new setting. While catholicism targeted the Irish for abuse, it also provided social and cultural self-sufficiency in the midst of the enemy. Until recently the parish was a cohesive community. James Carroll's *Prince of Peace* appreciates it as the focal point of Irish neighbourhoods, the gathering place for devotions, education, social and athletic events.[14] He and others have described gothic and baroque churches with plaster saints, gory Stations of the Cross, stained windows illustrating the New Testament, candle and incense smells, votive lights, mumbled Latin, and Gregorian chant. To sophisticates much of it was offensive, but to working and lower middle-class people the sounds, scents, and sights of the parish church were satisfying. For rich and poor, educated and ignorant the Church offered spiritual and psychological relief. In his family chronicle, *Mass for the Dead,* distinguished playwright, William Gibson, designates catholic liturgical and sacramental occasions as life signposts.[15] Mary McCarthy has credited the 'history and mystery' of catholicism with literary inspiration.[16]

Literature concedes catholicism's permanent imprint on the Irish-American psyche. In William Kennedy's *Legs*, John Thomas Diamond is a bootlegger, hijacker, drug dealer, and sadistic murderer. He publicly flaunts his chorus girl paramour, Kiki. Still, his wife Alice stays with him because as a good Irish catholic woman how could she expiate 'that black terribleness of marrying and loving evil, except by staying married to it?' Marcus Gorman, Diamond's religiously indifferent lawyer, is unable to escape the reasoning of St Thomas Aquinas. And he remains a product 'of the ecclesiastical Irish sweat glands, obesiant before the void, trying to discover something'.[18]

A literary consensus accepts the dominant catholic facet of the Irish personality but it shares with many writers in Ireland a conviction that Irish catholicism is an oppressive burden of peasant pietism, dogmatic authoritarianism, sexual puritanism, and anti-intellectualism. A large number of Irish-American writers have affirmed Michael Novak's description of Irish catholicism as a 'Celtic Heresy' and Philip Roth's observation that Jewish writers were fortunate to have escaped 'an Old Country link and strangling church like Italians, or the Irish or the Poles'.[19]

Writer critics of Irish catholicism have attributed frigidity, guilt, neuroses and psychoses, and gender segregation to its Jansenism. They blame much of Irish alcoholism on sexual frustration. Eugene O'Neill plays are saturated with sexual tension and guilt. Sexual incompatability and the inability to discuss it create friction between John and Nettie Cleary in Frank Gilroy's prize-winning play, *The Subject Was Roses*.[20] They also provoke and prolong the Davey family cold war in *World Without End, Amen*. Catholicism is central in all of Thomas J. Fleming's novels about the Irish in a New Jersey City, especially *The God of Love, Romans, Countrymen and Lovers, The Sandbox Tree, The Good Shepherd*, and *Promises to Keep*.[21] Admitting that catholicism once shielded the Irish cast adrift in urban, industrial America, Fleming says this service has become irrelevant and negative. Since the United States opened its door to diversity, the catholic mental ghetto has blocked entry. Fleming sees catholicism as alien authoritarianism in a liberal America. By emphasizing separateness against pluralism, it retards the progress of American catholics.

According to Fleming, catholic colleges and universities are irrelevant medieval detours from modern American realities. Their graduates enter another ghetto, the increasingly suburban parish. There they smugly attack materialism and secularism, congratulating themselves on superior virtue. But, says Fleming, catholic businessmen and professionals are as unscrupulous in their money hunt as other Americans. Catholic marriages feature indifference and strife. Roman rules have made women baby machines, entrapping wives and husbands in loveless, contentious unions. Compelled to sublimate the natural impulses of affection, they make love by the thermometer and the calendar and the Church calls it natural.

Many Irish-American fiction priests are fools or knaves. Edmund Farragan is a fool, as are priests in another MacHale novel, *Principatio*.[22] In William Kennedy's *Billy Phelan's Greatest Game* Martin Daugherty worries that his seminary-entering son might become like some clerics he has known: 'There was a suburban priest who kept a pet duck on a leash. One in Troy chased a nubile child around the parish house. Priests in their cups. Priests in their beggar's robes. Priests in their eunuch suits.'[23] *Moon Gaffney* priests are more knavish than clownish. 'Bingo Robbie' Malone recruits for the pro-fascist Christian Front. Another ultra-conservative bigot, Father O'Driscoll, gives wrong information on the rhythm system to Mount Murphy College students so that they become pregnant on their honeymoons and produce more souls for Christ. In Fleming's *The Sandbox Tree*, Father Denton Malone is also chaplain at a catholic women's college. He is a religious vocation recruiter who tortures Mount Saint Monica students with his sexual neurosis. Priest fascination has inspired but limited J.F. Powers. His highly regarded short stories and national Book Award novel, *Morte D'Urban,* satirize builder priests who invite money changers into the temple.[24] They enjoy good food and drink, expensive cars, tailored clothes, and golf at the country club. Their font of information and wisdom is *The Reader's Digest.* Oblivious to poverty, social injustices, and papal pronouncements on them, they preach against fornication, adultery, contraception, filthy books and movies, and communism.

Although catholic liberals of the 1940s and 1950s identified Powers as well as Sylvester with their points of view, Powers is more of a modern Chaucer than an Erasmus or Marsiglio of Padua. His intention is church purification rather than change. He criticizes the sanctimonious, superficially learned, patronizing, arrogant, smug liberal priest as well as the rotarian type. Post-Vatican II catholicism has not been attractive to Powers. A few writers have avoided stereotyping by analyzing the ambiguities of the priest's role as both spiritual and secular leader. Matthew Cardinal Mahan in Fleming's *The Good Shepherd* decides to emphasize the spirit of christianity rather than its rigid laws. He soft-peddles contraception and invites the divorced back into communion with the Church. Radical young priests in the archdiocese decide that Mahan is too tentative. His initiatives strike the older conservative clergy and the Vatican bureaucracy as dangerously radical. The Cardinal travels to Rome to explain his conviction that the Church must adjust to human nature and a better educated laity. He dies there a defeated man. Monsignor Desmond Spellacy in John Gregory Dunne's *True Confessions* is more real in his complexity than Mahan. Consciously, if not easily, he distinguishes between the cities of God and man. As chancellor of the Archdiocese of Los Angeles, trouble shooter and hatchet man for the cardinal, Desmond has to build quickly and cheaply the churches and schools badly needed in a rapidly expanding post-World War II metropolitan area. To do this he works with Jack Amsterdam, vicelord turned contractor. In a vigilante raid on evil and hypocrisy, Desmond's homicide detective lieutenant brother, Tom, once Amsterdam's bagman, pins a false murder charge on his ex-boss. The scandal blocks Desmond's rise to auxiliary bishop. Instead he ends up in a poor desert parish where he finds satisfaction and peace performing as a priest.[25]

Edwin O'Connor's Pulitzer Prize-winning *The Edge of Sadness* is a sensitive examination of clerical life. Father Hugh Kennedy is so involved with the tasks of his middle-class parish, St Stephen's, that he neglects to cultivate spirituality. Thus, when his father, who is also his best friend, dies he turns to whiskey, not God. Alcoholism forces his removal from St Stephen's and a four-year Colorado rest cure. The bishop calls Hugh back to the city and assigns him to Old St Paul's, a collapsing inner-city parish. He is content, viewing St Paul's as an interlude, a preparation for another comfortable Irish parish. Since Hugh is indifferent to the run-down parish and its polyglot population, his naive, platitudinous, dense curate, Stanley Danowski, ministers to the urban outcasts. Kennedy begins by patronizing the young Pole, then realizes his assistant is teaching him a lesson in priestly deportment. Associations with the Carmody family bring Hugh back into Irish social relationships. Charley, the eighty-one year old, cruel tongued, emotionally cold family patriarch has acquired a fortune from property, mainly apartment rentals. His children, John and Helen, were childhood friends of Hugh. John is pastor of St Raymond's, Hugh's idea of a parish, but is psychologically harassed by its burdens: the demands of clubs and societies, obsequious interventions on his privacy, details of maintaining the physical plant. Desperately he asks the bishop's permission to enter a monastery. The bishop replies that the contemplative life is not for world-escapers, that priests should seek God in other men, not in isolation. Hugh commiserates with his friend but he is told that he has shirked the duties of his calling. John's rebuke leads to self-recognition. When John dies of stress ulcers, the bishop offers Hugh his parish. Without hestitation Kennedy decides to stay put, realizing that catholicism should transcend ethnic tribalism, that priests must serve all men in all places, even the most wretched of God's creatures.[26]

Although catholicism is the essential feature of Irish-America, its association with politics gets more attention. In contrast with their technological limitations, the Irish arrived in the United States relatively competent in politics. Daniel O'Connell's Catholic Emancipation and Repeal of the Union organizations and Charles Stewart Parnell's Home Rule movement educated them in public opinion mobilizing and political tactics. By the close of the nineteenth century they controlled most American industrial cities. Authorities conceded that they were 'the best politicians in the country . . . with unequalled power of political

organization,' with a 'genius for municipal government or at least for getting political office'.[27] Literature has interpreted Irish-American politics
through its practitioners.

Joseph Dinneen's *Ward Eight* and Edwin O'Connor's *The Last Hurrah*
examine the Irish political style more imaginatively and perceptively than
academic history.[28] Dinneen drew Hughie Donnelly from model Michael
Lomasney, late nineteenth- and early twentieth-century Boss of Boston's
West End. He had counterparts in other cities such as New York's George
Washington Plunkitt and Chicago's Johnny Powers. Donnelly protects his
constituents, finding them jobs and housing, making sure they have food
on the table. He solves personal and family problems. When there are legal
difficulties he provides bail and counsel. When there is sickness he sends a
doctor. If his charges die poor he wakes and buries them. Hughie super-
vises graft but little of it reaches his pockets. What does is justified as small
return for large service. Hughie wants loyalty not money. When Italians
begin replacing the Irish in the ward he brings them into the party, forging a
multi-ethnic coalition. *The Last Hurrah's* aging Frank Skeffington is running for another term as Mayor of a New England city. Corruption has
blemished his many years in office but, like Donnelly, he gives most of
what he gets. While his public works projects are expensive, often unnecessary, they mean employment and recreation and medical facilities for
the needy. Handsome, witty, and charismatic, a conscientious wake, wed-
ding, church social, and public function attender, Skeffington has blended
Irish, Italians, and Jewish voters into a powerful force. His enemies are
also mighty. Wealthy Anglo-Potestant Amos Force, newspaper publisher,
and banker Norman Cass, are determined to destroy the Irish chieftain.
Skeffington's foes are also found in the Irish community. His successful
contemporaries, the cardinal, and Harvard-educated Roger Sugrue, blame
him for confirming the Irish political stereotype. Young college-educated
liberal organizer, Jack Mangan, acknowledges Skeffington's intelligence
and charm, but regards him as a political fossil. Foes of Skeffington
coalesce behind Kevin McCluskey, a dimwit with attributes attractive to
the new television prompted voter: Jesuit education, military service, and a
photogenic family. They are sure that he will be their puppet. Much to
Skeffington's surprise, he loses badly. Mangan interprets the results as less
a victory for the McCluskey forces than for Franlin D. Roosevelt's New
Deal which assumed Irish political machine services.

The long political career of James Michael Curley inspired O'Connor's
Skeffington. James Carroll's *Mortal Friends* and Edward R.F. Sheehan's
The Governor offer less romantic and flattering portraits of Boston's

colourful Mayor.[29] Instead of leading catholics toward cooperation with Anglo-Protestants, Curley manipulated their inferiority complexes into conflict with Yankees, freezing their mobility, hampering the progress of a great city. As were the overwhelming majority of pre-1970s Irish, Donnelly and Skeffington were Democrats. Yet, in parts of Pennsylvania and Ohio the Irish adapted to the invincibility of the Republican Party. Two interesting fictional Irish politicians wore Republican labels; Mary Deasy's Aloysius O'Shaughnessy of Caroli, Ohio and John O'Hara's Mike Slattery from Gibbsville, Pennsylvania. They provided the same kind of services and demonstrated the same kind of organizational abilities as did Skeffington and Donnelly.[30] A year before the publication of *The Last Hurrah* Richard J. Daley commenced a twenty-one year reign as Chicago's mayor. Contradicting O'Connor's thesis, he persuaded Washington to filter federal funds through the Cook County Democratic machine, making it more powerful than ever before. His achievement suggests that declining Irish urban political power had more to do with their migration to the suburbs than with the national welfare state.

Suburbanization symbolized Irish-America's economic and social progress which altered its politics from power obsession to purpose awareness. This became obvious when Irish politicians became more visible on the state and national levels. Roosevelt rewarded Irish loyalty to the Democratic Party with many influential appointments to federal office. Irish bureaucrats, senators, congressmen, and supreme court justices helped revitalize America's economic and social structures. John F. Kennedy's 1960 election to the presidency completed the Irish-American political climb from the ghetto to national power. Much of Kennedy's Irish catholicism was cultivated image, but his charm, intelligence and world popularity filled Irish and other American catholics with pride. Fitzie in Edward Hannibal's *Chocolate Days, Popsicle Weeks* expresses their new self-esteem: 'He was us not them'.[31] Not only did Kennedy's presence in the White House finally integrate catholics into the United States, it also made Americans feel good about themselves. This favourably reflected on the Irish. *The Last Hurrah* featured the entertainment quality of Irish politics, but Kennedy was real and on a national stage. In *Fogarty and Company,* Joe Flaherty keened the final Dallas curtain: 'What was lost with Kennedy was not so much substance but style . . . The truth was that America could ill-afford to squander its stylish sons . . . Kennedy had been a relief, a pleasure to have your cocktail with as he appeared on the evening news, a respite from all those goddam Grant Wood people who have been running the country for years.'[32]

Thomas J. Fleming's New Jersey Irish political novels emphasize the change from power concerns to pragmatic idealism. *All Good Men* is about a 1951 election matching Dave Shea, thirty-year Mayor and machine boss, with party renegade, Matty Blair.³³ A coalition of Anglo-Protestant reformers and Italians, Poles, and blacks resentful of Irish dominance support Blair. Over-confidence and isolation from changing currents of public opinion doom Shea. Even his most talented and realistic lieutenant, Ben O'Connor, county commissioner and leader of the 13th ward, barely carries his fief. Like Skeffington, Donnelly, Slattery, and O'Shaughnessey, Ben entered politics because, except for the Church, it was the only opportunity path for bright Irish lads in anti-catholic America.

Disabled by a gangrenous leg, Ben enlists the campaign assistance of his cynical, purposeless son Jake, ex-navy veteran of World War II and law-school graduate. Once involved Jake's political instincts are aroused. While he has inherited his father's vocation, he is determined to apply the power he achieves to more idealistic goals than perpetuating the machine.

Jake in *King of the Hill,* financed by Paula Stapleton, from one of the city's most distinguished Anglo-Protestant families, leads reform Democratic opposition to the Blair administration which is more corrupt and less serviceable than its Shea predecessor.³⁴ In *Rulers of the City*, Jake, married to Paula, now an uncomfortable catholic, is in his fourteenth year as progressive mayor. His liberalism is pragmatically Irish catholic, seeking the probability of improvement rather than the impossibility of perfection. But Paula is rigidly Anglo-Protestant liberal, convinced that there are solutions to all social problems and conflicts. Their marriage is endangered by Paula's insistence, as federal judge, that black children must be bussed to public schools in a catholic neighbourhood. Jake does not share the prejudices of his Irish, Italian, and Polish constituents but he understands their anxieties. He also wants to become senator. Therefore, he seeks alternatives to the court order. A personal experience with mob violence and reflections on the Irish experience in urban America persuade Jake to comply with judge Stapleton's decree. At a St Patrick's Day banquet he reminds the Irish that their ancestors suffered discrimination. He urges them to lead the crusade for civil rights. At the novel's conclusion, Jake is certain that America's future demands a blending of Anglo-Protestant optimism and idealism with Irish caring and political genius, a combination symbolized in his union with Paula.³⁵

In *Erin's Daughters in America,* Hasia Diner describes Irish-American women as more successful than Irish-American men or other women in the United States.³⁶ Irish-American fiction does not pay tribute to this accomplishment. It describes Irish-American women as emotionally and morally stronger, more stable, practical, industrious, conservative, and dependable but less imaginative, sensitive, poetic, adventurous, in general less interesting or exciting than Irish-American men. Few women in Irish-American fiction are multi-dimensional. Wives are docile and long suffering as Alice Diamond in *Legs* and Annie Phelan in Kennedy's *Ironweed* and *Billy Phelan's Greatest Game*; or emotionally unstable as Janice Fitzpatrick in *Chocolate Days, Popsicle Weeks*; or matriarchs such as Mary Flaherty in Farrell's Danny O'Neill novels and Julia Devlin in Elizabeth Cullinan's *House of Gold*.[37] Typical of fictional Irish matriarchs, Julia intimidates her husband and imprisons her children in neurotic love and devotion. Sexually, Irish women in novels, short stories, and plays tend to be prudish or whorish. Diner points to the significance of Irish-American nuns as educators, nurses, and providers of social services. As college presidents and directors of hospitals they were among the first women to hold administrative positions in the United States. Still in literature, with only a few exceptions, for example sister Agnes Marie in Fleming's *The Sandbox Tree* and *The Good Shepherd* and Sylvester's mother Thomas in *Moon Gaffney*, they instil neurotic sexual guilt. The main character in Christopher Durang's superficial, cheap shot Obie Award play, *Sister Mary Ignatius Explains it All For You,* destroys student egos and libidos. Throughout *Chocolate Days, Popsicle Weeks* sister Mary Mustentoucher whispers sexual prohibitions in Fitzie's brain. In John Powers's non-maliciously humorous *The Last Catholic in America* and *Do Patten Leather Shoes Really Reflect Up?* nuns join with priests and brothers in trying to dampen the sexual fires of young Chicago Irish catholics.

Elizabeth Cullinan and Mary Gordon have contributed to Irish-American literature without expanding the fictional complexity of their own sex. Isobel Moore in Gordon's *Final Payments* enters the world after years of caring for a tyrant father. As Wilfrid Sheed observes, she approaches life tentatively as a nun just out of the convent. Simple choice confuses her. Without a sense of self, Isobel gives herself to insensitive men.[39] Felicitas in Gordon's *The Company of Women* does not improve on Isobel. She had a cliché affair with and a child by a hippie Columbia University professor. Then she and daughter join her mother and two other women as disciples of father Cyprian, a rather old-fashioned priest.[40] Gordon set out to write two novels about women but her one-dimensional male characters such as professor Moore and father Mulcahy in *Final Payments* and father Cyprian in *The Company of Women* are still stronger and more fascinating than the heroines. Anne Clark in Cullinan's

A Change of Scene promises more than Isobel or Felicitas. She is a New York television executive on a Dublin sabbatical. Despite career achievements, Anne has little self-confidence and tumbles into bed with feckless, immature Irish males.[41] Sissie Sullivan, Flaherty's *Tin Wife*, supposedly is liberated but not in action. Retaliating for husband Eddie's infidelities she has a one-afternoon affair with his best friend. Her involvement with the women's movement includes a lesbian incident. Compared with her husband's conservative views, Sissie's liberalism is trite sloganism. Eddie dies in bed with a Hispanic police widow. His superiors announce that he collapsed chasing a drug dealer. When Sissie learns the truth she decides to blackmail the department into a posthumous bravery medal for Eddie and a Columbia University scholarship for daughter, Eileen. Instead of preparing for the encounter with the police commisisoner by sharpening her wits, Sissie dresses to emphasize the voluptuousness of her body.

*   *   *

Lagging behind the shifting reality of its subject, literature has distorted as well as illuminated Irish-America. Since the early 1960s the majority of Irish-Americans have blended into the suburban middle-class. They are not limited by the perspectives of neighbourhood parishes. Most mix comfortably with other nationalities and religions. Their social liberalism is second only to Jewish-Americans. Catholicism has little influence over them. A majority have rebelled against the Church's positions on contraception and divorce. Many would even make exceptions to its prohibition of abortion. Their sexual attitudes and conduct do not deviate much from the American norm. In the choice between competing loyalties to Roman authoritarianism and American liberalism, Irish-America has selected the latter. Because of their penchant for autobiographical examinations of childhood and adolescence, few writers have caught up with evolving Irish-America. Concentration on eastern urban subjects is also a factor. In that part of the country the Irish have not made the same progress as in other regions.

Edwin O'Connor was more perceptive about Irish-America's past and intuitive concerning its future than most other writers. He realized that Irish-American politics was not peasant conservatism and that Irish leadership did not retard the americanization of catholics. O'Connor understood that Irish Catholic communalism and personalism had challenged Anglo-Protestant *laissez faire* indifference to urban poverty and that the anglicization aspects of Irish catholicism made it more appropriate to the United States than the Continental version. Despite power fascination and tribal lapses Irish priests and politicians led all catholics into an American adjustment. O'Connor, however, was not sanguine about the accommodation or the ultimate destination of the Irish journey in the United States. That explains his nostalgia in *The Last Hurrah* about a passing breed of politicians. Compared to the new media robots they had flair, colour, individuality, and rapport with voters. *The Edge of Sadness* anticipated an Irish-America without the art of conversation or a sense of continuity and a post-Vatican II shake hands with your neighbour, halleluja catholicism, bereft of history of mystery.

James Carroll's *Prince of Peace* counterpoints Fleming's alienated Irish-American catholicism. According to Carroll, catholicism and American foreign policy fused in obsessive cold war anti-communism. He observes that after 1945 arrogance replaced catholic defensiveness. Because they anticipated the 'Red Menace' before other Americans, Catholics proclaimed themselves the true patriots. While differing on domestic issues, Francis Cardinal Spellman and John Fitzgerald Kennedy shared the illusion that God's and America's work were the same. This blasphemy gave the disastrous Vietnam involvement a catholic flavour. Consequently, catholic America's apparent rise to the summit of influence actually was the beginning of its descent. Edward Hannibal's *Chocolate Days, Popsicle Weeks* is a rare fictional representation of Irish-American generational change. John 'Fitzie' Fitzpatrick of Sommerville, Massachusetts earns his Boston College tuition by working in an ice-cream factory, hence the novel's title. Fitzie graduates, marries Janice, a nurse, and fulfils his ROTC obligations as an army officer in Germany. He rejects a permanent military career and the traditional college-educated Boston Irish options — teaching, law, insurance. Fitzie tries and succeeds in the exceptionally competitive New York advertising business. Eventually, he, his wife, and children are integrated into the fun and games of Merrimac, a posh suburb. Fitzie's career mobility and obsession triggers tensions in his marriage, but Janice is inarticulate in her discontent. He remains superficially and negatively Irish in his heavy drinking, sexual guilt, and hostility to Anglo-Protestants but not in his connections with his past and post-Vatican II catholicism. Increasingly Fitzie's commitments are to middle-class values rather than religion or nationality.

It is a long way from Dunne's Bridgeport to Hannibal's Merrimac, from the Bridgeport people who forged steel, slaughtered livestock, laid railway track, carried hods, drove horse-carts, loaded and unloaded ships and barges, put out fires, preserved the peace, tried to liberate Ireland with blarney and picnics, scrubbed floors, waited tables, taught children, and nursed the sick, to the Merrimac hucksters of the American consumer economy. Perhaps the actual and literary Irish trek from city to suburbs has been a journey from someplace to noplace. Is Fitzie's fate the future of Irish-America? Separated from a catholicism that was its culture and psychology as well as its religion, can Irish ethnicity survive the suburban melting pot? If not, can the significant Irish contribution to American literature long outlast its source? [42]

NOTES AND REFERENCES

1. Jack Dunphy, 'Prologue', *John Fury* (New York: Harper and Brothers, 1946).
2. The high quality of emigrants compared to those who remained at home is a thesis of Philip Taylor, *The Distant Magnet,* paperback ed. (New York: Harper and Row Publishers, 1971).
3. For more detailed discussions of Irish-American history see William V. Shannon, *The American Irish* (New York: Collier Books, 1974); Andrew M. Greeley, *The Irish-Americans: The Rise to Money and Power* (New York: Harper and Row Publishers, 1981); Lawrence J. McCaffrey, *The Irish Diaspora in America* (Washington, D.C.: The Catholic University of America Press, 1984).
4. *The Chicago Evening Post*, 27 July 1868.
5. This estimate of the John Boyle O'Reilly school of Irish-American literature is found in Charles Fanning, 'Finley Peter Dunne and Irish-American Realism', in Daniel J. Casey and Robert E. Rhodes (eds), *Irish-American Fiction* (New York: AMS, 1979).
6. Charles Fanning, *Finley Peter Dunne and Mr. Dooley: The Chicago Years* (Lexington: The University of Kentucky Press, 1978); *Mr. Dooley and the Chicago Irish* (New York: Arno Press, 1976); and 'Finley Peter Dunne and Irish-American Realism', op. cit.
7. The Studs Lonigan trilogy and the O'Neill-O'Flaherty pentalogy or the Washington Park novels are *Young Lonigan* (1932), *The Young Manhood of Studs Lonigan* (1934), and *Judgement Day* (1935); *A World I Never Made* (1936), *No Star is Lost* (1938), *Father and Son* (1940), *My Days of Anger* (1943), and *The Face of Time* (1953), Vanguard Press, New York published Farrell.
8. Charles Fanning and Ellen Skerrett, 'James T. Farrell and Washington Park: The Novel as Social History', *Chicago History,* VIII, 2 (Summer, 1979), pp 80-91; and Charles Fanning, 'The Literary Dimension', in Lawrence J. McCaffrey, Ellen Skerrett, Michael Funchion, and Charles Fanning, *Chicago's Irish* (Champaign: University of Illinois Press, In Press).
9. Harry Sylvester, *Moon Gaffney* (New York: Henry Holt & Co., 1947).
10. Tom McHale, *Farragan's Retreat* (New York: The Viking Press, 1971).
11. Jimmy Breslin, *World Without End, Amen* (New York: The Viking Press, 1973).
12. Joe Flaherty, *Tin Wife* (New York: Simon and Schuster, 1983).
13. Patrick O'Farrell, *Ireland's English Question* (New York: Schocken Books, 1971), p. 306.
14. James Carroll,< *rince of Peace* (Boston: Little Brown & Co., 1984).
15. William Gibson, *Mass for the Dead* (New York: Atheneum, 1968).
16. Mary McCarthy, *Memories of a Catholic Girlhood* (New York: Berkley Publishing Corporation, 1957).

17. William Kennedy, *Legs,* paperback ed. (New York: Penguin Books), p. 179.
18. *Ibid.*, p. 257.
19. Michael Novak, *The Rise of the Unmeltable Ethnics* (New York: MacMillan Publishing Co., Inc., 1973); Philip Roth, *The Anatomy Lesson* (New York: Farrar, Strau & Geroux, 1983), p. 74.
20. Frank D. Gilroy, *The Subject Was Roses* (New York: Random House, 1965).
21. Thomas J. Fleming, *The God of Love* (Garden City, New York: Doubleday & Co., Inc., 1963); *Romans, Countrymen and Lovers* (New York: William Morrow & Co., 1969); *The Sandbox Tree* (New York: William Morrow & Co., 1970); *The Good Shepherd* (New York: Doubleday and Co., 1974); *Promises to Keep* (New York: Doubleday & Co., 1978).
22. Tom McHale, *Principatio* (New York: Viking Press, 1970).
23. William Kennedy, *Billy Phelan's Greatest Game* (New York: Penguin Books, 1983), p. 18.
24. J.F. Powers, *Morte D'Urban* (New York: Doubleday & Co., Inc., 1962); *Prince of Darkness* (Garden City, N.Y.: Doubleday & Co., 1947); *Presence of Grace* (Garden City, N.Y.: Doubleday & Co., 1956); *Look How the Fish Live* (New York: Knopf, 1975).
25. John Gregory Dunne, *True Confessions* (New York: E.P. Dutton, 1977). The 1980 movie version with script by Dunne and Joan Diddion is better than the novel.
26. Edwin O'Connor, *The Edge of Sadness* (Boston: Atlantic-Little Brown Books, 1961).
27. Alan J. Ward, *Ireland and Anglo-American Relations, 1899-1921* (London: Weidenfeld and Nicolson, 1969), p. 93. Ward quotes Cecil Spring Rice, British Ambassador to the United States. John Paul Bocock, 'The Irish Conquest of Our Cities', *The Forum,* XVII (April 1984), p. 195.
28. Joseph Dinneen, *Ward Eight* (New York: Harper and Brothers Publishers, 1936); Edwin O'Connor, *The Last Hurrah* (Boston: Atlantic-Little Brown Books, 1956). In 1958 John Ford directed a reasonably good version of O'Connor's book. Irish-American politics has not attracted much attention from playwrights. However, William Alfred's *Hogan's Goat* (New York: Farrar, Strauss and Geroux, 1968) is an interesting play about late nineteenth-century Brooklyn Irish politics.
29. James Carroll, *Mortal Friends* (Boston: Little, Brown and Co., 1978); and Edward R.F. Sheehan, *The Governor* (New York: World Publishing Co., 1970).
30. Mary Deasy, *O'Shaughnessy* (New York: Doubleday and Co., 1957); and John O'Hara, *Ten North Frederick* (New York: Random House, 1955). Unlike most Irish fictional politicians, O'Shaughnessy is an unpleasant person.
31. Edward Hannibal, *Chocolate Days, Popsicle Weeks* (Boston: Houghton Miflin Company, 1970), pp 79. 80.
32. Joe Flaherty, *Fogarty and Company* (New York: Coward, McCann & Geohegan, 1973), pp 116, 117.
33. Thomas J. Fleming, *All Good Men* (New York: Doubleday & Co., 1961).
34. Thomas J. Fleming, *King of the Hill* (New York: New American Library, 1965).
35. Thomas J. Fleming, *Rulers of the City* (Garden City, N.Y.: Doubleday and Company, Inc., 1977).
36. Hasia R. Diner, *Erin's Daughters in America: Irish Immigrant Women in the Nineteenth Century* (Baltimore: John Hopkins University Press, 1983).
37. William Kennedy, *Ironweed* (New York: Viking Press, 1983); Elizabeth Cullinan, *House of Gold* (Boston: Houghton Mifflin Co., 1969).

38. John R. Powers, *The Last Catholic in America* (New York: Saturday Review Press, 1973), and *Do Patten Leather Shoes Really Reflect Up?* (Chicago: Regnery, 1975). The last mentioned was converted into a successful long-running musical comedy.

39. Mary Gordon, *Final Payments* (New York: Random House, 1978). Wilfrid Sheed, *The Good Word and Other Words* (New York: Penguin Books, 1980), pp 259-65.

40. Mary Gordon, *The Company of Women* (New York: Random House, 1980).

41. Elizabeth Cullinan, *A Change of Scene* (New York: W.W. Norton, 1982).

42. Except when I quote from Kennedy's *Legs* where I use the 1984 Penguin Books edition, I cite original publishers and dates to give readers perspective on the times the author's represent.